FIGHTERS
1914-1945

Hamlyn
LONDON · NEW YORK · SYDNEY · TORONTO
in association with Phoebus

CONTENTS

Published 1978 by
The Hamlyn Publishing Group Limited
London . New York . Sydney . Toronto
Astronaut House, Feltham, Middlesex,
England

ISBN 0 600 33636 0

Made and printed in Great Britain
by Waterlow (Dunstable) Limited

Written by Bill Gunston
Illustrated by John Batchelor
Edited by Christy Campbell
Designed by Stuart Perry

Bill Gunston is an aviation historian
who has spent many years flying and
writing about all types of aircraft. With
the experience of a flying instructor
behind him, he joined the editorial staff of
Flight International in 1951 and was
appointed Technical Editor in April 1955.
In 1964 he moved on to become the
Technology Editor of *Science Journal*
until in December 1970 he became a
freelance writer and editor. As well as
countless articles he has written 27 books
for aerospace publishers throughout the
English-speaking world. He is Assistant
Compiler of Jane's *All the World's
Aircraft*, and European Editor of the
Australian journal *Aircraft*.

John Batchelor, after serving in the
RAF, worked in the technical publications
departments of several British aircraft
firms, and went on to contribute on a
freelance basis to many technical
magazines. Since then his work for
Purnell's History of the World Wars
Specials has established him as one of the
most outstanding artists in his field.

INTRODUCTION

When Europe mobilised for war in August 1914, powered flight was only eleven years old. In a matter of months the Western Front turned to stalemate and the pattern of fighting in the air above the trench-lines was set – unarmed two-seat reconnaissance aircraft spotting for the guns, whose massed firepower was directed by the airborne observers' reports.

With offensive armament limited to duck-guns or rifle, mechanical failure rather than enemy action was the greatest hazard for the first warplanes. When the first synchronised machine-gun was taken aloft, however, a new breed of aircraft was born – the single-seat fighter designed to deny airspace to the enemy.

The principle remains the same, from 1915 to today; only the technology has changed. This book is a fascinating description of the development of fighter aircraft from the first experiments in the earliest days of the First World War, through the trials of four years of warfare and the period of development between the Wars, to the Second World War when fighter performance, engines and armament were tested in combat.

Some types, including the Spitfire and Bf 109, were 'stretched' successfully and were still fighting at the end of the war. Other new designs like the P-47 Thunderbolt and Hawker Tempest relied on brute power for high performance, yet the true classics of the wartime years were the superbly balanced designs such as the Fw 190 and P-51 Mustang which pushed piston-engined aircraft design to its limit.

New roles produced new aircraft – like the stalking night fighters and the many successful adaptations of fighter aircraft for ground attack.

All are amply covered in this authoritative and colourful book with chapters on the Battle of Britain, the air war over Russia and the Pacific, night fighters, fighter technology, engines and armament. From the first air battles over Flanders in 1914 to the first combat jets defending the crumbling Reich, *Fighters 1914–1945* tells the exciting story of fighters at war. John Batchelor's illustrations show off the machines to perfection and Bill Gunston charts the battles and the design developments with his expert text.

A CONCEPT EMERGES

On 5 October, 1914, a Voisin LA, called a Type III by the French *Aviation Militaire,* was droning lustily over a Western Front that had yet to degenerate into the bloody stalemate of trench warfare. The Voisin is a biplane pusher, with a strong steel framework but not possessed of a sparkling performance. The engine was put at the back of the nacelle so that the crew, comprising a pilot and an observer in the extreme nose, should have a better view. The Voisin's role was reconnaissance, though by October 1914 it had become the custom to carry small bombs in the front cockpit and throw them over the side in the vague hope of hitting suitable targets. But on the whole the business of reconnaissance was routine, and it was also practised by the hated Boche.

Suddenly the observer Louis Quénault spotted an enemy aircraft, an Aviatik with the distinctive black crosses. His pilot, Joseph Franz, opened the throttle and they closed the range. It was Quénault's big moment. Pivoted to the edge of his cockpit was a Hotchkiss machine gun, and as the Aviatik came within range he opened up with clip after clip of ammunition. Soon the Aviatik was spinning down out of control, to crash in a pyre of smoke. Eventually the smoke had dispersed and the little incident was but a memory to those who had witnessed it. But its ripples spread and multiplied, and reverberated in a thousand offices, parliaments, factories and front-line messtents. It was precisely what a very few people – virtually all of them not 'qualified' to express an opinion – had been predicting for four or five years. Air warfare was a concept so radically new that the official military mind had found it singularly hard to grasp.

By 1909 the flying machine was no longer part of mythology, laughed to scorn by newspaper editors and the general public alike. In the summer of that year vast crowds had flocked to Reims to watch the world's first great aviation meeting. Blériot boldly flew across the Channel to England. Nobody could scornfully claim that these things were delusions or fakes. The aeroplane had unquestionably arrived, and – though a few claimed that, like the horseless carriage, it was a mere flash in the pan, doomed soon to fade from the scene – most people thought it more likely that each new year would bring more and better aeroplanes capable of doing useful jobs. Visionaries published stories and sketches of future aerial travel – and future aerial warfare.

German Army officers experiment with an Otto, 1913. In the earliest days of military flying the observer was the officer and the pilot or 'chauffeur' was the NCO

Nor was the concept of air warfare confined to paper. The US Army was widely chastised for its sluggish reaction to the achievements of the Wright Brothers, but in fact it was years ahead of all other military services in forming an embryo 'air force' (the Aeronautical Section of the Signal Corps in 1907) and issuing a detailed specification for a military aircraft, in the same year. The US Army was not concerned with particular missions; it rightly judged that the ability to fly was at that time a worthwhile end in itself. But the enthusiasm of its young officers ran somewhat ahead of the old staff officers in Washington – whom the young pilots scathingly called 'mossbacks' – and, without any authority from above, experiments began in 1910 to see what warlike things could be done in the air. In August of that year Lt Jake Fickel, of the 29th Infantry at Governor's

Maurice Farman Longhorn, the almost ubiquitous training and reconnaissance machine of the first Allied airmen

Albatros L.1, B-type reconnaissance biplane – like the Farman an easy prey for an armed aircraft

Albatros-built Taube *– the 'dove'-like monoplane built by several German and Austrian manufacturers*

Island, New York, went to the public Air Meet at Sheepshead Bay. There he persuaded two famous aviators, Glenn Curtiss and Charles Willard, to let him try air-to-ground firing with a rifle. The civilian pilots had been apprehensive about the recoil, and also pointed out that, as there was no proper seat, their previous passengers had needed both hands to hold on with. But Fickel set up a ground target and, on many runs, scored many hits.

This was nothing more than a rather dangerous escapade by an enthusiast. The only official report, apart from word-of-mouth, was in a letter by Fickel to brother-officer Henry Arnold, who later became chief of the whole US Army Air Corps. Fickel commented that 'you have to allow for the motion of the plane'. It was easiest, he said, when you were in a direct line with the target so that you passed overhead. Shooting to either side was difficult. Fickel had tried in practice what would later be called deflection shooting. How to aim a gun was to be central to almost every part of air combat right up to the present day. There was just one time, in the 1950s, when it seemed likely that the ability to shoot straight would no longer be important to the fighter pilot. A combination of radar, autopilot and rockets appeared to do the job automatically, and later the guided missile seemed to render the gun obsolete. Today we know better, and to a considerable degree the top-scoring fighter pilots of any future conflicts will still be the good shots.

In August 1910 two other US Army officers did something which rather put poor Fickel in the shade. Lt Paul Beck and 2nd Lt Myron T Crissy went to a shop in San Francisco, bought some $2\frac{1}{2}$-in pipe and made the world's first aerial bomb. They also put fins on a live 3-in artillery shell. Then they flew over a big Air Meet at San Francisco's Tanforan racecourse and startled – if not physically endangered – the crowds with the world's first live aerial bombing raid. The bombs worked, exploding with very satisfying bangs.

By this time developments were taking place in aerial communications. The US Army experimented with an air-to-ground Morse system, with a wing-mounted device rather like a modernised Red Indian smoke-signal generator. Compressed air was released by a pilot-actuated valve to blow past a can of lamp-black, emitting short blobs of black soot for dots and long ones for dashes – provided the turbulent slipstream did not disperse the signal before they could be read. Far more significant was the pioneer experiment of Canadian J A D McCurdy, at the 1910 Sheepshead Bay meet: he had successfully transmitted messages by air-to-ground radio.

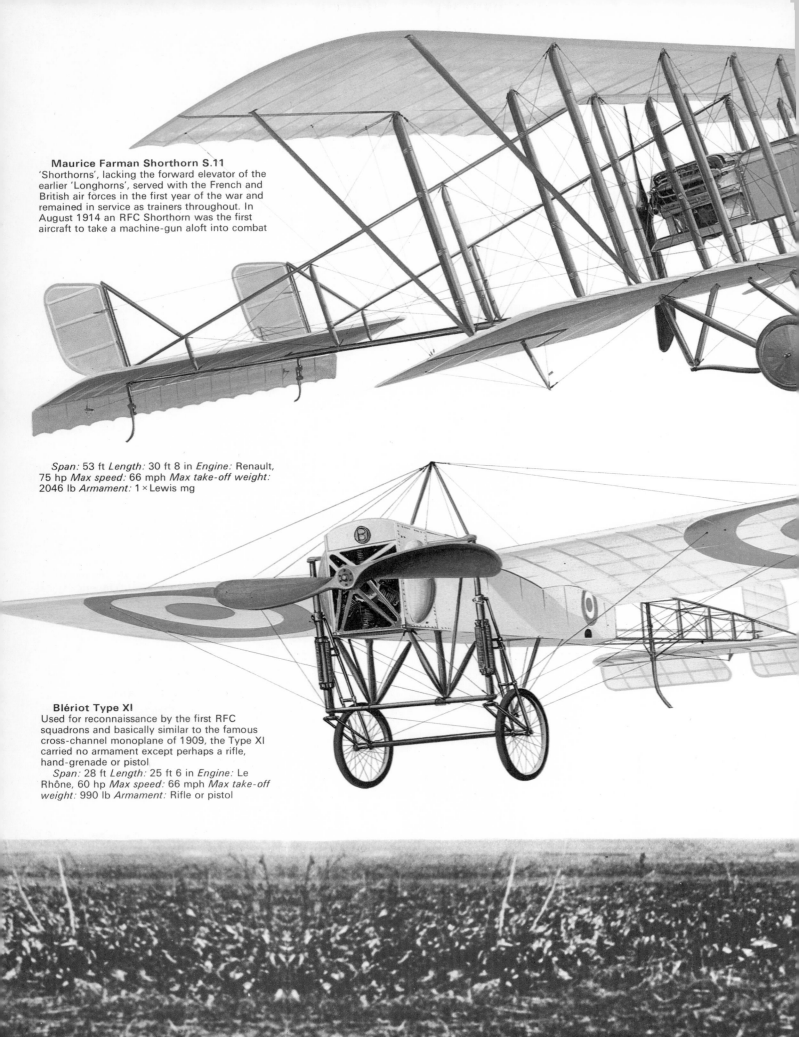

Maurice Farman Shorthorn S.11
'Shorthorns', lacking the forward elevator of the
earlier 'Longhorns', served with the French and
British air forces in the first year of the war and
remained in service as trainers throughout. In
August 1914 an RFC Shorthorn was the first
aircraft to take a machine-gun aloft into combat

Span: 53 ft *Length:* 30 ft 8 in *Engine:* Renault,
75 hp *Max speed:* 66 mph *Max take-off weight:*
2046 lb *Armament:* 1 × Lewis mg

Blériot Type XI
Used for reconnaissance by the first RFC
squadrons and basically similar to the famous
cross-channel monoplane of 1909, the Type XI
carried no armament except perhaps a rifle,
hand-grenade or pistol
Span: 28 ft *Length:* 25 ft 6 in *Engine:* Le
Rhône, 60 hp *Max speed:* 66 mph *Max take-off
weight:* 990 lb *Armament:* Rifle or pistol

Early arrivals to organised air warfare – men of No 1 Squadron RNAS pose around their airfield klaxon, late 1914

Unarmed Albatros takes off from a Flanders airfield. Any aircraft that might shoot it down, even with a 12-bore duck-gun, would be amongst the first fighters

In 1911 a former US Army officer, Riley E Scott, arrived at the world's first military air base at College Park, Maryland, with the world's first bombing system. It comprised a frame designed to be readily attached to a Wright or Curtiss, on which could be hung two aerial bombs. The frame carried an inclined telescope, with a graticule marked on one of the lenses, and a fixed sheet of numbers which related the passage of the target down the telescope scale to the speed and altitude of the aircraft. Probably the chief problem was that there were no reliable airspeed indicators or altimeters, and estimates were inaccurate. But the Riley Scott bombsight was at least a workable device which, once it had been calibrated by trial and error by a pilot used to judging speed and height, gave

encouraging results. Riley Scott took it to Europe, and at Villacoublay won the Michelin Prize of $5000 by extremely accurate bombing of marked-out ground targets from heights of 200 and 800 metres. Later the Riley Scott was the basis for the first production bombsight.

In 1911 war flared up between Turkey and Italy in Tripolitania. It was the first opportunity for aircraft to demonstrate whether or not they were of military value. The Italians had several aircraft in North Africa, and on 22 October, Capt Piazza took off in a Blériot on the world's first combat mission. He landed after having spent a full hour studying the Turkish positions, and his report was extremely detailed. Unlike the observer in a balloon he was able to fly over and around the

enemy, and the picture he gathered was as full as one could wish. Further reconnaissance missions followed, and on 1 November, Lt Gavotti flew over the Turkish camp at 2500 ft and dropped four bombs by hand. Though he had no Riley Scott sight, he caused casualties and consternation, and provoked an angry reply alleging a criminal act. In 1912 there was plenty of air activity in the Balkan War. Turkish-held Adrianople was bombed several times, and the air-minded Bulgars not only had pilots of their own but hired mercenaries with their own aircraft. Sakoff, a Russian, appears to have been the first bomber pilot to return to base with bullet holes in his machine. One mercenary, the American Bert Hall, knew of the Riley Scott sight and went into action with a locally made copy. He did much better than the Russian aviators who merely hung their 22-lb bombs from their feet with a slip knot and released them with a sharp kick! Later one of the Russians, Kolchin, was shot down and killed by Turkish rifle fire. He was the first aviator to be killed in air warfare.

Britain, France and Germany all had embryonic air forces by 1910, and in 1911 officers in all three countries had practised firing rifles in the air. The Briton, Capt Brooke-Popham of the Air Battalion, Royal Engineers, was promptly ordered to cease such a practice, but about 18 months later official sanction was given for him, as a major commanding No 3 Sqn of the new Royal Flying Corps, to practice shooting at kites from a Henry Farman. The hazards to people on the ground are obvious, and instead of being a serious matter of training and research the firing of guns in the air seems to have been regarded as sport for senior officers. It required that the marksman should take both hands off the control column for several seconds at a time, so in rough air it was a tricky business. Pilots kept personal score by putting a dab of coloured paint on the bullets taken aloft, which left a ring round any hole in the kite. Such a practice never became official.

Active Combat

In the United States Col Isaac N Lewis was finding no success in marketing the outstanding machine gun, designed around the turn of the century by Samuel McClean, which he had improved and which now bore his name. The Lewis gun was in fact the best in the world in 1912 for aerial use, because it was light and compact, had a high rate of fire, was reliable, and was fed by a handy drum of 47 or 97 rounds. In June 1912 Lewis visited College Park and got one of his guns mounted on a US Army Wright. Lt Tom Milling did the flying, and the CO, Capt Charles de Forest Chandler, blasted away with the new gun at a ground target made of cheesecloth. The results were excitingly good, and the gun made a most favourable impression. But the 'mossbacks' in the War Department insisted that there was absolutely no question of the aeroplane ever carrying guns and engaging in active combat. In any case, even if it ever did, the standard Army machine gun was the Benet-Mercier, not the Lewis. Unfortunately when the Benet-Mercier was mounted on a Wright it got in the way of the pilot's control column, because it had an 18-in ammunition feed sticking out on one side and an equally long ejection chute on the other.

Other experiments were going on in many countries to see how useful aeroplanes, and

airships, might be as carriers of guns and droppers of bombs. One of the longest-established air units was the airship *(Luftschiff)* branch of the Imperial German Navy. This used the well-tried Zeppelin airships, which, compared with early aeroplanes, carried much heavier loads and could fly further. Though still frail and extremely vulnerable in severe weather, the Navy Zeppelins were manned by courageous and efficient crews and directed by officers who never doubted that in wartime their mission would be an active bomb-dropping one, as well as ocean reconnaissance. By 1912 they were possibly the first air service in the world to indulge in bomb-dropping practice as a routine matter of training, and their effectiveness became considerable because they dropped heavy bombs with increasing accuracy. The German Army, which used Zeppelins and Schütte-Lanz ships, saw its role mainly as front-line reconnaissance and possibly bombing in support of its ground troops, and learned the hard way that airships do not survive long over battlefields.

When The First World War began on 4 August, 1914, all these things were public knowledge. Altogether it added up to a substantial body of experience of air warfare, yet to most of the general staffs and members of governments air warfare was still something written about by semi-lunatics. Almost universally the official

Morane-Saulnier Type L
The Type L is probably the most famous parasol monoplane of its time, and was the first to carry a machine-gun firing forward through the propeller disc. Steel wedges deflected bullets that hit the blades, and this innovation was discovered by the Germans when a Type L flown by Roland Garros was shot down at Courtrai in April 1915. Within weeks the Germans had deployed synchronised machine-guns as a response
Span: 36 ft 9 in *Length:* 22 ft 6¾ in *Engine:* Gnome seven-cylinder or Le Rhône 9C nine-cylinder air-cooled rotary, 80 hp *Max speed:* 72 mph at 6500 ft *Max take-off weight:* 1440 lb *Armament:* 1×8-mm Hotchkiss or 0.303-in Lewis mg

view was that the aeroplane might have some use as a reconnaissance vehicle, because it might be able to have a closer or more varied look at the enemy than would be possible with a tethered balloon. Even this was a reluctant admission, and many officers – who, of course, were all officers in an established army or navy, because no

The Royal Flying Corps, established in 1912, began work with a series of Royal Aircraft Factory products including the B.E.8

An Albatros B-type was still enough of a novelty to attract the curious gaze of German officers

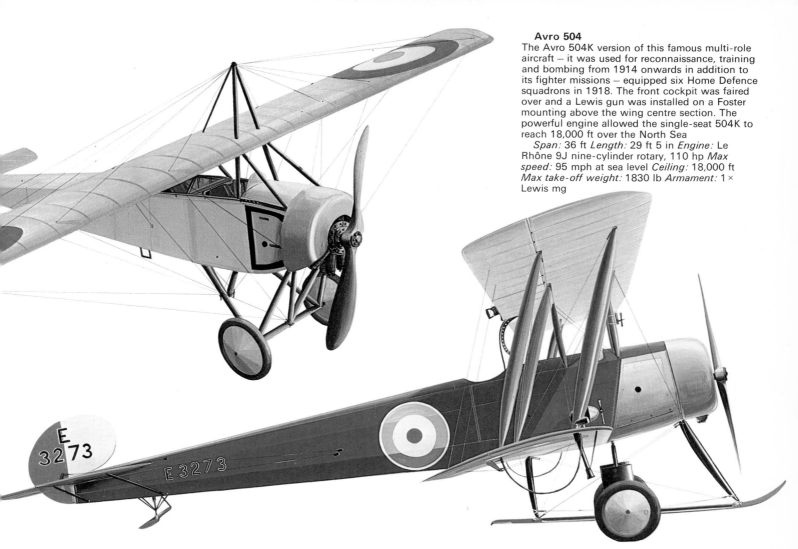

Avro 504
The Avro 504K version of this famous multi-role aircraft – it was used for reconnaissance, training and bombing from 1914 onwards in addition to its fighter missions – equipped six Home Defence squadrons in 1918. The front cockpit was faired over and a Lewis gun was installed on a Foster mounting above the wing centre section. The powerful engine allowed the single-seat 504K to reach 18,000 ft over the North Sea
Span: 36 ft *Length:* 29 ft 5 in *Engine:* Le Rhône 9J nine-cylinder rotary, 110 hp *Max speed:* 95 mph at sea level *Ceiling:* 18,000 ft *Max take-off weight:* 1830 lb *Armament:* 1 × Lewis mg

such thing as an air force existed – regarded the aeroplane as being similar to the submarine as something that no gentleman would wish to be associated with. This was especially the case in Britain, where the Air Battalion, and from 1912 the Royal Flying Corps, had had to get along on budgets so meagre that its handful of enthusiastic officers had often met official bills out of their own pockets. Even in Germany, where military aviation funding was at least twelve times greater, there was no official grasp of the concept of air warfare whatever.

Even when one makes allowance for the fact that in the years before 1914 elderly men had not yet got used to a world of rapid technological change, the failure to plan for an aerial war is difficult to comprehend. Today the subject of forecasting – not just the weather but the future of almost every human activity – is a highly developed art, science and big business. People of all kinds, and certainly people in military uniform, need to know what is probably, or even possibly, going to happen in the years ahead. Had there been any forecasters before the First World War, other than the writers of fiction, air warfare would have immediately been identified in stark reality.

In the absence of knowledge of their motives it would be wrong to pour scorn on the important people of the pre-1914 era who dismissed the whole notion of air warfare as ridiculous. It may be that their minds could not accept so new an idea. It may be that they had watched the flying of the early aviators and, rightly judging that some could only just get off the ground,

were short-sighted enough to conclude that the aeroplane would never be able to carry a gun or a bomb. Perhaps they considered the aeroplane would always be a rare and exotic species, and that machines belonging to opposing sides would be unlikely to meet. Yet, no matter how one tries to view things through pre-1914 eyes, the absence of any official action to plan for aerial warfare remains an enigma.

It was especially surprising in Britain. The British had for generations felt totally secure in their island, guarded by the unchallenged might of the Royal Navy.

When Blériot landed his frail flying machine in the grounds of Dover Castle in 1909 it was a profound shock. 'No Longer an Island' proclaimed the newspaper headlines, and more than any other event this caused the British to look at their own non-performance in aviation. Three years later an ominous throbbing along the Thames heralded the visit of a large airship, whose lights were seen by many Britons. Later the Admiralty admitted it was 'not one of our ships'. It could only be a Zeppelin, and Zeppelins could do a lot of damage. Yet not one anti-aircraft gun was ordered, and not

Mechanical failure was a greater danger than enemy action in the earliest days, as this crashed Farman testifies

A B.E.2c displays one of the earliest forms of British marking, a simple red disc on a white background on the upper wing with a Union Jack on the tail

one aeroplane was bought with a gun. No action whatsoever was taken to provide any form of air defence.

Nine months earlier, when the Royal Flying Corps was formed, it was announced that its strength was to be '131 aeroplanes', but in December 1912, two months after the Zeppelin's nocturnal visit, the Secretary of State for War admitted the RFC possessed 14 aeroplanes, of which three were under repair. In August of that year the War Office had organised a Military Aircraft Trials competition to decide upon the best aeroplane for the RFC. Far and away the best was the BE.2 designed and built at the government's own Royal Aircraft Factory at Farnborough; but the RAF (factory) had no authority to build aircraft and its superintendent was one of the judges, so the winner had to be an obsolete and un-suitable machine (Cody's large biplane nicknamed 'The Cathedral'). Even in 1912 this was outclassed and had no chance of flying useful military missions; but the very idea of a 'military mission' was thought not to exist, despite all the shooting and bomb-ing that had already been done by a few enthusiasts.

When war did finally break out the puny Royal Flying Corps was hastily ordered to despatch aircraft to France. What was to happen if they should meet a Zeppelin coming the other way? This was a fair enough question, and a prospect which could have been discussed and armed against at any time in the previous two years. The answer was that, as there was no other method, they should attempt to destroy the Zeppelin by ramming it. Admit-tedly at this time other RFC machines were carrying out the first operational patrols over the Thames estuary with observers carrying rifles, and canvas bandoliers con-taining 50 rounds of ammunition. But as 'fighter' aircraft such machines were un-impressive; one could have done better in 1911, and a quick answer was needed.

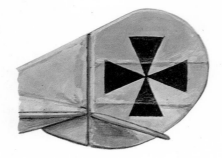

Germany

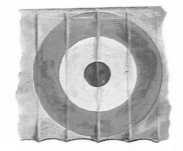

France

Britain

National Markings: 1914

Up to this point nobody had apparently thought about the problem of aircraft recognition until inability to tell one machine from another had already caused trouble. The first aeroplane buffs, many of whom were schoolboys, could tell at a distance not only what type an aeroplane was but which particular machine it was, and probably who owned it. Such capability was not possessed by those in positions of authority, nor by the ordinary private soldier with an itchy trigger finger. One of the first RFC machines to reach France had to land at Senlis, short of its destination. As the aircraft bore no national markings the pilot was arrested, and though he protested in what must have been recog-nised as English he was locked up in the town gaol – according to published reports, for a week. It was mainly because of this comic-opera situation that the RFC and Royal Naval Air Service (RNAS) were required to display some form of national marking. France had adopted a tricolour roundel and Germany the Croix Paté – often called the Maltese cross. As a temp-orary measure the RFC sewed small Union Jacks on the fuselage or nacelle, but before long much larger 6-ft Union Jacks were painted on the wings and smaller flags on the tail. Later, in 1915, the British adopted the French roundel and rudder strips, and then reversed the colours so that the British and French machines, though obviously Allied, could be distinguished from each other. The Union Jack had, it was said, too much similarity to the German cross.

In France the problem of aircraft recog-nition was judged so important that it resulted in an across-the-board regula-tion regarding aircraft design. German aeroplanes had tractor (front-mounted) pro-pellers, so French aircraft, especially bombers, were by General Staff decree designed as pushers. By this brutish but effective rule the French, at least, hoped to avoid mistaken identity.

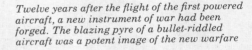

Twelve years after the flight of the first powered aircraft, a new instrument of war had been forged. The blazing pyre of a bullet-riddled aircraft was a potent image of the new warfare

THE OPENING ROUNDS

Before the First World War it had been difficult enough just to build a reliable and safe flying machine. But in 1914–15 this aim was no longer enough. First, aircraft had not only to fly but to carry armament which could be used effectively. Secondly, the armament had to be developed. Thirdly, tactics had to be worked out so that the new species of combat aircraft could be used in the most efficient way.

In only one respect was the designer's task made easier. By 1914 several families of aero-engine had sufficient background of flight experience for the propulsion of the aircraft to be no longer a problem. The Central Powers – Germany and Austria-Hungary – almost completely standardized on a range of water-cooled engines with four or six cylinders in line, developed directly from pre-war car engines. The Benz, the Mercedes and the Austro-Daimler were the chief members of a closely related and highly refined family of engines which had been tempered in the fire of Grand Prix racing. They were robust and reliable, but massive. They needed heavy water cooling systems, and the radiator caused extra drag when it was simply bolted on the side of the fuselage. By late 1915 most German and Austro-Hungarian fighting scouts had the radiator recessed inside the upper wing, with a cooling-water pipe sloping up to it from the front cylinder. This reduced drag, but the water circuit was vulnerable, and if a bullet hit the radiator the pilot was drenched in near-boiling water.

The 1914 Mercedes Grand Prix engine was also used in Britain. The winner of the British Grand Prix was towed up to Derby and given to Rolls-Royce, with instructions that the famous car company should build an aero-engine, using the proven Mercedes

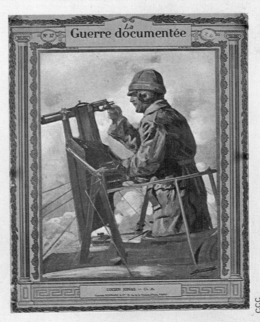

The perils of actually fighting from the first military aircraft are amply illustrated in this contemporary French print of a Hotchkiss-armed Deperdussin

technology where they thought it would help. The result was a six-in-line called the Hawk, used for blimps (non-rigid airships) and a few aircraft, and a much better engine called the Falcon with two banks of Hawk cylinders arranged in vee formation. It was to become a famed fighter engine, and the bigger V12 Eagle was one of the most powerful Allied engines used in large numbers in the war, rated at up to 375 hp. There were many satisfactory water-cooled in-line and vee engines used by the Allies, most of them of French design.

Throughout the war a very large role was also played by the rotary engines derived from the Gnome of 1907. These had broken away entirely from established automobile practice and offered aviators an engine which, for its power, was much lighter and in some ways simpler. A drawback of the Gnome was that it was machined from high-strength steel forgings, and though beautifully made it was time-consuming and expensive to construct. It also behaved as a powerful gyroscope, because the fact that the whole engine (apart from the crankshaft) spun round with the propeller was a mixed blessing. It kept the cylinders cool, but made rapid flight manoeuvres difficult, especially in small aircraft with a single large engine. As will be explained, several rotary-engined aircraft became notorious for being able to turn like lightning in one direction, while being most reluctant to turn the opposite way. This powerfully influenced the way a pilot handled his aircraft in combat, and sometimes made his actions predictable. The rotaries were also liable to fling their castor-oil lubricant from every small crack in their rotating parts, particularly from the valve gear (which differed fundamentally between types, some having a flap-valve in the piston itself). Even today one can whiff burned castor-oil near any surviving rotary, and it was an odour familiar to most fighter pilots of the First World War.

At first it did not make very much difference whether the engine was put in front of the crew, in the so-called Blériot arrangement, or behind a short nacelle, in the so-called Farman arrangement (this nomenclature was responsible for the British B.E. designation for early tractor aircraft and F.E. for early pushers). In the pre-1914 era few aircraft could exceed 70 mph and neither configuration seemed to have a marked performance advantage. The Central Powers displayed a Teutonic love of standardization and throughout the war made virtually every one of their aircraft of the tractor type. The French initially had a preponderance of pushers, because this gave the crew a good view and, by late 1914, because it made it easier to mount a machine gun. The British went into production with both tractors and pushers, but most of the earliest fighting scouts were pushers. Important examples included the Airco D.H.1 and 2, the F.E.2 and the Vickers 'Gunbus', the last two of which were designed long before the war.

The tragedy with these machines is that so much time was wasted in getting them into service. A R Low and G H Challenger designed the Vickers Type 18 'Destroyer' in early 1913, and it was exhibited at the 1913 Aero Show at Olympia with a Maxim machine-gun in the nose. The design was then refined in a succession of further prototypes until the E.F.B.5 (Experimental Fighting Biplane) was ordered for the RFC. These had a much handier gun, the new Lewis, but were not impressive performers, being just able to work up to a maximum of 70 mph and taking half an hour to climb to a ceiling of about 9000 feet. The very first 'fighter squadron' in history was RFC No 11, which arrived in France with the F.B.5 Gunbus in July 1915. The original F.E.2a was also designed in early 1913, in this case at the Royal Aircraft Factory at Farnborough. Like the Vickers it was a two-seater, the gunner (called the observer, because the intention had been to build an armed reconnaissance machine) occupying the front cockpit where his Lewis could sweep the whole sky in the forward hemisphere. No urgency appears to have been put behind development or production, and it was not until a year later, in August 1914 (after the start of the war), that 12 were ordered. These F.E.2a aircraft had a poor British engine, the 100-hp water-cooled Green, and an unimpressive performance. By 1915 the decision had been taken to fit the 120-hp Beardmore, and this resulted in a very useful machine – though still no great performer, with a maximum speed of 80 mph and ceiling of 9000 feet. Many 'Fees' had a second Lewis on a tall pillar behind the observer to cover the upper rear. Later these tough machines became night bombers and even night fighters. The original F.E. designer, Geoffrey de Havilland, produced a rather smaller fighter/reconnaissance aircraft in early 1915, the D.H.1. Powered by either the 70-hp Renault or (D.H.1a) 120-hp Beardmore, it was a very manoeuvrable machine and with the Beardmore was a much better performer than the 'Fee'; only 73 were delivered, however. The D.H.2 was a small single-seater with quite

Vickers F.B.5 Gunbus
The F.B.5 achieved distinction by being the aeroplane operated by the world's first single-type squadron formed specifically for air combat: No 11 Sqn, Royal Flying Corps, in July 1915. The Gunbus did not have an outstanding performance, and its engine was unreliable, but the type achieved a considerable reputation with the Germans. By the spring of 1916 the F.B.5 was outclassed by Fokker's monoplanes and began to be retired
Span: 36 ft 6 in *Length:* 27 ft 2 in *Engine:* Gnome Monosoupape, 100 hp, or Clerget 9Z, 110 hp *Max speed:* 70 mph at 5000 ft *Ceiling:* 9000 ft *Max take-off weight:* 2050 lb *Armament:* 1 ×0.303-in Lewis or Vickers mg, occasionally with supplementary Lewis gun or rifle

Mercedes In-line Six-cylinder Engine
German designers concentrated on in-line engines rather than rotary or radial layouts. The Mercedes powered such aircraft as the Fokker D. VII and Albatros D.V
Power: 180 hp at 1400 rpm

good performance on the 100 hp of a Gnome Monosoupape (Monosoupape = single valve, the other valve being in the crown of the piston).

Flying a D.H.2 in RFC No 5 Sqn during early trials on the Western front in July 1915 was a full-time job. Though the aircraft itself was fine, the pilot also had to aim his forward-pointing Lewis gun. Pilots argued over whether the dominant hand (in most people the right) should fly the aircraft or aim and fire the gun. In either event it left no hand free to work the throttle or do anything else, and changing ammunition drums was even more tricky. In most early D.H.2s the gun was pivoted on the left side, but many pilots (not necessarily the left-handed ones) found it better on the right. But the best answer was staring everyone in the face, and some time in February 1916 the first unit fully equipped with the production D.H.2, RFC No 24 Sqn, hit on the idea of simply fixing the gun to fire straight ahead. This for the first time gave the Allies an effective dogfighter, and by 1916 such a thing was desperately overdue.

One of the greatest puzzles of the genesis of fighter aircraft is why, when so many people had given thought to the matter of fighter armament and come up with an answer, nobody in any official position in any country took any action whatsoever. By far the biggest single advance was the machine-gun fixed to fire ahead past the blades of a tractor propeller. This could be done in several ways. The crudest was merely to fix steel deflectors on each blade at the correct radius, but this had several drawbacks. It imposed numerous severe shocks on the wooden blade, which might eventually lead to failure; the deflectors and attachment holes themselves weakened the blade and impaired its efficiency; and the ricocheting bullets posed a significant hazard. A much better solution was to link the mechanism of the gun with the engine so that it could fire only if there was no propeller blade about to pass across the line of fire. In general, blades passed ahead of the gun at a faster rate than the gun could fire bullets. A typical 1914 machine gun fired 550 rounds per minute, but a 1914 aero-engine ran at 1000–1500 rpm (which had to be multiplied by two or four depending on the number of blades on the propeller). As early as 1913 Franz Schneider of the German LVG company and Lt Poplavko of the Imperial Russian Air Service had devised and published rather crude interrupter gears and actually tested them. Schneider, at least, took out a patent. In

Drum-fed Hotchkiss arming a Voisin

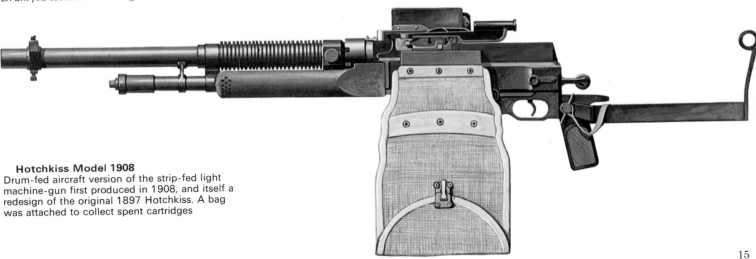

Hotchkiss Model 1908
Drum-fed aircraft version of the strip-fed light machine-gun first produced in 1908, and itself a redesign of the original 1897 Hotchkiss. A bag was attached to collect spent cartridges

1914 the British Edwards brothers took out a patent for a better system, and demonstrated a working model to the War Office, while in France Raymond Saulnier, of the famed Morane-Saulnier aircraft company, linked the gun trigger with a special two-lobed cam on the engine (on the crankshaft, although it was a rotary) and demonstrated it actually working.

Despite all this, there was no support whatever for any such scheme from a single official in any country. Aircraft designers, who may not have known what others had achieved, thus had to fall back on a grotesque array of aircraft configurations to try to build a fighter. At Farnborough the mass-produced B.E.2c – virtually the standard equipment of the 1914–15 RFC, but in no sense a fighter – was turned into the B.E.9 by swapping the observer and the engine. The result was a pathetic travesty of a fighter, with the observer sitting in a separate cockpit carried on struts and wires in front of the great four-blade screw. Dubbed 'The Pulpit' by RFC 16 Sqn, it was potentially lethal to its observer, who could not communicate with the pilot and would have been cut to pieces or crushed in any bad nose-over landing, such as then were frequent. An even stranger answer was found by Louis Becherau, technical director of the French Spad company, in the Spad A2. This had a front cockpit that could be bodily hinged down to permit access to the engine. When clipped in place the front gunner's nacelle was fastened by two pins engaging in trunnions on the upper wing and by a ball-race fixture on a front extension of the propeller shaft! Small numbers proved most unpopular with the French and Russians, and later there was even a more powerful series designated A3, A4 and A5, some of which had flight controls and a gun in both cockpits so that either man could fly the aircraft or fire at the Hun.

F.E.8

Designed, like the D.H.2, to counter the Fokker monoplanes on the Western Front, the first F.E.8 flew in October 1916. It had some success but was soon outclassed by new tractor types and it was the last of the pusher scouts

Span: 31 ft 6 in *Length:* 23 ft 8 in *Engine:* Gnome, 100 hp *Max speed:* 94 mph *Max take-off weight:* 1346 lb *Armament:* 1 × Lewis mg

de Havilland D.H.2
Geoffrey de Havilland's pusher fighting scout equipped the Royal Flying Corps' No 24 Sqn, which became the RFC's first single-seat fighter unit to see combat (in February 1916). Once the D.H.2's unforgiving handling characteristics had been mastered it became a useful addition to the fighter force, but the superiority of the new German Albatros and Halberstadt tractor biplanes was emphasised when the 24 Sqn commander, Maj Hawker, fell to von Richthofen's guns in November 1916
Span: 28 ft 3 in *Length:* 25 ft 2½ in *Engine:* Gnome Monosoupape, 100 hp, or Le Rhône 9J, 110 hp *Max speed:* 93 mph at sea level *Ceiling:* 14,000 ft *Max take-off weight:* 1440 lb *Armament:* 0.303-in Lewis mg

One solution to the problem of firing a machine-gun in the line of flight was the pusher layout. The Lewis-armed D.H.2 could just hold its own against the Fokker E.III with its synchronised machine-gun

The need to develop aircraft to shoot down Zeppelins led to equally strange arrangements. In Lincoln the firm of Robey & Co, which made large numbers of aircraft to others' designs, teamed with J A Peters to build two rather different prototypes of a three-seat anti-Zeppelin fighter. Basically they were conventional biplanes, of quite good design and performance; the odd part was that the armament was carried in large streamlined nacelles, each housing a gun and gunner, on the left and right upper mainplanes. Of course, thousands of combat aircraft were built with guns pivoted or fixed to the upper wing, even after methods had been found to fire safely past the propeller. Sometimes the pilot had to grip the rear of the gun and aim it up at the belly of the enemy, while he flew (probably in violent manoeuvres) with the other hand. In other cases the gun was fixed to the upper wing at an inclination that would clear the propeller. In many aircraft, such as the Sopwith Dolphin and the Parnall Scout, one or more machine guns were fixed firing up at an oblique angle from the fuselage, presaging the *Schräge Musik* type armament used by Luftwaffe night fighters from 1943. One of the best schemes was the British Foster mount, comprising a curved rail arching in a quadrant from the upper wing to the cockpit of a single seater. A Lewis gun could be pulled back down this rail until it was almost pointing straight up, with the breech right in front of the pilot. The pilot could fire it in this position, but the reason for the rail was to facilitate changing ammunition drums. The reloaded gun could then be pushed back up the rail to its normal position firing ahead, just above the tips of the propeller blades.

There were many other schemes, all intended to enable a machine-gun to be fired accurately from a fast aircraft. Dufaux in France and Gallaudet in the United States put the propeller on a hub rotating around the main structural member of the fuselage, just behind the wing, driving through gears. Thus the advantages of a pusher, with clear field of fire ahead, could be combined with a high-speed streamlined form. Of course with two engines there was no problem, and one could have machine-gunners from nose to tail. There were not many twin-engined fighters in the First World War, but the Caudron R.11 was very successful and used in large numbers, while there were numerous prototypes by other companies. A cunning arrangement by Mann & Grimmer in Britain was the single-engined twin-pusher. A 100- or 125-hp Anzani radial engine in the fuselage nose was installed back to front, driving a shaft on which were two gearwheels. These in turn drove chains turning pusher propellers carried on struts between the wings. Thus the nose was left free for a manually aimed Lewis; had the scheme been taken further, one might in a more powerful machine have had a regular battery of fixed guns firing ahead. Another scheme was to accept the tractor propeller on the nose and put the gunners on each side of it, as was done in the Armstrong Whitworth F.K.12. This strange-looking fighter had a Lewis gunner in left and right nacelles projecting well ahead of the propeller – where they could have shot at each other!

Many companies, including Nieuport in France, Lloyd and various Brandenburg C.I types in Austria-Hungary and Sage in

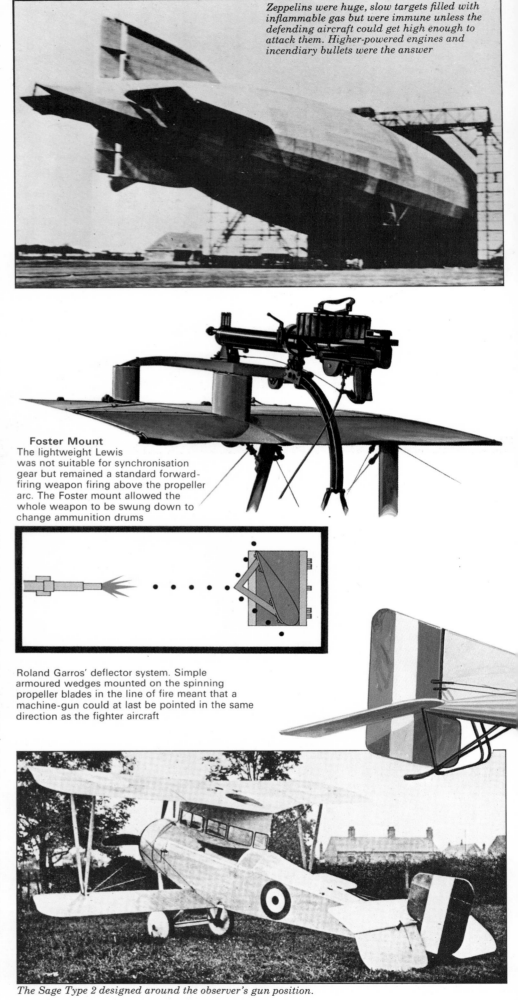

Zeppelins were huge, slow targets filled with inflammable gas but were immune unless the defending aircraft could get high enough to attack them. Higher-powered engines and incendiary bullets were the answer

Foster Mount
The lightweight Lewis was not suitable for synchronisation gear but remained a standard forward-firing weapon firing above the propeller arc. The Foster mount allowed the whole weapon to be swung down to change ammunition drums

Roland Garros' deflector system. Simple armoured wedges mounted on the spinning propeller blades in the line of fire meant that a machine-gun could at last be pointed in the same direction as the fighter aircraft

The Sage Type 2 designed around the observer's gun position.

Business end of an RFC Morane, the Lewis machine-gun and 'Garros-wedges' clearly showing

Britain, all arranged for a gunner to stand upright in a deep fairing (sometimes it was virtually a cabin) to fire a gun mounted above the upper wing, usually with the mounting having limited depression to avoid hitting the propeller. There was yet another possibility. From as early as 1912 engineers and inventors had investigated the possibility of arranging a gun to fire through the hub of the propeller. Many early fighters – including the first scheme for one of the best fighters of the entire war, the S.E.5 – were planned to have a machine-gun or even a large-calibre cannon mounted close beside or between the cylinder blocks of a geared engine, and with the barrel passing through the gearbox and hollow propeller shaft. This became common only in the years after 1918, but there was one really remarkable fighter of early 1917 that solved the problem in a novel way. The ace Charles Nungesser asked Armand Dufaux if he could build a small high-speed fighter capable of mounting a heavy-calibre cannon firing ahead. Dufaux's answer was to use two rotary engines mounted sideways in the nose driving the hollow propeller shaft through bevel gears, with the big gun down the centreline.

But all these clever and not-so-clever schemes were destined to be mere side issues. The mainstream of fighter development was to centre on the gun arranged to fire safely past the blades of a propeller, and like so many other human achievements it was ignored until it was adopted by the enemy. By the outbreak of war there cannot have been anyone interested in the subject who did not know at least some of the patents and firing trials that had related to interrupter gears or synchronising gears, but no action was taken. The way such armament finally came about was circuitous. In his pre-war trials on the ground Saulnier had got a good mechanism working but had been completely thwarted by

Morane-Saulnier Type N

The Type N made its public debut just before the outbreak of the First World War, being flown by Roland Garros. After Garros was shot down and captured while flying the first Morane-Saulnier Type L fitted with a forward-firing machine-gun, his close friend Eugene Gilbert of Escadrille MS.23 named his Type N *Le Vengeur* (Avenger) and set out to continue his friend's work. The French *Aviation Militaire* was sufficiently impressed by the Type N's abilities to order a limited number, and the aircraft also served with the Royal Flying Corps

Span: 26 ft 8½ in *Length:* 19 ft 1½ in *Engine:* Le Rhône 9C, 80 hp *Max speed:* 90 mph at sea level *Max take-off weight:* 976 lb *Armament:* 1 ×8-mm Hotchkiss, 0.303-in Vickers or 0.303-in Lewis mg

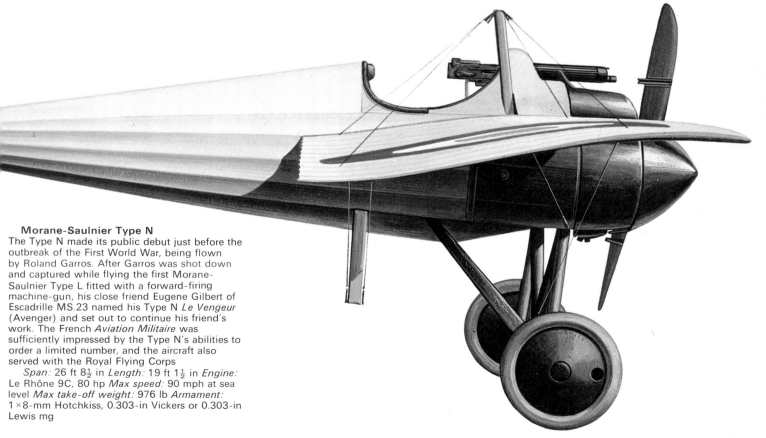

the Hotchkiss ammunition, which was prone to 'hang fire' – a moment's delay before the round fired – and this was enough to hit the propeller blade with the scheme Saulnier had devised. After trying to find an answer Saulnier gave up and resorted to 'brute force and ignorance' by simply fitting the propeller with deflectors.

Morane-Saulnier's brilliant pilot Roland Garros, who had done more than anyone to spread the fame of the company from 1912 onward, joined the Aviation Militaire and obtained permission to try out the bullet-deflector idea in flight. His main contribution was to reshape the propeller with a narrow portion in line with the gun, so that the deflector could be smaller. He experimented for months, sometimes with catastrophic results, until after patient work by his mechanic Jules Hué he had a system that worked reliably. This was in February 1915. Features of the definitive deflectors included a channel shape, to guide the bullets, and strong braces linking them to the propeller shaft; it was also important to use copper or thick-jacketed bullets that did not shatter when they hit the wedge-shaped deflector. Garros returned to his combat unit in March 1915 eager to try out his new forward-firing gun. The French authorities still showed no interest, and even cancelled an order to convert more Morane-Saulnier Type L parasol monoplanes to carry such a gun. But Garros flew as often as he could, and on 1 April, 1915, chanced on a formation of four Albatros two-seaters. The German crews doubtless saw the little Morane but gave it little thought as it dived at them. Then, as if by magic, machine-gun fire spurted out in front of it. After three clips from his Hotchkiss the first Albatross was spinning down in flames. The others beat it for home, and reported what had happened. On 15 April Garros got another Hun and on the 18th a third (many reports insist that he scored five confirmed victories between 1 and 18 April, 1915). But on 18 April, he foolishly made a low-level bombing mission on Courtrai railway station; hit by ground fire, he force-landed and only partly succeeded in burning his aircraft.

Deadly Fokker
The Germans were intensely interested in Garros' aircraft. The gun and engine/propeller installation were removed and set up as a display exhibit to study how it worked. The Dutch aircraft designer Anthony Fokker was shown the Garros gear and ordered to fit a copy on his new monoplane. But Fokker did better than this. He had tried to design aircraft for Britain, but been turned down. In Germany he flew a copy of the Morane-Saulnier Type H in 1913. His copy, called M.5, was developed with short-span wings (M.5K) and long-span (M.5L). By 1915 both were in small-scale service, but as they could not carry armament they were not especially useful. Fokker at once saw how ideal his nimble monoplane would be as a carrier of a forward-firing gun. In his autobiography he claimed to have invented synchronising gear, but what actually happened is that his team of engineers – who knew of Schneider's pre-war scheme – decided that a proper synchronising gear was better than mere deflectors. Within a week they had designed, built, tested, improved and fully developed a simple interrupter gear that was to bring about a dramatic change in

fortunes in the air war.

It so happened that Fokker's mechanism, which normally fired one round for every two revolutions of the propeller (ie, four blades), arrived just as the Imperial Aviation Service was being completely overhauled and turned into a much more dynamic and aggressive force by the new *Feldflugchef*, Major Hermann von der Leith-Thomsen. The Fokker with the forward-firing gun was put into urgent mass-production (numbers were still modest, but they were measured in hundreds, where before there had not even been tens). It was called the E.I (E=Eindecker=monoplane), and the first to reach the Western front was given to an exceptional pilot, Oswald Boelcke, in June 1915. By July the E.II was in service, with an Oberursel rotary (similar to the French Le Rhône) of 100 hp, instead of only 80 hp. Though still light and seemingly flimsy aircraft, they were deadly, especially in the hands of such pilots as Boelcke, Max Immelmann, Ernst Udet and most of the future aces of the Imperial Aviation Service.

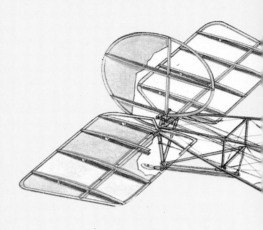

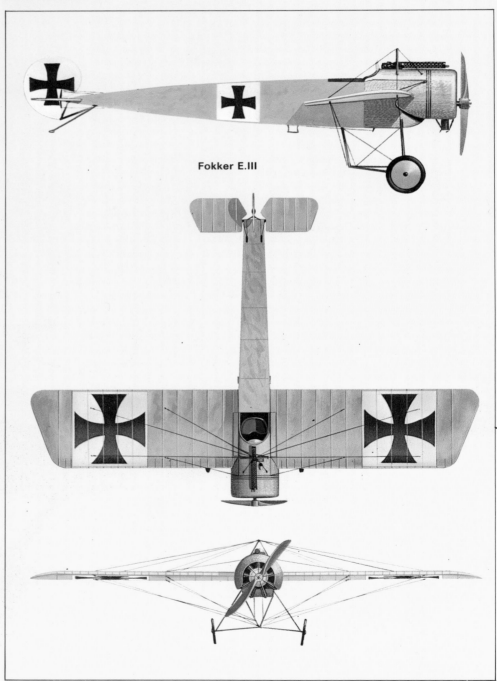

Fokker E.III

20

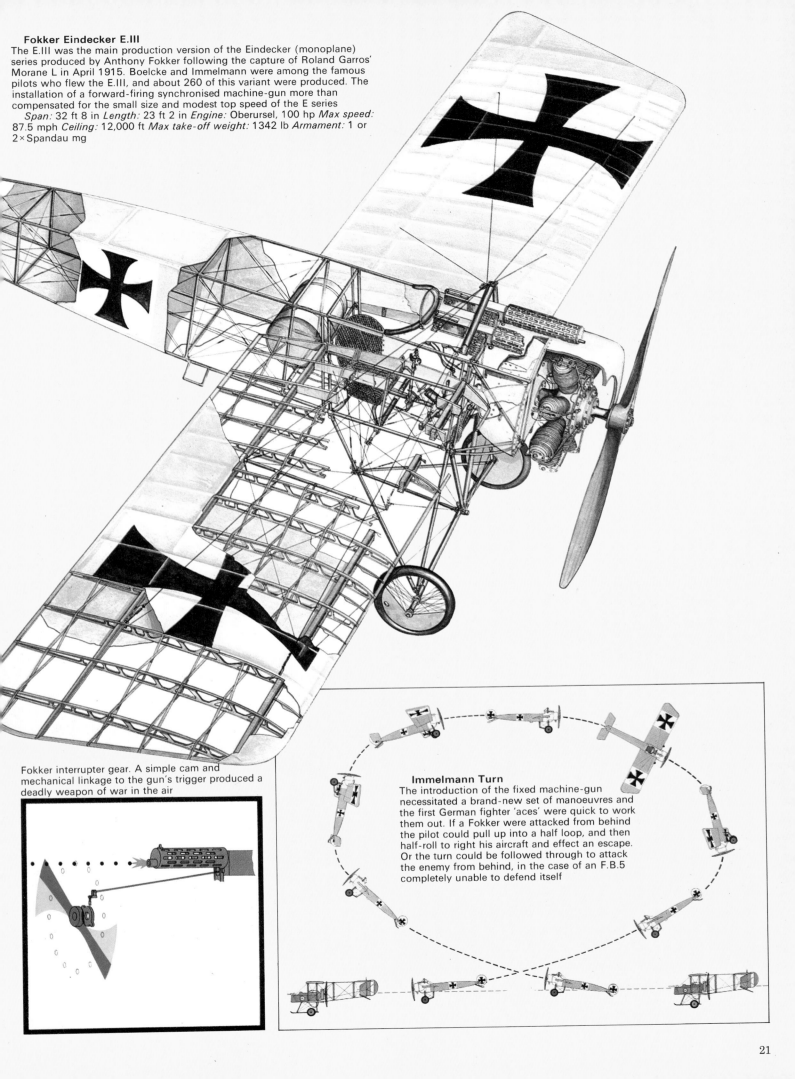

Fokker Eindecker E.III

The E.III was the main production version of the Eindecker (monoplane) series produced by Anthony Fokker following the capture of Roland Garros' Morane L in April 1915. Boelcke and Immelmann were among the famous pilots who flew the E.III, and about 260 of this variant were produced. The installation of a forward-firing synchronised machine-gun more than compensated for the small size and modest top speed of the E series

Span: 32 ft 8 in *Length:* 23 ft 2 in *Engine:* Oberursel, 100 hp *Max speed:* 87.5 mph *Ceiling:* 12,000 ft *Max take-off weight:* 1342 lb *Armament:* 1 or 2×Spandau mg

Fokker interrupter gear. A simple cam and mechanical linkage to the gun's trigger produced a deadly weapon of war in the air

Immelmann Turn

The introduction of the fixed machine-gun necessitated a brand-new set of manoeuvres and the first German fighter 'aces' were quick to work them out. If a Fokker were attacked from behind the pilot could pull up into a half loop, and then half-roll to right his aircraft and effect an escape. Or the turn could be followed through to attack the enemy from behind, in the case of an F.B.5 completely unable to defend itself

FORGING THE WEAPONS

On 1 August, 1915, the RFC raided the home base of *Fliegerabteilung* 62 at Douai. This happened to be the E.II squadron that had led all others in receiving new equipment, and its pilots included Boelcke and Immelmann. The two outstanding Germans took off, chased the raiders and brought one down (it would have been two, but Boelcke's gun jammed). This can fairly be described as the day the fighter came into existence. From then onwards a quite small number of Fokker monoplanes completely turned the tables on the Allies, who were bringing to the front thousands of hastily trained young aircrew and thousands of almost defenceless aircraft. The most numerous RFC type was the B.E.2c, which not only could not defend itself but was so strongly stable that it could not be manoeuvred out of the line of fire. By October the life-expectancy of an Allied pilot on the Western front had been reduced to a week or two – unless his aircraft was kept on the ground by unserviceability or bad weather. Newspapers wrote of the 'Fokker scourge', while the British Parliament described the enormous numbers of replacement RFC pilots as 'Fokker fodder'. What was not explained was why the Allies had consistently refused to show any interest in fighter armament.

The Eindecker itself was merely a pleasant little platform on which to mount a machine gun. With a speed of 83 mph it was only just fast enough to catch most Allied machines, and its success came increasingly from carefully planned tactics, bold flying and the skill of its pilots. 'Beware the Hun in the Sun' was a vital piece of advice as early as January 1916, and though the German pilots (and the Austro-Hungarians, who also used the E-types) had yet to work out how to operate as a team, they individually learned techniques that would save time, maximise the time their guns could be brought to bear on a target, and increase their own chances of survival. At this time no pilots had parachutes, very few aircraft

had armour or any other protection, and everything depended on the pilot's own alertness (in all directions), vision from the cockpit, aircraft performance and manoeuvrability, and the reliability of his guns. On the whole the last factor was poor. Especially in the air, guns frequently jammed, as explained in a later chapter. The pilots who could handle all these factors, and never forget any of them for a moment, were those who racked up scores of victories. Until the Fokker E-type there had never been any real 'fighter pilots'. Suddenly Germany realized that the public and front-line troops wanted heroes, and in Boelcke and Immelmann they found them. The two aces, the first in the world, later split and worked in different sectors in friendly rivalry. Eventually Immelmann, who gave his name to the climbing 180° turn formed by a half-loop followed by a half-roll, plunged to his death on 28 June, 1916, with 15 victories to his credit. The great Boelcke was killed after a mid-air collision on 28, October, 1916, with 40 victories.

The little monoplane that struck terror into the Allied flyers, a mere copy of a 1913 French machine, eventually drove home to the Allied leaders that fighting aircraft were important. Without a synchronised gun, the only available aircraft were the Gunbus, the D.H.2, the 'Fee' and, probably best of all, the French Nieuport XI. Called the *Bébé* (Baby) when it entered Aviation Militaire and RNAS service in mid-1915, the trim Nieuport was one of a long and very important series of combat aircraft designed by Gustave Delage. The XI was possibly the smallest major warplane in history, with very compact dimensions and a gross weight of only 1058 lb, compared with about 1400 lb for the Fokker monoplanes. Thus, though it had only an 80-hp Le Rhône

rotary engine, it could reach almost 100 mph, and it was as nimble as anything in the sky. The only drawback was that the Lewis machine gun had to be mounted above the upper wing to clear the propeller, and the pilot had to fly with one hand, sight while looking straight ahead and reach up with one arm in the full blast of the slipstream to grasp the pistol grip and fire. Changing drums was not normally tried.

Hanriot HD.1
The HD.1 appeared slightly later than the Spad 7.C1 and failed to impress the *Aviation Militaire* sufficiently to be selected as a replacement for the earlier type. Despite this setback, however, the HD.1 was adopted by the Italians and was built in substantial numbers by Nieuport Macchi
Span: 28 ft 6½ in *Length:* 29 ft 2 in *Engine:* Le Rhône 9Ja, 110 hp; Le Rhône 9Jb, 120 hp; Le Rhône 9Jby, 130 hp; or Clerget 9B, 130 hp *Max speed:* 115 mph at sea level with Le Rhône 9Jb *Ceiling:* 20,000 ft *Max take-off weight:* 1330 lb *Armament:* 1 × Vickers 0.303-in mg

The redoubtable Cdr Samson RNAS and his Nieuport XI

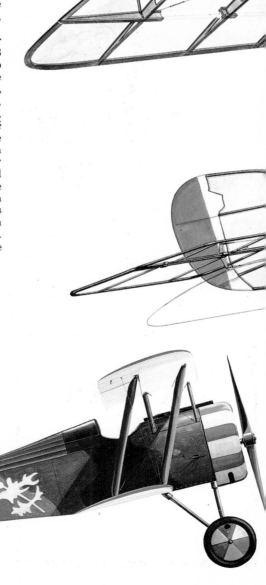

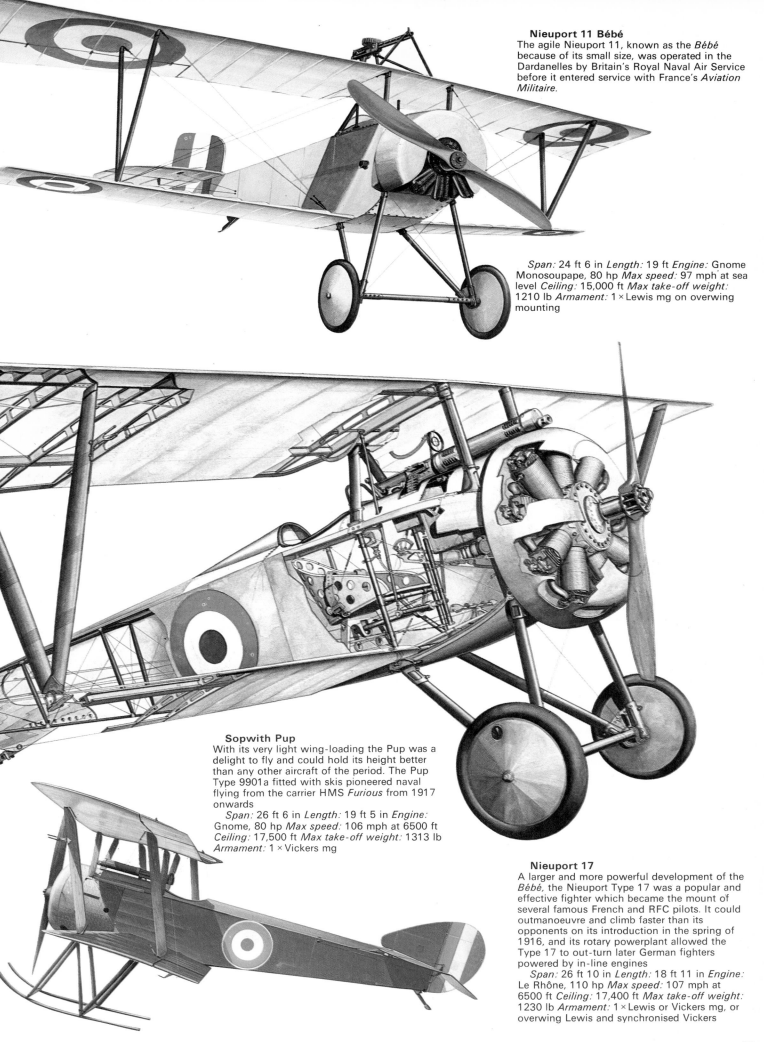

Nieuport 11 Bébé
The agile Nieuport 11, known as the *Bébé* because of its small size, was operated in the Dardanelles by Britain's Royal Naval Air Service before it entered service with France's *Aviation Militaire.*

Span: 24 ft 6 in *Length:* 19 ft *Engine:* Gnome Monosoupape, 80 hp *Max speed:* 97 mph at sea level *Ceiling:* 15,000 ft *Max take-off weight:* 1210 lb *Armament:* 1 × Lewis mg on overwing mounting

Sopwith Pup
With its very light wing-loading the Pup was a delight to fly and could hold its height better than any other aircraft of the period. The Pup Type 9901a fitted with skis pioneered naval flying from the carrier HMS *Furious* from 1917 onwards
Span: 26 ft 6 in *Length:* 19 ft 5 in *Engine:* Gnome, 80 hp *Max speed:* 106 mph at 6500 ft *Ceiling:* 17,500 ft *Max take-off weight:* 1313 lb *Armament:* 1 × Vickers mg

Nieuport 17
A larger and more powerful development of the *Bébé,* the Nieuport Type 17 was a popular and effective fighter which became the mount of several famous French and RFC pilots. It could outmanoeuvre and climb faster than its opponents on its introduction in the spring of 1916, and its rotary powerplant allowed the Type 17 to out-turn later German fighters powered by in-line engines
Span: 26 ft 10 in *Length:* 18 ft 11 in *Engine:* Le Rhône, 110 hp *Max speed:* 107 mph at 6500 ft *Ceiling:* 17,400 ft *Max take-off weight:* 1230 lb *Armament:* 1 × Lewis or Vickers mg, or overwing Lewis and synchronised Vickers

At this time fighters were still lightly built and powered by small engines. Though most were reasonably safe in normal flight, the stresses imposed in the new art of dogfighting were still partly unknown. Even local damage from a single bullet could cause total collapse of primary structure, or the fabric to peel from a wing, while the basic flying characteristics of many aircraft were highly dangerous. Some had engines prone to catch fire without help from the enemy, while others were almost impossible to recover from a spin. About three-quarters of the primary structural members – more in some aircraft, fewer in others – were of wood, and in many aircraft the wood itself was below nominal strength, faulty or even too short for the part and thus connected by joints of untried strength. Gradually the strength of airframes and materials became better understood in precise numerical terms, but this was counterbalanced by the fact that, as the war continued, the best structural hardwoods were used up and poorer materials took their place.

With the earliest fighting scouts it made quite a difference whether the pilot was a big man or a small one. A single machine-gun and ammunition represented as much as one-tenth of the total laden weight, and the recoil of a Lewis on the upper wing could tilt the nose up sufficiently to cause the bullets to pass harmlessly above the enemy. Two guns was often too much, and after Immelmann had burdened his E.III with three Spandaus he thought better of it and removed one. The obvious next stage in fighter development was to increase engine power, to carry heavier loads, climb faster and more steeply and reach higher speeds.

It was here that the traditional rotary engines began to show their limitations. Though at the 80–100-hp level they were neat and light, as power was increased they began to become more complex and relatively heavier, and their spinning mass exerted such a powerful gyroscopic effect as to dominate the aircraft in which they were fitted. Even the 130-hp Clerget 9B made the otherwise excellent Sopwith F.1 Camel an exceedingly tricky machine to fly, and with the inexorable demand for more power the future for rotaries was not promising. The original engines were mostly of nine cylinders, and it was found possible to squeeze 11 into a single row and push power up to 200 hp. Some engine manufacturers developed two-row rotary engines, while others worked hard to wring more power from each cylinder. One of the latter was Lt W O Bentley (later to be famed for his cars) who in 1917 produced a nine-cylinder rotary rated at 230 hp yet posing less of a gyroscopic problem than the Clerget. Such engines remained in mass production to the end of the war, because they combined the essentials needed.

Albatros D.III
The D.III, with a narrow-chord lower wing and V-shaped interplane struts *à la Nieuport* to improve visibility, enjoyed a brief period of ascendancy in the spring of 1917 before it came up against the new British fighters
Span: 29 ft 6¼ in *Length:* 24 ft *Engine:* Mercedes, 160 hp *Max speed:* 109 mph at 3200 ft *Ceiling:* 18,000 ft *Max take-off weight:* 1950 lb *Armament:* 2×Spandau mg

Roland C.II
The dumpy Roland C.II, nicknamed *Walfisch* (Whale), had a substantial endurance – thanks partly to its low drag, achieved by keeping interplane bracing to a minimum – and was employed as a long-range escort in addition to its primary role of reconnaissance. The type entered service in early 1916, and nearly 300 were built in all
Span: 33 ft 10¾ in *Length:* 24 ft 8 in *Engine:* Mercedes, 160 hp *Max speed:* 103 mph *Max take-off weight:* 2885 lb *Armament:* 1 × Parabellum mg plus, in some aircraft, Spandau mg

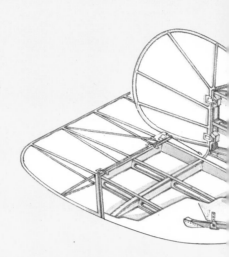

Lt Danhuber in his Albatros D.Va. Accessibility of the guns was an important factor if they jammed

Albatros D.V
The D.V was developed as a successor to the D.III, the D.IV having suffered from being fitted with the unreliable Mercedes geared 160-hp engine. The D.V was structurally weak but was built in substantial numbers to fill the gap left by the Pfalz D.III and Fokker Triplane, neither of which came up to expectations. The final D.Va variant was still in service at the time of the Armistice

Span: 29 ft 6½ in *Length:* 24 ft *Engine:* Mercedes, 180 hp *Max speed:* 117 mph at 3200 ft *Ceiling:* 20,500 ft *Max take-off weight:* 2000 lb *Armament:* 2×fixed Spandau mg

Engine designers knew in their hearts that the future belonged to the in-line and the static radial. At first there had been few static radials, one of the types to get into production being the Salmson (Canton-Unné) which had water-cooled cylinders. Nearly all the non-rotary engines had cylinders arranged in line, the Central Powers never departing from their generous and reliable four- and six-cylinder engines and the Allies building large numbers with six, eight or 12 cylinders in vee formation. Three of the most important early builders, the Royal Aircraft Factory (RAF), Beardmore and Renault, were gradually eclipsed by the Hispano-Suiza and Rolls-Royce companies which succeeded brilliantly in pushing up the power of a single engine to 300 hp and beyond. In 1917 the United States entered the war and a consortium of car manufacturers, assisted by Allied engineers, very quickly designed an advanced V12 which was soon in production on an unprecedented scale at a power of 400 hp. This engine, the Liberty, was no short-term lash-up and many were in service in the 1930s.

With ample power available, fighters became larger, faster and more heavily armed. As described in the next chapter, numerous schemes were perfected for synchronising fixed guns, and by 1916 the usual forward-

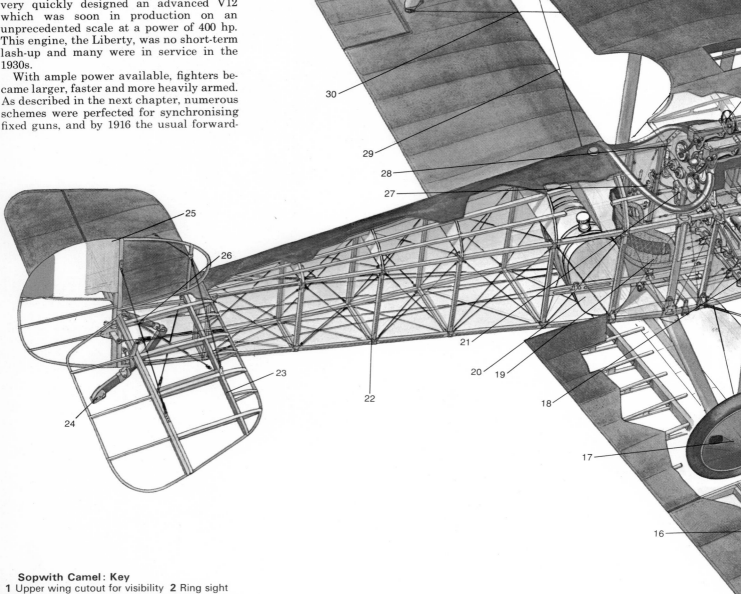

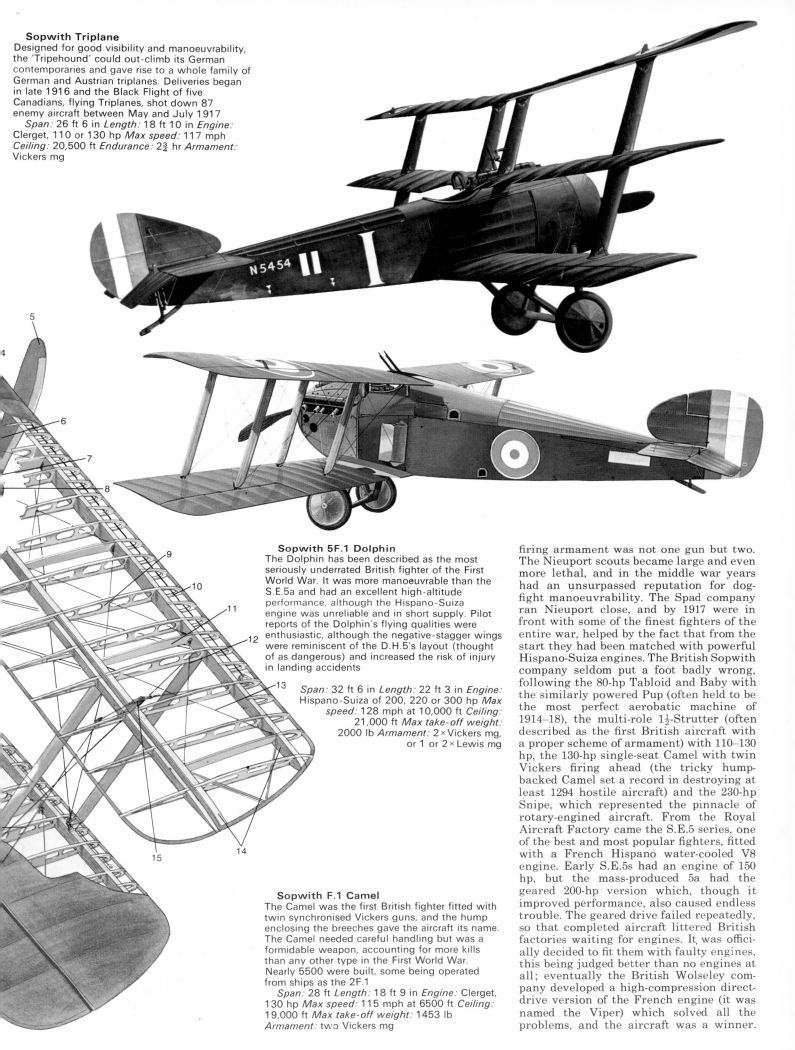

Sopwith Triplane
Designed for good visibility and manoeuvrability, the 'Tripehound' could out-climb its German contemporaries and gave rise to a whole family of German and Austrian triplanes. Deliveries began in late 1916 and the Black Flight of five Canadians, flying Triplanes, shot down 87 enemy aircraft between May and July 1917
Span: 26 ft 6 in *Length:* 18 ft 10 in *Engine:* Clerget, 110 or 130 hp *Max speed:* 117 mph *Ceiling:* 20,500 ft *Endurance:* 2¾ hr *Armament:* Vickers mg

Sopwith 5F.1 Dolphin
The Dolphin has been described as the most seriously underrated British fighter of the First World War. It was more manoeuvrable than the S.E.5a and had an excellent high-altitude performance, although the Hispano-Suiza engine was unreliable and in short supply. Pilot reports of the Dolphin's flying qualities were enthusiastic, although the negative-stagger wings were reminiscent of the D.H.5's layout (thought of as dangerous) and increased the risk of injury in landing accidents
Span: 32 ft 6 in *Length:* 22 ft 3 in *Engine:* Hispano-Suiza of 200, 220 or 300 hp *Max speed:* 128 mph at 10,000 ft *Ceiling:* 21,000 ft *Max take-off weight:* 2000 lb *Armament:* 2 × Vickers mg, or 1 or 2 × Lewis mg

Sopwith F.1 Camel
The Camel was the first British fighter fitted with twin synchronised Vickers guns, and the hump enclosing the breeches gave the aircraft its name. The Camel needed careful handling but was a formidable weapon, accounting for more kills than any other type in the First World War. Nearly 5500 were built, some being operated from ships as the 2F.1
Span: 28 ft *Length:* 18 ft 9 in *Engine:* Clerget, 130 hp *Max speed:* 115 mph at 6500 ft *Ceiling:* 19,000 ft *Max take-off weight:* 1453 lb *Armament:* two Vickers mg

firing armament was not one gun but two. The Nieuport scouts became large and even more lethal, and in the middle war years had an unsurpassed reputation for dog-fight manoeuvrability. The Spad company ran Nieuport close, and by 1917 were in front with some of the finest fighters of the entire war, helped by the fact that from the start they had been matched with powerful Hispano-Suiza engines. The British Sopwith company seldom put a foot badly wrong, following the 80-hp Tabloid and Baby with the similarly powered Pup (often held to be the most perfect aerobatic machine of 1914–18), the multi-role 1½-Strutter (often described as the first British aircraft with a proper scheme of armament) with 110–130 hp, the 130-hp single-seat Camel with twin Vickers firing ahead (the tricky hump-backed Camel set a record in destroying at least 1294 hostile aircraft) and the 230-hp Snipe, which represented the pinnacle of rotary-engined aircraft. From the Royal Aircraft Factory came the S.E.5 series, one of the best and most popular fighters, fitted with a French Hispano water-cooled V8 engine. Early S.E.5s had an engine of 150 hp, but the mass-produced 5a had the geared 200-hp version which, though it improved performance, also caused endless trouble. The geared drive failed repeatedly, so that completed aircraft littered British factories waiting for engines. It was officially decided to fit them with faulty engines, this being judged better than no engines at all; eventually the British Wolseley company developed a high-compression direct-drive version of the French engine (it was named the Viper) which solved all the problems, and the aircraft was a winner.

During the first quarter of 1916 the Sopwith design team, while delighted at the outstanding combat manoeuvrability of the Pup, considered how this might be improved further. The ability to roll or turn quickly had never before been very important in aircraft design, but by 1916 this had been recognised as central to the very concept of a fighter, especially one whose armament was fixed to fire ahead. Sopwith's designers, led by Herbert Smith, thought it worth trying a triplane version of the Pup, and the prototype Triplane flew in May 1916 and, with a Vickers gun added, was tested on the Western front the following month. Its unusual appearance emphasised its excellent manoeuvrability and rate of climb, and though only 266 were built – all used by the RNAS – the nimble Triplane had a fantastic impact on the enemy. General von Hoeppner, commander of the Imperial Air Service, went into raptures over it, and within days almost every fighter builder in the Central Powers was trying to build an 'answer'. Eventually 14 German and Austro-Hungarian fighter triplanes were developed, but the only one to see extensive service was Fokker's Dr.I (Dr. = Dreidecker = three-winger). Fokker had been so desperate to find out about Sopwith's machine that he

had – so the story goes – improperly arranged for his factory to receive the wreck of the first RNAS Triplane to be shot down. In fact Fokker's brilliant designer, Reinhold Platz, was not sold on the triplane at all, and in any case produced a totally different machine which in its original form did not have interplane struts (later a single, streamlined strut was added to link the three wings). Like the Sopwith, the Dr.I was extremely manoeuvrable, and though it was smaller and lighter it carried two guns. Yet, like the Sopwith, it was made in only modest numbers. It was never completely outclassed, and the greatest of all First World War aces, Manfred von Richthofen, was flying a Dr.I when he met his death on 21 April, 1918. But the triplane and the numerous quadruplanes played only a minor part in the overall conflict.

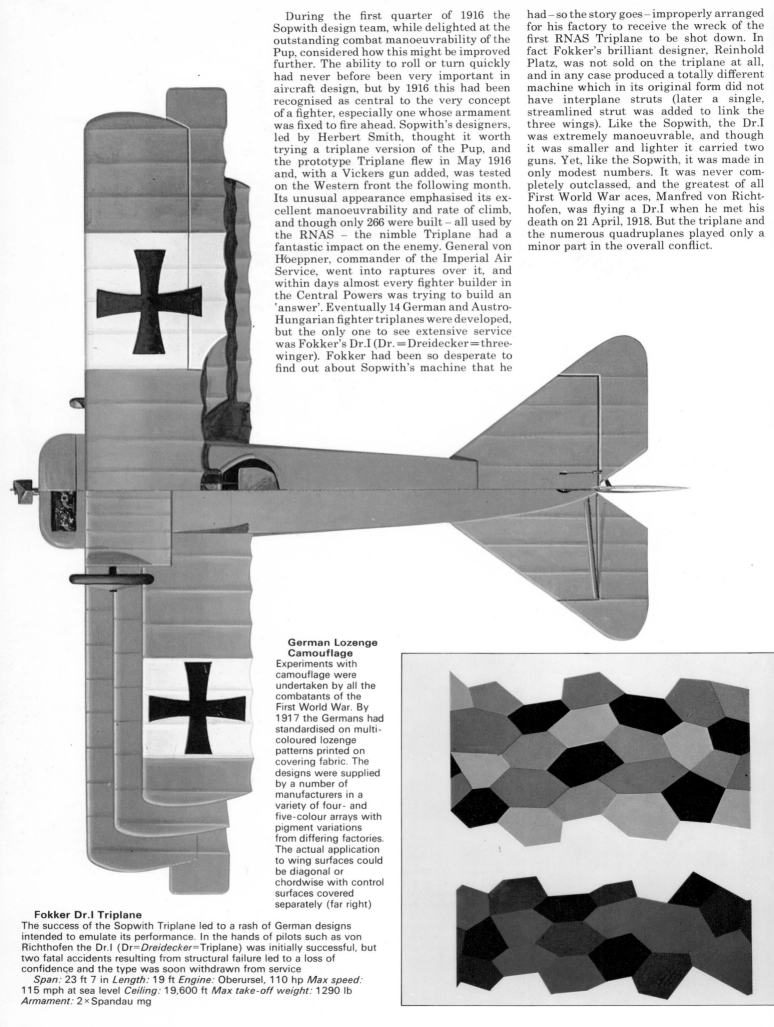

German Lozenge Camouflage
Experiments with camouflage were undertaken by all the combatants of the First World War. By 1917 the Germans had standardised on multi-coloured lozenge patterns printed on covering fabric. The designs were supplied by a number of manufacturers in a variety of four- and five-colour arrays with pigment variations from differing factories. The actual application to wing surfaces could be diagonal or chordwise with control surfaces covered separately (far right)

Fokker Dr.I Triplane
The success of the Sopwith Triplane led to a rash of German designs intended to emulate its performance. In the hands of pilots such as von Richthofen the Dr.I (Dr=*Dreidecker*=Triplane) was initially successful, but two fatal accidents resulting from structural failure led to a loss of confidence and the type was soon withdrawn from service
Span: 23 ft 7 in *Length:* 19 ft *Engine:* Oberursel, 110 hp *Max speed:* 115 mph at sea level *Ceiling:* 19,600 ft *Max take-off weight:* 1290 lb *Armament:* 2 × Spandau mg

The moments before take-off at a Fokker Dr.I-equipped Jasta

Halberstadt D.II

The D.II came into service in 1916 just as the Fokker monoplanes were losing their ascendancy. For a time the D.II outclassed any Allied opposition, combining the climb and handling of a biplane with a synchronised machine-gun. The Allies soon caught up, however, and the frail tail assembly was a weakness. The D.II had disappeared from the Western Front by May 1917

Span: 28 ft 11½ in *Length:* 21 ft 5 in *Engine:* Argus As II, 120 hp *Max speed:* 90 mph
Armament: 2 × Spandau mg

The great von Richthofen discusses the qualities of the Fokker Dr.I with his fellow officers. The aircraft's climb and manoeuvrability made it a favourite mount of the most skilful pilots

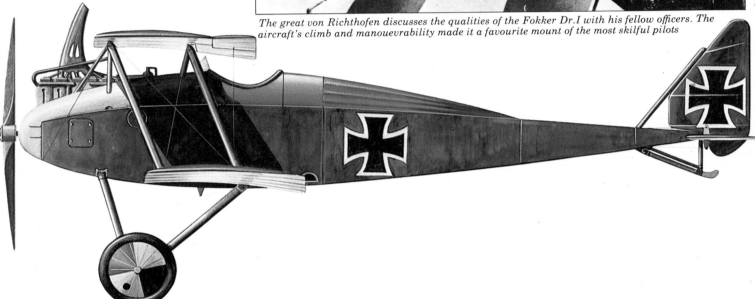

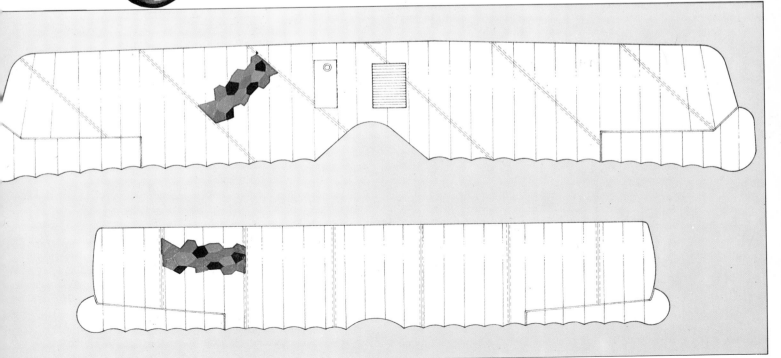

Ground Attack Fighters: Keeping the enemy's head down

By 1917 the pattern of aerial warfare was set – Reconnaissance aircraft spotting for the guns while ever more potent fighters duelled for air superiority. Then the Germans led the way with a new concept – ground-attack fighters spearheading offensives by actually engaging battle on the front line – and British designers were quick to follow

Far more important were the improved two-seat fighters which emerged in 1916–17. The Germans introduced the CL category of two-seat fighters in early 1917 which led to an excellent series of tough and versatile machines. Though naturally bigger and more ponderous than the single-seaters, the 'Hannoveranas', the Halberstadt CL series and the all-metal Junkers monoplanes were quite manoeuvrable, difficult to shoot down and worthy opponents in battle. Carrying various bombs and grenades they also operated in the dangerous close-support role low over the battlefield and at times succeeded in inflicting severe casualties on Allied troops and lowering their morale. Sopwith tried to develop a good aircraft in the same class, but in the Hippo and Bulldog only scored near-misses. The company did achieve great success with a similar design on a slightly smaller scale, the single-seat Dolphin which often had as many as four

machine-guns, and also with heavily armoured derivatives of the small single-seaters designed specifically for 'trench fighting' (ie, close support), the Salamander being the most notable. But by far the most important of all First World War two-seat fighters was the Bristol Fighter.

A Halberstadt CL.II is bombed up with bundles of fragmentation grenades, ready for a close-support mission

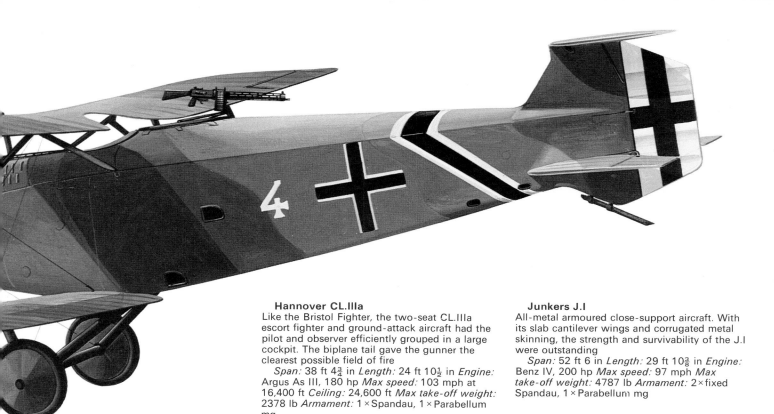

Hannover CL.IIIa
Like the Bristol Fighter, the two-seat CL.IIIa escort fighter and ground-attack aircraft had the pilot and observer efficiently grouped in a large cockpit. The biplane tail gave the gunner the clearest possible field of fire
  Span: 38 ft 4¾ in *Length:* 24 ft 10½ in *Engine:* Argus As III, 180 hp *Max speed:* 103 mph at 16,400 ft *Ceiling:* 24,600 ft *Max take-off weight:* 2378 lb *Armament:* 1 × Spandau, 1 × Parabellum mg

Junkers J.I
All-metal armoured close-support aircraft. With its slab cantilever wings and corrugated metal skinning, the strength and survivability of the J.I were outstanding
  Span: 52 ft 6 in *Length:* 29 ft 10⅜ in *Engine:* Benz IV, 200 hp *Max speed:* 97 mph *Max take-off weight:* 4787 lb *Armament:* 2 × fixed Spandau, 1 × Parabellum mg

A Hannover CL.IIIa (foreground) on the airfield of a Schlasta (Schlachtstaffel – Battle-Squadron), as the German ground-attack units were known

Looking like a curious throwback when it first appeared in 1917, the Vickers FB.26 Vampire might have been a formidable ground-attack aircraft if it had been developed. The pusher layout made several further comebacks during the 1920s

de Havilland D.H.5

The marked back-stagger of the D.H.5 was designed to give the pilot the best possible view, but the loss of aerodynamic efficiency made it difficult to fly. The first batches reached France in 1917 but they were soon relegated to escort work and ground-attack

Span: 25 ft 8 in *Length:* 21 ft 9 in *Engine:* Le Rhône, 110 hp *Max speed:* 102 mph at 10,000 ft *Ceiling:* 16,000 ft *Max take-off weight:* 1492 lb *Armament:* 1 × Vickers mg

With the Ludendorff offensive of March 1918, the Schlastas came into their own. Here a CL.III flies over the troops it is supporting

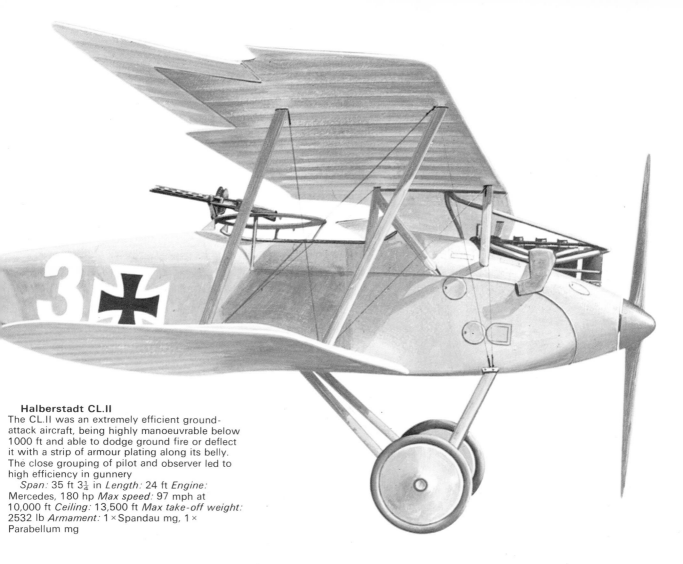

Halberstadt CL.II

The CL.II was an extremely efficient ground-attack aircraft, being highly manoeuvrable below 1000 ft and able to dodge ground fire or deflect it with a strip of armour plating along its belly. The close grouping of pilot and observer led to high efficiency in gunnery

Span: 35 ft 3¼ in *Length:* 24 ft *Engine:* Mercedes, 180 hp *Max speed:* 97 mph at 10,000 ft *Ceiling:* 13,500 ft *Max take-off weight:* 2532 lb *Armament:* 1 × Spandau mg, 1 × Parabellum mg

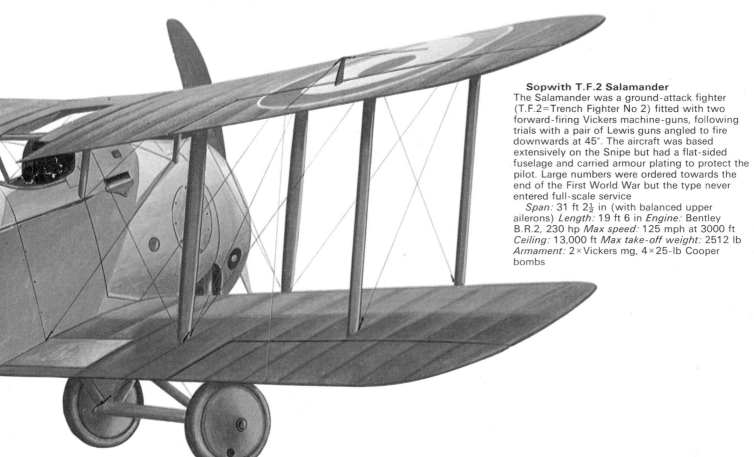

Sopwith T.F.2 Salamander

The Salamander was a ground-attack fighter (T.F.2 = Trench Fighter No 2) fitted with two forward-firing Vickers machine-guns, following trials with a pair of Lewis guns angled to fire downwards at 45°. The aircraft was based extensively on the Snipe but had a flat-sided fuselage and carried armour plating to protect the pilot. Large numbers were ordered towards the end of the First World War but the type never entered full-scale service

Span: 31 ft 2½ in (with balanced upper ailerons) *Length:* 19 ft 6 in *Engine:* Bentley B.R.2, 230 hp *Max speed:* 125 mph at 3000 ft *Ceiling:* 13,000 ft *Max take-off weight:* 2512 lb *Armament:* 2 × Vickers mg, 4 × 25-lb Cooper bombs

The Bristol Fighter

Perhaps the best general-purpose aircraft of the First World War, the Bristol Fighter was outstandingly strong, manoeuvrable and efficient in air combat

This was originally planned as an improved reconnaissance type, but entered production with the 190-hp Rolls-Royce Falcon engine as a fighter, with a fixed Vickers and free Lewis. At first it proved easy meat, because pilots flew straight and level and relied on the observer's gun. Later it was discovered that the tough Bristol could be flung about in a dogfight, and that the observer could still get in shots even under these conditions. Fitted with various engines of 190 to 400 hp, the splendid F.2B version soon gained such a reputation that German fighters would never attack a formation of three or more – so the Bristols deliberately flew in pairs or singly to try and bring the Hun to battle. Squadron after squadron in 1917–18 established complete mastery of local airspace with this quite large two-seater, which succeeded so well simply by having no faults. It was unbreak-

able in combat manoeuvres, the crew were close and could talk, the armament was wholly satisfactory and performance was very good. To show what a Bristol could do, one Canadian crew, Lt (later Maj) A E McKeever and Sgt (later Lt) L F Powell, shot down 30 enemy aircraft in the second half of 1917.

Eventually there were more than 3000 Bristols in action, but by 1918 the main dogfighters were the Camel, S.E.5a, Spad VII and XIII, and the formidable German Albatros D.III and D.V and Fokker D.VII. The German scouts were not exceptional, but merely good conventional machines boldly flown by experienced and aggressive pilots. It says much for the skill of the German designers and pilots that these aircraft were not outclassed even by the time of the Armistice, despite the fact that the Germans lacked engines suitable for fighters giving more than 185 hp. There were small numbers of more powerful engines, including advanced rotaries, but the best fighter of all, the D.VII, usually had only 160 hp. Yet this was the type singled out for special attention by the Allied disarmament control commission in 1918–19. Every D.VII had to be handed over to the Allies; but with a bright young man like Fokker behind it the next stage is not hard to guess.

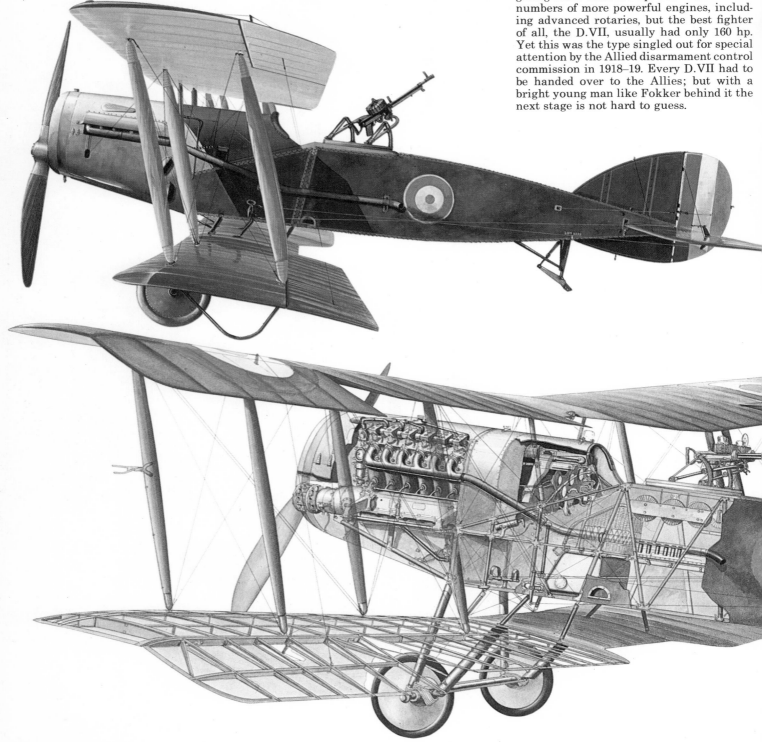

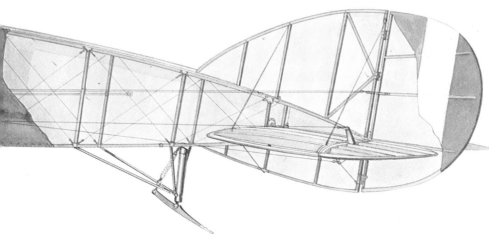

Bristol F.2B Fighter

The F.2B version of the "Brisfit" was fitted with a Rolls-Royce Falcon of up to 275 hp, conferring a performance superior to that of many single-seat contemporaries. The Bristol Fighter was designed to be operated as a conventional fighter with the addition of a sting in the tail in the form of the free-mounted weapons. The type remained in RAF service until 1932

Span: 39 ft 3 in *Length:* 26 ft 2 in *Engine:* Rolls-Royce Falcon of 190, 220 or 275 hp *Max speed:* 125 mph at 3000 ft *Ceiling:* 22,000 ft *Max take-off weight:* 2590 lb *Armament:* 1 × Vickers mg, 1 or 2 × Lewis mg

BIRDS OF PREY

The trenchbound armies of the First World War saw the duels of the airmen at a distance – unless they crashed earthwards, usually in flames. This Camel has crashed almost intact, however, emphasising the structural strength of this machine

Most of the armament carried by aircraft in the First World War was to some degree an improvisation; indeed, even the supposed properly designed armament schemes often failed to work properly (or at all) until they had been completely changed by pilots and fitters in the front-line squadrons. At the same time, the major powers did set up capable research establishments where such questions as aircraft armament were debated and improved. The whole technology of military aviation, and the flying machine itself, was advancing at an unnatural pace, and in this chapter it is necessary to stop for a moment and look at some of the problems.

We are concerned mainly with armament, but what had to be done was to turn the aeroplane from a dangerous and temperamental toy, that with luck could usually be flown in good weather, into a reliable weapon-platform or reconnaissance vehicle that could be flown without fail at a given time no matter what the weather. In fact the true night and all-weather machine could not be achieved until many years later, but advances were nevertheless enormous. Flying by night had been attempted as early as 1910, and the equipment later included an electric accumulator (in large aircraft it was recharged by a small windmill-driven generator) and cockpit lighting, some form of airfield lighting such as flares made from petrol-soaked asbestos carried above the ground in small containers, and searchlights whose crews were skilled in using the lights to convey information. In some

John Batchelor

In 1918, 297 Nieuport 28s were purchased from France as equipment for the first US fighter squadrons. This beautifully preserved example is flown at Chino, California

Imperial War Museum

The Canadian ace Capt W Bishop demonstrates how to change a drum on a Lewis-equipped Nieuport 17

Lewis Gun (left)
Designed by Col I N Lewis (US Army rtd) in 1911, the lightweight gas-operated Lewis was an ideal aircraft weapon and was manufactured in Britain by BSA. The Lewis was taken aloft in 1912 and first used in combat in August 1914. The 'Scarff' ring for observers was standard until well into the Second World War and the Foster mount made it a

standard forward-firing weapon without the synchronising gear of a fuselage-mounted Vickers
Weight: 27 lb *Rate of fire:* 600 rpm

An RFC squadron lines up with its S.E.5a fighters - one of the best British fighters of the war. The Lewis guns on their Foster mounts are clearly visible but the squadron codes have been obscured by the censor

Vickers F.B.12

The pusher layout effectively expired with the D.H.2 and F.E.8 but Vickers produced a rotary-engine powered pusher fighter prototype, the F.B.12, in late 1916. Thirty were ordered in November but poor performance and improved tractor types curtailed any further development
Span: 29 ft 7 in *Length:* 21 ft 10 in *Engine:* Le Rhône, 80 hp *Max speed:* 86 mph at 6500 ft *Ceiling:* 14,500 ft *Max take-off weight:* 1447 lb *Armament:* 1 × Lewis mg

cases searchlights could illuminate hostile aeroplanes or airships, for interception by fighters, while in others the lights could give position information or even send simple prearranged messages. But everyone had to learn the hard way. RFC Lt Slessor, who 40 years later became Chief of the Air Staff, tried to land after a primitive night anti-Zeppelin mission in 1915 but found the airfield shrouded in dense white mist. The airfield searchlight crew decided to help, but instead of aiming at where he was going they pointed the beam right at him. He was, of course, blinded and was no longer able to see even brief glimpses of the ground.

A year later bold pilots of RFC 44 Sqn flew the Camel on night patrol, and from 1916 onwards this very demanding little aircraft became an important night fighter. Why was the Camel difficult to fly? The reasons centred on the engine, which imparted such a strong gyroscopic force that the Camel had to be 'flown' constantly. It could turn like lightning to the right, but in turning to the left the pilot had to fight the effect of the engine (so Camel pilots sometimes turned left by making a 270° turn to the right). Enemy pilots were not slow to do what they could to take advantage of this lopsided characteristic, though the Camel and other rotary-engined machines were never to be taken lightly. The tricky handling of light scouts powered by large spinning engines was, of course, fundamental and incapable of much improvement.

Other basic areas of technology where very considerable progress was made by 1918 concerned flight control and stability, instruments, navigation and pilot equipment. In 1914 the fact that aircraft often appeared to get out of control and spiral straight down to the ground was the subject of apprehensive discussion among pilots. Not until British test pilots deliberately investigated spinning was the problem solved. Lt Wilfred Parke, a Naval pilot, had recovered from a spin in August 1912 but the deadly locked-in situation was not mastered until deep study, rounded off by courageous trials by F A Lindemann (later Lord Cherwell, Britain's Chief Scientist in the Second World War). This removed the terror of spinning, so that by winter 1917–18 it could even be taught to pupils along with a foolproof method of recovery. At the same time the instruments in the cockpit were made more accurate, giving better and more immediate indications of what the aircraft and engine were doing – but still with severe limitations. By 1918 the pilot could safely fly in clear weather, and navigate with map and magnetic compass (and in large aircraft with a mariner's type sextant and plotting charts), but he was in peril if he entered cloud or met fog. Inexplicable

crashes gradually rammed home the lesson that pilots could either lose control in a cloud or lose their orientation. Once they could no longer tell which way was up, they became totally disoriented and could come out of cloud in a screaming dive and discover the ground above them. Unless there was plenty of room to recover, they would just hit the ground. As for pilot equipment, this had from the earliest days included goggles and warm windproof clothing, and during the First World War Sir Geoffrey Taylor solved the basic design problems for a safe parachute (though air forces did not in general adopt this life-saving device until long after 1918).

Almost every other facet of the design of combat aircraft could also be described as a lash-up, but the central factor where fighters are concerned has always been armament. At first there were only infantry weapons, small grenades, bombs and mortars, and a few larger quick-firing guns mainly of naval origin. The standard service rifle was unwieldy, being rather long and difficult to aim in an airstream going past at 60 to 100 mph, yet it was the only authorised RFC weapon at the outbreak of war. Most handguns, such as pistols and revolvers, were so inaccurate and difficult to aim in

air combat as to be of very limited value, though the long-barrelled German pistols (especially the Mauser) could be aimed much more accurately when clipped to their wooden holsters, turning them almost into low-power rifles.

Until 1914 little thought had been given to armament actually attached to the aircraft. In any case the most likely weapon, the machine-gun, was still considered rather new and ungentlemanly, and the machine-guns adopted as standard army weapons were almost all large and cumbersome, and needed water to cool the barrel. One of the very few reasonably light guns was the Benet-Mercier, the standard machine-gun of the US Army Signal Corps, and was thus the world's first 'fighter armament', but simply did not fit. The Wright biplanes sat the pilot and machine-gunner side-by-side, and the Benet-Mercier had a long rigid ammunition feed projecting on one side and an equally long ejector chute on the other. No matter which way round the pilot and gunner sat the gun fouled the control columns and made flight impossible. Later the neat drum-fed Lewis was admitted, and this compact air-cooled weapon was made in larger numbers than any other for air use in the First World War.

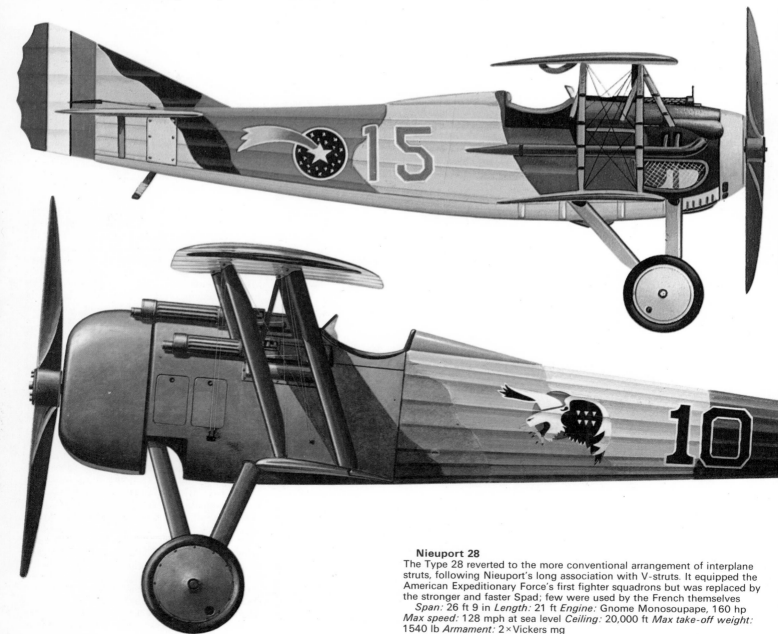

Nieuport 28
The Type 28 reverted to the more conventional arrangement of interplane struts, following Nieuport's long association with V-struts. It equipped the American Expeditionary Force's first fighter squadrons but was replaced by the stronger and faster Spad; few were used by the French themselves
Span: 26 ft 9 in *Length:* 21 ft *Engine:* Gnome Monosoupape, 160 hp
Max speed: 128 mph at sea level *Ceiling:* 20,000 ft *Max take-off weight:*
1540 lb *Armament:* 2 × Vickers mg

Italy entered the war in 1915 with some experience of air fighting – over Tripoli in 1911. Macchi built under licence the Nieuport XI seen equipping this Squadriglia in 1917

Ansaldo SVA.5

The SVA series of fighters (Savoia-Verduzio-Ansaldo) represented the best of Italy's indigenous wartime fighter aircraft. If not quite up to other Allied types, it served successfully as a bomber and scout and some remained in service until the mid-1930s

Span: 29 ft 10¼ in *Length:* 26 ft 7 in *Engine:* SPA 6A, 220 hp *Max speed:* 143 mph *Max take-off weight:* 2315 lb *Armament:* 2×Vickers mg

Spad S.13

By the last year of the First World War the Spad 13 was the standard French fighter, having succeeded the smaller and less powerful S.7. The S.13 was strong and fast, although less manoeuvrable at height than its German contemporaries. Nearly 8500 were built, and the type remained in service with the *Aviation Militaire* until 1923. The S.13 was also operated by Italy and Belgium; it would have been built in large numbers in the United States had the war continued

Span: 26 ft 11 in *Length:* 20 ft 8 in *Engine:* Hispano-Suiza, 200 hp *Max speed:* 130 mph at 6500 ft *Ceiling:* 22,300 ft *Max take-off weight:* 1815 lb *Armament:* 2×Vickers mg

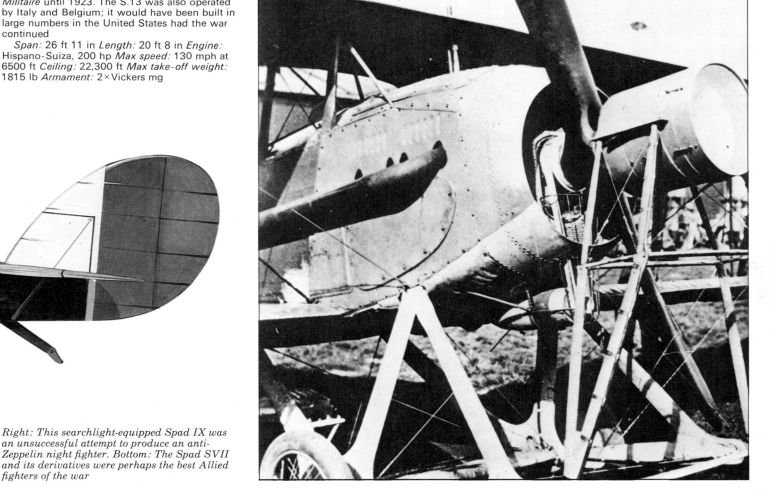

Right: This searchlight-equipped Spad IX was an unsuccessful attempt to produce an anti-Zeppelin night fighter. Bottom: The Spad SVII and its derivatives were perhaps the best Allied fighters of the war

Fortunately the RFC and RNAS were both permitted to use the Lewis at an early date, before August 1914. Two years earlier the first trials were held at Farnborough with a B.E., and later with a prototype F.E.2, carrying a weighty Maxim machine gun, but fortunately such a weapon was never issued to the RFC. Instead the light gas-operated Lewis was standardised, and it was used both with and without the fat air-cooling casing that was necessary on non-flying Lewises. The latter invariably had a 47-round drum magazine, but in aerial use a deeper 97-round drum was often used. This enabled longer bursts, or more bursts, to be fired without changing drums, but the actual task of changing the heavy drums was no joke in a single-seater. It was no joke to the observer either, if the aircraft was wildly manoeuvring in a dogfight, but the single-seat fighter pilot had to change drums with the Lewis pulled down from its

Above: The observer on a German two-seater services his Parabellum machine-gun. Below: An RFC wall chart on just how to attack a two-seater and avoid giving the rear gunner his chance

INCORRECT METHOD.
THE NATURAL INCLINATION OF THE ATTACKER, IF INEXPERIENCED, IS TO TURN IN THE SAME DIRECTION AND FOLLOW.
THIS RESULTS IN GIVING THE ENEMY JUST THE OPPORTUNITY HE DESIRES.

2ND POSITION
SCOUT FOILS ENEMY'S ATTEMPT BY IMMEDI-ATE TURN IN OPPOSITE DIRECTION.

1ST POSITION
ATTACKING MACHINE DIRECTLY BEHIND & BELOW OPPONENT.

3RD POSITION
REGAINS FAVOURABLE ATTACKING POSITION BY TURNING TOWARDS ENEMY.

2ND POSITION
ENEMY MACHINE BANKING IN AN ATTEMPT TO BRING HIS GUN TO BEAR ON SCOUT

1ST POSITION
ENEMY'S GUN UNABLE TO BEAR ON SCOUT.

3RD POSITION
ENEMY MACHINE COMING OFF HIS BANK AS MANO-EUVRE HAS FAILED.

4TH POSITION
ATTACKING MACHINE AGAIN IN POSITION UNDER ENEMY'S TAIL.

4TH POSITION
ENEMY'S GUN AGAIN UNABLE TO BEAR ON SCOUT.

A HOSTILE TWO-SEATER WHEN ATTACKED FROM BEHIND AND BELOW ALMOST INVARIABLY TURNS WITH A VIEW TO BRINGING THE OBSERVER'S GUN TO BEAR ON THE ATTACKER.
THIS MANOEUVRE CAN BE EFFECTIVELY COUNTERED BY TURNING AT FIRST IN THE OPPOSITE DIRECTION AND THEN, TAKING ADVANTAGE OF SUPERIOR SPEED AND HANDINESS, TURNING AFTER THE ENEMY AND AGAIN COMING UNDER HIS TAIL.

Pfalz D.XII
The D.XII saw only a few weeks' action in the
autumn of 1918 as a substitute for the Fokker
D.VII, which was in short supply. It could
withstand considerable punishment but was
sluggish, had a poor rate of climb and was
difficult to maintain
Span: 29 ft 6 in *Length:* 20 ft 11 in *Engine:*
Mercedes, 160 hp *Max speed:* 120 mph at sea
level *Ceiling:* 18,500 ft *Max take-off weight:*
1960 lb *Armament:* 2×Spandau mg

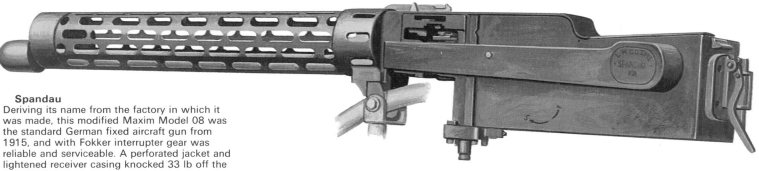

Spandau
Deriving its name from the factory in which it
was made, this modified Maxim Model 08 was
the standard German fixed aircraft gun from
1915, and with Fokker interrupter gear was
reliable and serviceable. A perforated jacket and
lightened receiver casing knocked 33 lb off the
weight of the weapon

Parabellum
An early modification of the Maxim to provide a
lightweight aircraft gun for flexible mountings,
the 7.92-mm gun was standard on nearly every
German two-seater
Weight: 22 lb *Rate of fire:* 700 rpm

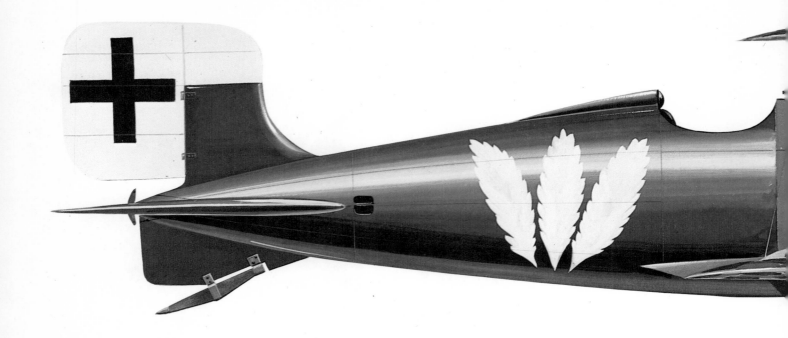

Foster mount into a high-speed airflow while he also tried to fly the aircraft (indeed, he was likely to be engaged in a fierce dogfight). Sometimes the sheer mass of the 97-round drum, combined with 'g' and wind loads, would almost break the pilot's wrist.

Many Lewis were fixed obliquely, firing outwards past the tractor propeller, or upwards. Observers began with plain spigot mounts, some aircraft having as many as four spigot sockets around the cockpit into which the gun could be placed. RFC Capt L A Strange devised a series of mounts, one of which fired obliquely ahead, so that the pilot had to formate on the enemy's quarter (diagonally behind) or else crab along with full rudder from astern; another was a cranked pillar for a Lewis fired by an observer. Many aces, such as Albert Ball, tried various armament schemes and often seemed unable to decide what was best. For observers there was soon no doubt; two-seat fighters, and other aircraft with manually aimed guns, universally adopted the ring mount devised by Warrant Officer F W Scarff of the Admiralty Air Department. The Scarff No 2 ring mount was developed with the help of Sopwith and first used on the 1½-Strutter. It at last allowed the observer to aim freely throughout his entire arc of fire and was a standard fitment in many air forces well beyond 1939. The Bristol F.2B and many other types, including French and American fighters, often had Scarff mounts for twin Lewis, or for the American 0.30-in Marlin or Browning.

Scarff was also one of the inventors of a synchronising gear for fixed guns. Once Fokker's engineers had perfected the mechanical interrupter gear used in the E-series monoplanes, there was no longer any question but that the myopic Allied top brass would swiftly follow suit. One of the earliest Allied synchronising gears was developed by Vickers (Challenger). It was purely mechanical, and so were those developed by Ross, by Sopwith in partnership with Kauper, and Scarff in partnership with the Russian Lt-Cdr Dibovski. In France several schemes, notably the Alkan, followed similar arrangements, answering the urgent need for linkages that would work reliably. But a much better scheme was developed

later in 1916 by a Romanian mining engineer, Georges Constantinesco, in partnership with an Artillery officer Maj G C Colley. The Constantinesco CC gear was not mechanical but hydraulic, linking a motor on the gun trigger by sealed oil pipes with plungers driven by the engine. The pilot had to pump up a suitable pressure in the piping, after which the CC gear linked the engine and gun smoothly and (after some months of trouble in the S.E.5 and 5a, the first installation in service) reliably. One advantage was that the same basic CC gear could be used for almost any kind of engine and any kind of gun, or any number of guns. With modifications, this gear remained standard with many air forces until the Second World War.

Most of the fixed machine guns of the Allies were Vickers, based on the Maxim. This famous name encompassed a great variety of sub-types and calibres from 6.5- to 11-mm, but all were fed by a long belt of ammunition usually joined by metal links. The dominant free gun was the Lewis, designed by an American and made chiefly in Belgium, but another extremely important gun was the Hotchkiss. This was virtually the same as the Benet-Mercier, and thus had the same drawback of being fed by short clips of, usually, 25 rounds. Revelli made a family of guns in Italy, but these were little used in aircraft until the 1920s. By far the most important family of guns of the Central Powers were those based on the Maxim, and they thus had an action identical to that of the Vickers. The basic fixed fighter gun was the MG 08/15, commonly called the Spandau from the armoury near Berlin where it was first made. On board Zeppelins it was used as a free gun with the same water-cooling jacket as the ground guns, but for combat aeroplanes a simple slotted casing admitted cooling air. Ammunition was the standard German 7.92-mm (0.311-in) rimless type. The German observer gun was a development commonly called the Parabellum, after the code-name for the Deutsche Waffen und Munitionsfabriken where it was developed. It was not easy to make the basic Maxim action any better, but the air-cooled Parabellum was notably lighter, fired at up to 700 rds/min and was

Siemens-Schuckert D.IV
Tough, manoeuvrable and with a very high power-to-weight ratio, the D.IV had an incredible rate of climb but arrived too late and in too few numbers to restore Germany's declining fortunes on the Western Front
Span: 27 ft 4¾ in *Length:* 18 ft 8½ in *Engine:* Siemens-Halske Sh IIIa, 200 hp *Max speed:* 119 mph *Ceiling:* 26,240 ft *Max take-off weight:* 1620 lb *Armament:* 2 × Spandau mg

German pilots confer moments before take-off. By mid-1918 the Allies had wrested almost complete mastery in the air over the Western Front

Fokker D.VII
The D.VII won a design competition for a single-seat fighter in January 1918 and reached the front only four months later. Advanced features included a thick-section cantilever wing, fuselage of welded steel tubing and car-type radiator. These combined to give good high-altitude manoeuvrability and resistance to battle damage combined with docile handling qualities, although the top speed was not impressive
Span: 29 ft 3½ in *Length:* 22 ft 9 in *Engine:* Mercedes, 160 hp *Max speed:* 117 mph at 3200 ft *Ceiling:* 20,000 ft *Max take-off weight:* 1936 lb *Armament:* 2×Spandau mg

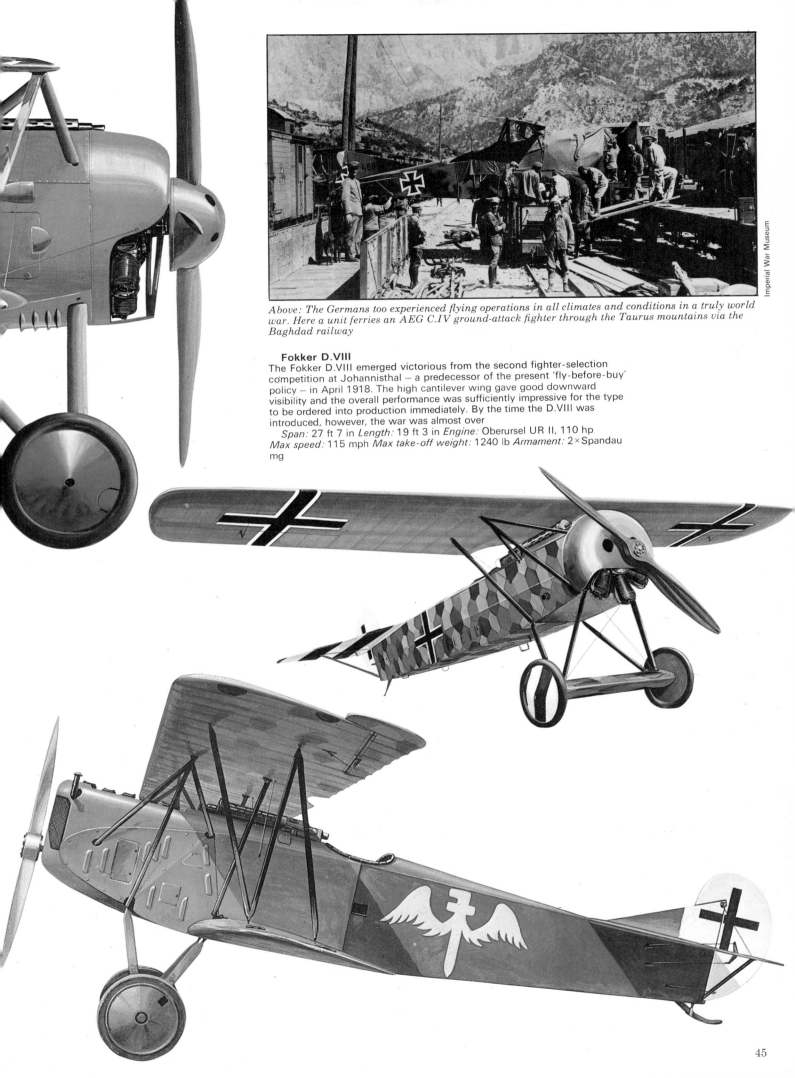

Above: The Germans too experienced flying operations in all climates and conditions in a truly world war. Here a unit ferries an AEG C.IV ground-attack fighter through the Taurus mountains via the Baghdad railway

Fokker D.VIII

The Fokker D.VIII emerged victorious from the second fighter-selection competition at Johannisthal – a predecessor of the present 'fly-before-buy' policy – in April 1918. The high cantilever wing gave good downward visibility and the overall performance was sufficiently impressive for the type to be ordered into production immediately. By the time the D.VIII was introduced, however, the war was almost over

Span: 27 ft 7 in *Length:* 19 ft 3 in *Engine:* Oberursel UR II, 110 hp *Max speed:* 115 mph *Max take-off weight:* 1240 lb *Armament:* 2 × Spandau mg

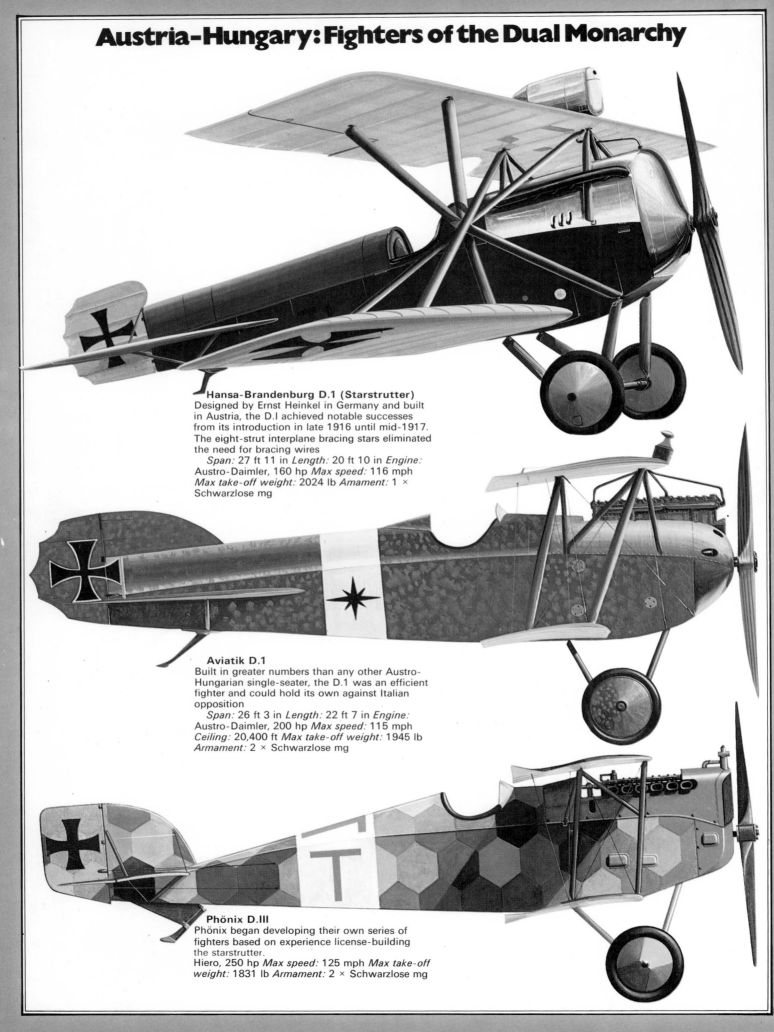

Austria-Hungary: Fighters of the Dual Monarchy

Hansa-Brandenburg D.1 (Starstrutter)
Designed by Ernst Heinkel in Germany and built in Austria, the D.I achieved notable successes from its introduction in late 1916 until mid-1917. The eight-strut interplane bracing stars eliminated the need for bracing wires
Span: 27 ft 11 in *Length:* 20 ft 10 in *Engine:* Austro-Daimler, 160 hp *Max speed:* 116 mph *Max take-off weight:* 2024 lb *Amament:* 1 × Schwarzlose mg

Aviatik D.1
Built in greater numbers than any other Austro-Hungarian single-seater, the D.1 was an efficient fighter and could hold its own against Italian opposition
Span: 26 ft 3 in *Length:* 22 ft 7 in *Engine:* Austro-Daimler, 200 hp *Max speed:* 115 mph *Ceiling:* 20,400 ft *Max take-off weight:* 1945 lb *Armament:* 2 × Schwarzlose mg

Phönix D.III
Phönix began developing their own series of fighters based on experience license-building the starstrutter.
Hiero, 250 hp *Max speed:* 125 mph *Max take-off weight:* 1831 lb *Armament:* 2 × Schwarzlose mg

fed by a long fabric belt neatly wrapped in a large spool on one side. The only other aircraft machine gun of the pre-1918 era that deserves mention is the outstanding Gast, based on the British Bethel Burton of 1886 but re-patented by Carl Gast in Germany in 1916. Its action served left and right recoiling barrels, each of which locked and fired the other. Fed by twin drums clipped on from above as one unit, the Gast fired at the unprecedented rate of 1600 rds/min (with spring-loaded buffer, 1800). It was in very large-scale production in mid-1918, but it did not see action and the existence of the Gast was not even known to the Allies until 1921!

With a gun such as the Gast even a single second of well-aimed fire could be decisive. But from before 1914 a few far-seeing people had begun to debate the possible advantage of having a gun which, while firing more slowly, could destroy its enemy with one shot. This argument raged until long after the Second World War and has not been stilled even today. Certainly, in 1913–14 the French official view was that, should air combat ever come to pass, it would be better to have a large-calibre gun, and throughout the First World War the French were the leading exponents of the *Avion Canon*. The 37-mm Hotchkiss cannon, firing a shell weighing about 700 grams (1½ lb), was mounted for the first time in a pusher Voisin at the Paris air show in 1911, but apparently did not fly until 1913. The gun was first used in the primitive-looking but tough and quite popular Breguet de Chasse (Breguet fighter) types BUC and BLC in late 1915. This slow pusher did not have the performance to catch targets, though the 37-mm was effective against surface targets. Later Breguets were faster, and in the formidable Type 11 Corsaire there were twin gun nacelles, one having one or two machine guns and the other the cannon. The same gun was used in many other aircraft, and by 1918 had even been fired in the air in a number of small single-seaters (mainly advanced Spads) with the gun firing through the hub of the propeller. This was to remain a favoured type of cannon installation until the end of the piston era.

Britain made little use of guns of calibre larger than the traditional 0.303-in, and confined such use to trials with the Vickers

The Supermarine Nighthawk, an anti-Zeppelin fighter designed to fly standing patrols and intercept raiders

Maxim in the 0.45-in calibre, the Vickers 1-pdr 'Pom Pom' and a small range of unadopted guns, plus the only one to see operational service, the Coventry Ordnance Works (C.O.W.) 1½-pdr. This big and weighty gun was much longer and harder-hitting than the low-velocity Hotchkiss of similar 37-mm calibre, and was mainly confined to large aircraft, though it did form the main armament of the three-seat F.E.4 fighter. Likewise the Germans restricted their excellent Becker 20-mm cannon to bombers and Zeppelins, and would probably have done the same with their very advanced later cannon such as the Semag, Rheinmetall (Ehrhart) and Szakats.

There was yet another type of gun developed specifically for fighters: the recoilless type. Britain developed two important members of this family, the Davis and the Vickers-Crayford. The Davis fired normal shells (the most common model fired 900-gram, 2-lb projectiles) and simultaneously expelled propellant gases and the spent case to the rear to approximately cancel out the recoil. The Robey-Peters

prototypes were designed to carry at least one Davis 2-pdr, aimed by a gunner over whose shoulder passed the rear of the barrel with its venturi nozzle. Other Davis installations were fixed, two of them (AD Scout and Blackburn Triplane) having a pusher rotary engine just behind the gun! How these guns worked in such an installation has become a mystery. The gun by the Vickers works at Crayford was totally different, for it fired rocket-propelled shells. Two of the aircraft built to carry this fearsome weapon were the Royal Aircraft Factory N.E.1 and Vickers' own F.B.25, both of which were anti-Zeppelin night fighters. Another aircraft in this class, built to carry the Davis in the 1½-pdr size as well as two Lewis, was the Pemberton-Billing P.B.31E. This incredible aircraft, flown in February 1917, was intended to loiter for hours waiting for Zeppelins. A veritable flying fortress, it had two engines, four wings, an electric generating set and searchlight, a battery of gunners and a pilot who could hardly see out. Strange to think that the P.B. company was renamed Supermarine, so that this weird 'fighter' was an ancestor of the Spitfire.

Sopwith 7F.1 Snipe

The Snipe, intended as a replacement for the Camel, became operational only in September 1918 and therefore saw most of its service after the First World War. Electrical heating and oxygen equipment were standard, and the Snipe would have replaced Camels in home-defence squadrons and on shipboard duties if the war had continued. The type was finally withdrawn in 1927

Span: 31 ft 1 in *Length:* 19 ft 10 in *Engine:* Bentley B.R.2, 230 hp; Clerget 11Eb, 200 hp; or ABC Dragonfly, 320 hp *Max speed:* 121 mph at 10,000 ft *Ceiling:* 19,500 ft *Max take-off weight:* 2020 lb *Armament:* 2×Vickers mg, 4×25-lb Cooper bombs

THE TWENTIES

While those who survived the First World War danced the Charleston or bootlegged whisky into the United States, fighter technology progressed in different countries at paces that ranged from mediocre to very slow indeed. Paradoxically, the victorious Allies were those who led the race to be slowest, and their young air services (in the case of Britain, an independent Royal Air Force, which had to fight for its very existence) had to shrink to the stature of an exclusive flying club, where everyone knew everyone else. Airfields lay derelict, littered with hundreds of rotting airframes and rusting engines. Only relatively small numbers of equipment items were needed for the small peacetime air forces, and every penny and cent for defence was argued by governments before being grudgingly allocated. Yet in such countries as Japan and the Soviet Union nothing rated higher than fighter technology, and budgets grew annually. Even the defeated Germans found ways of advancing the art of fighter design, mainly under cover or in friendly states such as the Soviet Union, Sweden, Switzerland and Spain.

To young Fokker the Armistice meant only the slightest of hiccups. Under the noses of the Allied Control Commission, he packed up tons of aeronautical products, including more than 400 of the latest engines, about 120 Fokker D.VII aircraft and 20 of the new D.VIII monoplanes, and smuggled them across the frontier into his native Holland. There he established a prosperous and rapidly growing aircraft works building everything from fighters to airline transport aircraft. Others tried to do the same, but orders were few and competition fierce. For the engine-builders times were slightly better, because in the years following 1918 engines developed very greatly. First World War engines had been produced in a great hurry, to state-of-the-art designs that generally went back in concept to 1907–13. Reliability was exceedingly poor, and total life seldom greater than 100 hours and often only half as much. But in the new peacetime air forces engines had to work reliably for many years, often in extremes of climate. So new engines were developed, better planned and designed, and made of improved steels and other alloys. The concept of fatigue, which in 1918 had scarcely been identified, was reduced to precise numerical terms so that highly stressed parts could last for 1000 operating hours, or longer, without a hint of failure. The whole business of aircraft design and manufacture was put on a sound footing, with precise inspection of the designs, the raw material and the finished products. Structural breakup in flight, common in the First World War, became almost unheard-of, despite growing engine power, growing weights and progressive increases in speed, climb and ceiling.

One of the few wartime engines to remain important through the 1920s was the American Liberty. This had from the start shown that hasty design and rapid mass-production could still yield a superior product, and though it had failed to improve certain European combat types (notably the Bristol Fighter) the Liberty gave exemplary service in many others (such as the D.H.9a). In the American Packard Le Père LUSAC-II fighter a 425-hp Liberty gave sparkling performance despite large size, and had the war continued these machines would for the first time since the Wrights have shown the quality of US aeronautical products. Such encouragement was needed, because in 1917 the US government had grandly decided on central Federal control of aircraft design and production and got the potentially vast programme into a sad mess. In 1918 it turned the job back to industry, the LUSAC being a good result. Another, too late for the war, was the Thomas-Morse MB-3, designed to beat the Spad XIII which was the pride of the American Expeditionary Force which established a fine reputation on the Western front in 1918.

Though the MB-3 suffered from many faults, and had the same Hispano-Suiza engine as the Spad but made by Wright, it had an important influence on a little-known company in the far northwest of the United States. In 1920, a year after the prototype MB-3 had flown, the US Army decided to buy 200 (a remarkable number for the lean year 1920). The policy in the USA at that time was that the Army could put any production job out to the lowest bidder, no matter who had designed the item, and in this case the low bidder was a company called Boeing. Building the 200 improved MB-3A scouts established Boeing as a major force in aviation, and began one of the greatest families of fighters of the inter-war era. The US Army Air Service called fighters 'pursuits', and gave them numbered designations prefaced by 'PW', for 'pursuit, water-cooled engine'.

First flown in April 1918, the Westland Wagtail was so hampered by problems with its ABC engine that it missed the war and the prototypes served as flying testbeds

Packard-Le Père LUSAC II
Two-seat fighter which would have been the US equivalent of the Bristol Fighter had it appeared bef the armistice. Only 30 were built
Span: 41 ft 7 in *Length:* 25 ft 6 in *Engine:* Liberty 12A, 400 hp *Max speed:* 132 mph at 2000 ft *Ceiling* 20,000 ft *Max take-off weight:* 3746 lb *Armament:* Marlin mg, 2 × Lewis mg

Thomas Morse S-4C
Equipped almost entirely with French types, the American Expeditionary Forces received only a trickle of home-built designs before the armistice. One of these was the S-4C, a US-built fighter trainer of 1917. Experience with the S-4C gave the company a lead in designing the MB-3, produced in large numbers by Boeing
Span: 26 ft 6 in *Length:* 19 ft 10 in *Engine:* Le Rhône, 80 hp *Max speed:* 95 mph *Ceiling:* 15,000 ft *Max take-off weight:* 1374 lb

The Nieuport 29, the superlative fighter design of Gustave Delage built around an in-line Hispano-Suiza engine. It arrived too late to see combat but figured prominently in several post-war air races

Boeing's first original fighter design was the XPW-9 (X for experimental) of 1923. Boeing had no order for this new pursuit, but recognised that, in the tough aviation climate of the early 1920s, it would have to work hard to survive. The thing to do was demonstrate what the US Army did not fully appreciate: that the MB-3A represented a wartime technology that could be improved upon significantly. Like the Spads on which it was based, the Thomas-Morse fighters were made entirely of wood, with fabric covering. Boeing did not object to wooden wings, made efficiently by glueing and pinning, but considered the fuselage a poor structural concept. Traditional wartime fighters had a fuselage made from four strong longerons of hardwood, held together by numerous vertical and cross-members. The parts could not just be glued; they had to be linked by complicated fittings, usually of steel, which were attached by multiple bolts. The fittings also anchored steel bracing wires which had to be tightened after assembly. Not only was the construction complex and expensive but it resulted in a fuselage whose shape depended on the tightness of each wire. Throughout the service life of the aircraft, maintenance engineers – usually called airframe fitters, or riggers – had to crawl up and down the fuselage adjusting the tightness of the wires, to make the aircraft fly in a straight line and with proper loads on all the parts. But Fokker had perfected a way of making the fuselage of his wartime fighters from welded steel tubing. This was not new; the Wright brothers, who were bicycle makers, used the same method. What Fokker, and his designer Platz, did was make gas-welded joints in a complete fuselage while all the parts were held in their exact positions in a fixture. It was much cheaper, weighed about the same, and meant that the structure needed no maintenance because its shape never changed. But Boeing could see how even this could be improved.

When Frank Tyndall took off at Seattle in the Boeing Model 15 on 29 April, 1923, he was flying the newest fighter, technically, in the world. The fuselage was made of steel tubes joined by an improved method of welding with an electric arc. The engine was the new Curtiss D-12, rated at 435 hp. The water radiators were moved from the sides of the fuselage to a new position under the engine, with the air ducted through a kind of tunnel. The two guns, one of 0.30-in and the other of the hard-hitting 0.50-in calibre, were neatly fixed above the engine under the cowling. The wooden wings had more span than most earlier fighters, giving increased area for tighter turns. Boeing again copied Platz's methods in using a relatively thick high-lift section, with a wooden spar built up into a slender box. Though considerably larger than the Thomas-Morse, the Model 15 flew at 163 mph, compared with 140 (itself an excellent speed), and after testing by the Army at McCook Field it was accepted as the XPW-9. There followed a long series of production PW-9 fighters, and the similar FB-1 to FB-5 for the Navy and Marine Corps (FB= Fighter, Boeing).

Competition for Boeing came from Curtiss, who used their D-12 engine in the first of the famous Hawk series, the PW-8 of 1923. This was if anything even faster, partly because it had ply-covered wings with smooth and accurate profile, the skin of the upper plane incorporating completely flush

cooling radiators. The latter enabled the streamlined pointed-nose installation of a water-cooled in-line engine to be achieved without the drag of a radiator (which generally made the speeds of water-cooled and air-cooled radial-engined fighters about the same, despite the fact that radials seemed to be blunt and badly streamlined). Curtiss had perfected the skin radiator in racers of 1921–22, but in military service it gave too much trouble, besides being extremely vul-

nerable to gunfire. But on 23 June, 1924, one of the speedy PW-8 Hawks achieved fame by flying across America in a day. Lt Russell Maughan took off from Long Island and flew in stages, travelling with the Sun, until he reached San Francisco 21 hr 48 min later, an average of 117 mph including all the refuelling stops. From the PW-8 series came the long succession of Army Hawks (P-1 onwards) and the Navy F6C series.

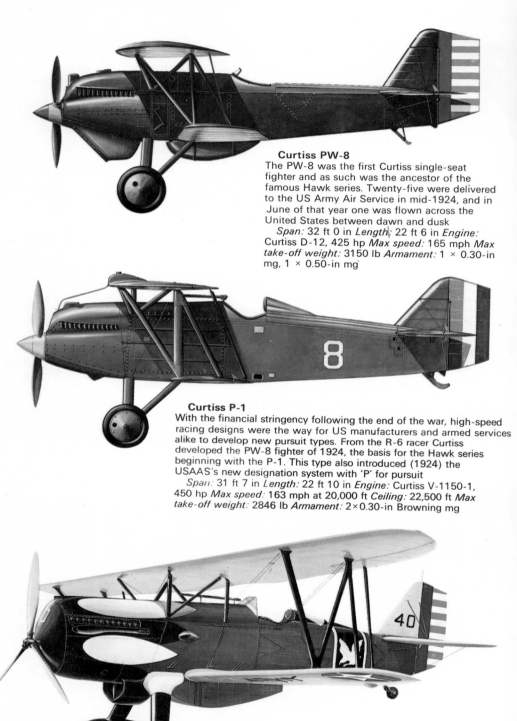

Curtiss PW-8
The PW-8 was the first Curtiss single-seat fighter and as such was the ancestor of the famous Hawk series. Twenty-five were delivered to the US Army Air Service in mid-1924, and in June of that year one was flown across the United States between dawn and dusk
Span: 32 ft 0 in *Length:* 22 ft 6 in *Engine:* Curtiss D-12, 425 hp *Max speed:* 165 mph *Max take-off weight:* 3150 lb *Armament:* 1 × 0.30-in mg, 1 × 0.50-in mg

Curtiss P-1
With the financial stringency following the end of the war, high-speed racing designs were the way for US manufacturers and armed services alike to develop new pursuit types. From the R-6 racer Curtiss developed the PW-8 fighter of 1924, the basis for the Hawk series beginning with the P-1. This type also introduced (1924) the USAAS's new designation system with 'P' for pursuit
Span: 31 ft 7 in *Length:* 22 ft 10 in *Engine:* Curtiss V-1150-1, 450 hp *Max speed:* 163 mph at 20,000 ft *Ceiling:* 22,500 ft *Max take-off weight:* 2846 lb *Armament:* 2×0.30-in Browning mg

Curtiss P-6E
The series of Curtiss Hawk P-6 fighters for the US Army culminated in the P-6E with an improved cooling system and spatted undercarriage. The 17th Pursuit Squadron made the machines famous with their painted claws on the spats and diving eagle insignia
Span: 31 ft 6 in *Length:* 22 ft 7 in *Engine:* Curtiss V-1570-23 Conqueror C, 600 hp *Max speed:* 198 mph *Ceiling:* 24,700 ft *Max take-off weight:* 3392 lb *Armament:* 2×0.30-in mg

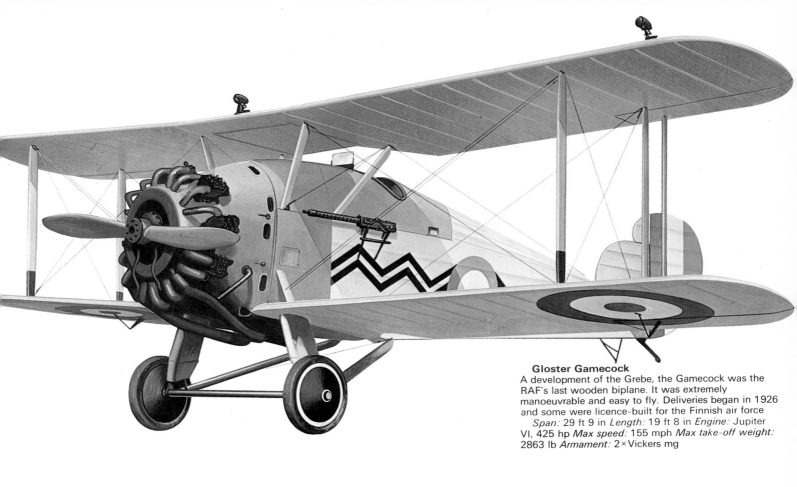

Gloster Gamecock
A development of the Grebe, the Gamecock was the RAF's last wooden biplane. It was extremely manoeuvrable and easy to fly. Deliveries began in 1926 and some were licence-built for the Finnish air force
Span: 29 ft 9 in *Length:* 19 ft 8 in *Engine:* Jupiter VI, 425 hp *Max speed:* 155 mph *Max take-off weight:* 2863 lb *Armament:* 2×Vickers mg

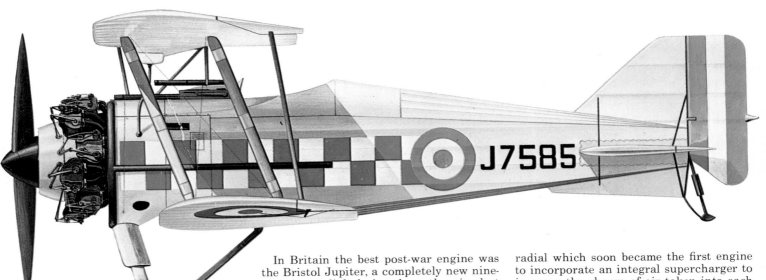

Gloster Grebe
The Grebe was, together with the Armstrong Whitworth Siskin, the first new fighter to be ordered into quantity production for the Royal Air Force after the First World War. The high-lift upper wing gave good take-off and climb performance, while the lower wing was designed for the minimum drag at cruising speeds. The total order was for 130 Grebes, some of which took part in parasite-fighter experiments with the R.33 airship
Span: 29 ft 4 in *Length:* 20 ft 3 in *Engine:* Armstrong Siddeley Jaguar, IVA, 425 hp *Max speed:* 151 mph at 5000 ft *Ceiling:* 23,000 ft *Max take-off weight:* 2622 lb *Armament:* 2 × Vickers mg

In Britain the best post-war engine was the Bristol Jupiter, a completely new nine-cylinder radial designed as the simplest possible engine in the 400–500-hp class. An earlier engine of the same layout, the ABC Dragonfly, had been selected in 1918 for almost all the new crop of fighters that were coming into mass-production at the Armistice. Had the war continued there would have been a crisis in British fighters, because the Dragonfly was not only a failure but its faults could not be cured, and over 1000 had been built when this was discovered. A few aircraft, such as the Badger and Nighthawk, were re-engined with the Jupiter, but it was not until 1923 that the RAF wanted any new post-war fighters and the choice fell on the Jupiter-engined Hawker Woodcock. Another type bought in quantity was the Armstrong Whitworth Siskin, developed from the Siddeley Siskin first flown with a Dragonfly in 1919. In this case the engine was the Siddeley company's own Jaguar, a neat 14-cylinder two-row

radial which soon became the first engine to incorporate an integral supercharger to increase the charge of air taken into each cylinder on each induction stroke. Unsupercharged engines naturally lose power as the aircraft climbs into thinner air, and this was especially serious for fighters, which need the highest possible performance at all heights. Supercharging enabled the full flight performance to be maintained up to high altitudes, giving such aircraft a pronounced edge in combat. In 1924 the RAF received the first Siskin III fighters, with a completely new structure made entirely from thin steel tubing and strip (but used in a direct replacement for wood, and with fabric covering). The Mk IIIA Siskin, with the supercharged engine, followed in 1927.

Two other RAF fighters of this period were the Gloucestershire (Gloster) Grebe, with Jaguar engine, and Gamecock, with Jupiter. Suddenly attracted by the 'streamlined' Curtiss D-12 engine, Fairey built a

fast bomber called the Fox that was faster than most fighters, and followed with the Firefly fighter later used by Belgium. But in 1927 the Jupiter radial was again chosen for the RAF's next standard fighter, the Bristol Bulldog. The water-cooled Rolls-Royce Kestrel was selected for RAF Hawker Fury single-seaters, and two-seat Demon fighters that succeeded the Bristol Fighter of 1917, but overseas customers chose the air-cooled radial engines. The RAF's final biplane fighters were the Gloster Gauntlet of 1935 and Gladiator of 1937, both powered by a development of the Jupiter called the Mercury. Like the Sopwith Snark of 1918 the Gloster company had fitted six machine-guns into the S.S.19 of 1932, but when the S.S.19 became the Gauntlet the armament reverted to the standard two Vickers guns that had been on almost every RAF fighter since the Camel. But there had been many interesting variations.

For example, in 1924 the Air Ministry issued Specification 4/24 for a heavy twin-engined fighter carrying two cannon. Between 1918 and 1935 no British aircraft was designed to carry any cannon other than the ponderous 37-mm C.O.W. gun, though plenty of smaller, faster-firing cannon were available from other countries. The two aircraft built to the 4/24 specification were poor designs, the Westland Westbury being a biplane and the Bristol Bagshot a braced monoplane, both having two Jupiters, and the cannon aimed by hand from the nose and a mid-upper cockpit. Soon the officials forgot about such machines, but with Specification F.29/27 in 1927 they suddenly asked for a cannon-armed single-seater. The result was the Westland C.O.W. Gun Fighter, a trim low-wing monoplane, and the archaic-looking Vickers 161 biplane pusher, both of which carried the heavy gun firing obliquely upwards at 55°. Again, once

built, these aircraft were forgotten.

Other countries had a wider choice of armament, and many used calibres of 0.5-in (12.7-mm), 20-mm and 23-mm, though the rifle-calibre gun remained by far the most common. The standard French fighters of the 1920s were the Loire-Gourdou-Leseurre LGL 32 and a family of Nieuport-Delage machines of which the main type was the ND 62 and its derivative the 622. The LGL was a tough high-wing monoplane with Gnome-Rhône-built Jupiter, while the ND 62 was a sesquiplane (biplane with the lower plane extremely small) with water-cooled Hispano-Suiza 12M engine. A small number of Wibault scouts also entered service, notable for their patented form of all-metal construction with light-alloy skin. Though the skin did not bear flight loads it was much stronger than fabric or ply, and was widely copied or built under licence (for example, by Vickers for fighters in Britain). In Japan all military aircraft before the 1930s were designed by Western engineers, almost all from Britain, while the Soviet Union was so engrossed in settling the protracted civil war and re-building the economy it had little time for breaking new ground in aviation (though Polikarpov's I-3 single-seat biplane fighter of 1927 reached the excellent speed of 186 mph).

Fokker continued to build fighters in Holland, but competition was severe. In newly created Czechoslovakia several companies built outstanding fighters. Fiat in Italy began a long series of C.R. (*Caccia Rosatelli*, ie fighter designed by Rosatelli) models, Emile Dewoitine produced an equally long series of outstanding high-wing monoplane fighters in France and Switzerland, and a brilliant Polish designer, Zygmunt Pulawski, chose the same layout for a series of PZL fighters that were even

better (beginning with the 195-mph P.1 of 1929). Meanwhile, in the United States in 1925 a team of gifted engineers broke away from the powerful Wright company and founded Pratt & Whitney Aircraft, building not aircraft but engines. Their first product was an outstanding 400-hp radial, named the Wasp. It transformed the fighter scene, sweeping away the pointed noses of the water-cooled engines and making the air-cooled radial dominant throughout military aviation. Boeing's PW-9 and FB fighters turned into the F2B, F3B and F4B for the Navy and Marines and P-12 family for the Army, while Curtiss developed a diverse family of Hawks of different sizes and shapes and eventually retractable landing gear in the 1930s.

Wibault W.11 experimental French parasol-winged fighter of 1928

Hawker Demon

A fighter version of the highly successful 1928 Hawker Hart day bomber, the Demon two-seat escort fighter went into service from April 1933. The Osprey was a navalised reconnaissance version for service with the fleet

Span: 37 ft 3 in *Length:* 29 ft 1 in *Engine:* Rolls-Royce Kestrel II, 581 hp *Max speed:* 181 mph at 15,000 ft *Ceiling:* 24,500 ft *Max take-off weight:* 4464 lb *Armament:* 2×Vickers mg, 1×Lewis mg

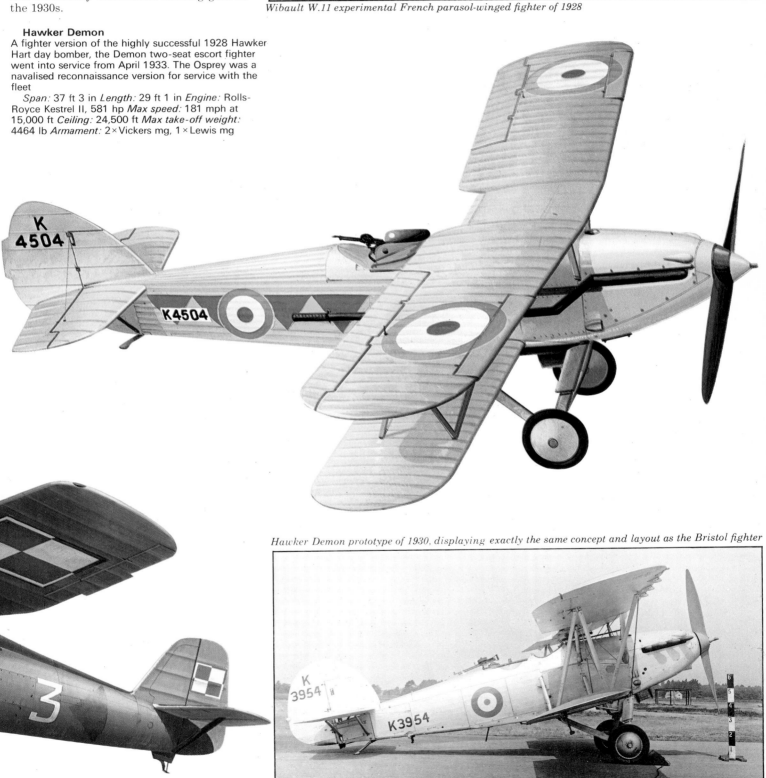

Hawker Demon prototype of 1930, displaying exactly the same concept and layout as the Bristol fighter

THE THIRTIES: TIME OF TESTING

The decade that led up to the Second World War was as crucial and uncertain as any in the whole of fighter history. None of the old problems had been resolved. Senior officers, procurement officials, chief designers and combat-ready pilots, all had firm views on what was best, often failing to listen to those whose views were in violent disagreement.

Sydney Camm, of Hawker Aircraft, liked water-cooled in-line engines because the aircraft built around them looked streamlined. Almost everyone in the United States ignored such engines, until the last Curtiss V-1570 Conqueror came off the line in 1935 and pointed-nose Americans were temporarily extinct. Italian pilots passionately clung to the traditional fabric-covered biplane, sacrificing speed, firepower and everything else for the best possible manoeuvrability and pilot view. Japan's rapidly growing army and navy air forces thought along similar lines, but had no objection to the new stressed-skin monoplanes. In the vast air fleets of the Soviet Union, fighters were sound and conventional, but at the test establishments were unconventional experiments that explored more radical ideas than in any other country. In Britain immense talent was seldom permitted to depart from tradition – the fabric-covered biplane with two Vickers machine-guns – though in industry and research airfields many new ideas were being tried. And in some countries, not including Britain, bigger fighters were continually appearing, either as long-range escorts for bombers or as vaguely conceived aerial battleships with guns pointing in all directions.

France was especially drawn towards the latter, despite the poor showing of the Blériot 127/2 of 1929 which in the early 1930s saw service with the *Aviation Militaire* (*Armée de l'Air* from 1933). Like the types which followed, the 127/2 was a lumbering monoplane with the appearance of a bomber, an unusual feature being the location of gunners in the tails of the long nacelles. Various *Multiplace de Combat* designs followed, but the next to serve in quantity

was the Potez 540, first delivered in 1934. This again looked like a bomber, and could also fly bombing and reconnaissance missions. In 1934 its speed of 193 mph was excellent for so large an aircraft, but like the Amiot 143 which followed it the ungainly Potez was really a bomber, and quite incapable of holding its own in air combat. There were numerous attempts in other countries to build large multi-seat fighters relying for their effectiveness not on manoeuvrability but on firepower, and the concept was resurrected in 1943 with special escort versions of the US Army Air Force heavy bombers. It was the exact opposite of the concept followed by the Italians and Japanese, in which everything possible was done to make the fighter lighter, even at the expense of leaving out all but the lightest armament.

Indeed, at intervals from 1915 onwards there have appeared 'light fighters' of one sort or another, intended either to have better manoeuvrability, or to be cheaper (and thus purchasable in greater quantity), or for various other reasons. In the jet era in the early 1950s there was a sudden crop of small lightweight fighters largely because the ordinary kind seemed to be getting impossibly large, complex and expensive, with the prospect that they could never be kept serviceable. But between the wars there were other reasons. France named its small fighter prototypes *Le Type Jockey*, but though many were built none was adopted as a standard type. The nearest miss was the beautiful little Caudron-Renault C.714, which was just getting into production at the very end of the 1930s after the start of the Second World War. Powered by a slender 450-hp Renault air-cooled V12 engine, this stemmed from a long line of extremely efficient little racers. Built cheaply of wood, the C.714 had four machine-guns in fairings under the wings, and might have been effective if it had been ordered earlier. Its speed and climb were comparable with those of the standard M.S.406 of the *Armée de l'Air*, which had twice the power.

On the flight line at Boeing's Seattle plant is this beautiful F4B-4 for the US Navy.

Arado Ar 68E
After the *Luftwaffe* came into the open in 1935, its chief fighters such as the Ar 68 and the He 51 stuck to the proven biplane formula despite the imminent appearance of the *Luftwaffe's* first monoplane fighters. Developed later than the He 51, the Ar 68 was little better and by 1940 they we relegated to training
  Span: 36 ft 1 in *Length:* 31 ft 2 in *Engine:* Junkers Jumo 210Ea, 680 hp *Max speed:* 202 mph at 13,125 ft *Max take-off weight:* 4435 lb *Ceiling:* 26,575 ft *Armament:* 2 × 7.9-mm MG 17 mg

Smithsonian Institution

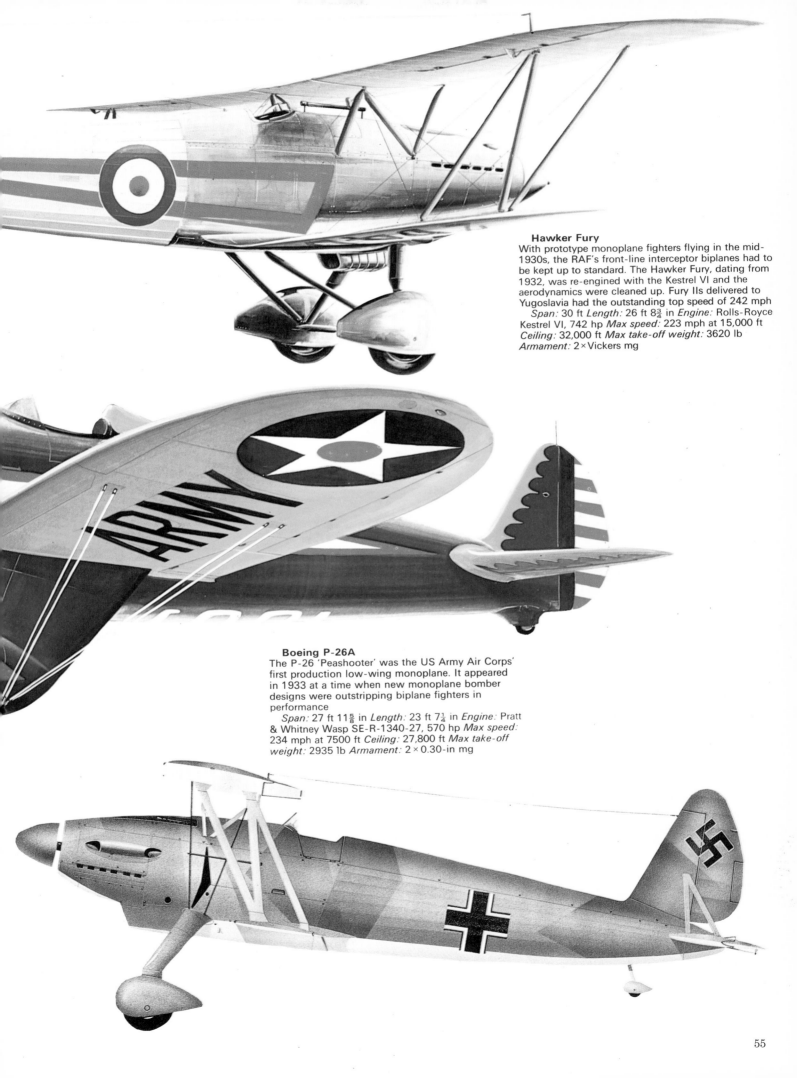

Hawker Fury
With prototype monoplane fighters flying in the mid-1930s, the RAF's front-line interceptor biplanes had to be kept up to standard. The Hawker Fury, dating from 1932, was re-engined with the Kestrel VI and the aerodynamics were cleaned up. Fury IIs delivered to Yugoslavia had the outstanding top speed of 242 mph
  Span: 30 ft *Length:* 26 ft 8¾ in *Engine:* Rolls-Royce Kestrel VI, 742 hp *Max speed:* 223 mph at 15,000 ft *Ceiling:* 32,000 ft *Max take-off weight:* 3620 lb *Armament:* 2×Vickers mg

Boeing P-26A
The P-26 'Peashooter' was the US Army Air Corps' first production low-wing monoplane. It appeared in 1933 at a time when new monoplane bomber designs were outstripping biplane fighters in performance
  Span: 27 ft 11⅝ in *Length:* 23 ft 7¼ in *Engine:* Pratt & Whitney Wasp SE-R-1340-27, 570 hp *Max speed:* 234 mph at 7500 ft *Ceiling:* 27,800 ft *Max take-off weight:* 2935 lb *Armament:* 2 × 0.30-in mg

Fighters over Spain: Dress rehearsal for a second round

Polikarpov I-15
Span: 29 ft 11½ in *Length:* 20 ft 7½ in *Engine:* M-25,
700 hp *Max speed:* 224 mph *Ceiling:* 32,800 ft
Max take-off weight: 3135 lb *Armament:* 4×7.62-mm
ShKAS mg

Polikarpov I-16
Span: 29 ft 6½ in *Length:* 20 ft 1¼ in *Engine:*
Shvetstov M-62, 1000 hp *Max speed:* 362 mph at sea
level *Max take-off weight:* 4564 lb *Ceiling:* 29,530 ft
Armament: 4×7.62-mm ShKAS mg

Messerschmitt Bf 109B-2
Span: 32 ft 6 in *Length:* 28 ft 7 in *Engine:* Jumo
210Da, 650 hp *Max speed:* 280 mph at 10,826 ft
Ceiling: 29,530 ft *Max take-off weight:* 4680 lb
Armament: 5×7.62-mm MG 17 mg

Polikarpov I-16

[W]hen the I-16 entered service in 1934 it was of [ex]tremely advanced conception, being the first [lo]w-wing interceptor monoplane with a retractable [un]dercarriage to enter service in any air force. It served [wi]th the Republicans in Spain, where it held its own [wi]th the first Bf 109s, and fought over China and [M]anchuria. The I-16 was a sitting target for the first [Lu]ftwaffe attacks of 1941, however, when thousands [we]re destroyed on the ground and in the air

Polikarpov I-15

[Fi]rst appearing in 1933, the I-15 went to Spain in [lar]ge numbers where it was dubbed *Chato* (The Flat-[no]sed One). The type fought in Finland and a few [su]rvived only to be shot down in droves during the [op]ening weeks of *Barbarossa*

Messerschmitt Bf 109B

[Sp]ain was the laboratory in which the new monoplane [fig]hters of the late 1930s could be tested in combat. [In] late 1937 the Bf 109 went to Spain, where its speed [an]d handling were shown to be excellent. The poor [ar]mament soon became apparent, though, and this was [in]creased on the subsequent C-series

Fiat C.R.32

[Ty]pical of the Italian fighter designers' preference for [ma]noeuvrability, the C.R. 32 fought in some numbers [ov]er Spain with the *Aviación Legionara* in the hands of [Ita]lian pilots and was supplied to the Nationalist [go]vernment itself. The type, which was widely [ex]ported, was still Italy's most important front-line [fig]hter in the Autumn of 1939

Span: 31 ft 2 in *Length:* 24 ft 5⅜ in *Engine:* Fiat [A.]30, 600 hp *Max speed:* 221 mph at 9480 ft *Ceiling:* [28],750 ft *Max take-off weight:* 4200 lb *Armament:* [2 ×]12-mm Breda-SAFAT mg

Other countries generally avoided being sidetracked into the 'light fighter' concept, though many examples were built. British prototypes included the Avro Avocet and Blackburn Lincock, both powered by Lynx engines of well under 250 hp. In Germany the careful plans for rebuilding the Luftwaffe in the early 1930s led to an RLM (Air Ministry) specification in 1933 for a 'home-defence fighter' which could also serve as an advanced trainer. In this case the concept was a good one. Germany lacked sufficient supplies of engines suitable for full-blooded fighters, but could build aircraft that could train fighter pilots to become proficient in air combat. Several aircraft were built to this requirement, all powered by the 240-hp Argus As 10C air-cooled inverted-V8 engine, and the winner was a parasol monoplane, the Focke-Wulf Fw 56 *Stösser* (Falcon). About 1000 were built, armed with one or two synchronised machine guns and racks for light bombs. Virtually unbreakable, the Fw 56 could be used for vertical dive-bombing, and its general combat capability was close to the limit attainable from 240 hp. One has only to compare its speed of 173 mph with that of more powerful machines in the First World War to appreciate its efficiency, and in countries such as Britain and the United States where defence funding was niggardly in the extreme it is remarkable that more was not done to explore the limits attainable with low-powered fighters.

Of course, everything hinged around the engine and armament, and these aspects are discussed in the relevant chapters. But there began in the 1930s a process of fundamental change. At the start of the 1930s the normal fighter was a fabric-covered biplane with two machine-guns and with a gross weight of about 3500 lb, while ten years later it was a stressed-skin monoplane weighing almost twice as much and with much heavier armament. This alone represented a complete revolution, and it ran parallel with the deeper revolution in all aircraft as the forces of civil or military competition made designers adopt the advanced ideas and techniques that others had demonstrated many years earlier. It is important now to list what these changes were.

Structurally, designers had had a series of choices since 1910. By that time pioneers in Switzerland and France had devised ways of making monocoque structures, a word which means that the strength is in the outer shell instead of in a large framework braced by wires both within and without. During the final years before 1914 this technique had been used to make beautifully streamlined fuselages for racing aircraft, but the structural methods at that time involved wrapping multiple layers of tulip-wood or mahogany, fastened by glue and hundreds of brass pins. Rather similar methods were later used in production of seaplane floats and flying-boat hulls, but only because there was no simple alternative. Fighters were made more cheaply by cruder methods that gave a tough structure that could easily be repaired after a combat or a minor crash. In any case, wings could not yet be made by such a method, though the Fokker fighters of Reinhold Platz had thick wings that were strong enough to need no external bracing. Fokker added struts to his triplane and D.VII mainly to please the officials (and perhaps the pilots).

During the 1920s the change to metal

structures had been accompanied by the emergence of all-metal stressed-skin aircraft in which the skin carried a major part of the loads. All-metal fighters had seen service in the First World War, notable examples being the Junkers D.I and CL.I. Likewise the mass-produced French Wibault 7 series of the 1920s excited widespread interest, yet curiously the modern type of stressed-skin airframe was introduced not on fighters but in slow flying boats and fast American airliners. It was Emile Dewoitine who built the first truly all-stressed-skin fighter, in 1931. Though French, he had become disenchanted with his own country in the 1920s because it would not buy his aircraft, and most of his fighters of that decade were parasol monoplanes built in Switzerland. But in 1930 Dewoitine began work on a bold low-wing cantilever (unbraced) fighter to meet the future need of the French air force and this, the D.500, flew on 19 June, 1932. It was notable in that the all-metal stressed-skin philosophy was applied to the ultimate, even the ailerons and tail control surfaces being skinned in light alloy. It was of generous size, so that despite having a long and bulky water-cooled engine it could manoeuvre as well as the best of the biplanes. In spite of having a prominent spatted landing gear, it was very fast; the D.500 and 501 reached 224 mph and the more powerful 510 about 250 mph. By no means least it could carry a Hispano 20-mm cannon and up to six machine-guns. This showed the way things were going.

In the United States Boeing made the switch in pursuit design from biplane to monoplane with the Model 248, flown in March 1932. But they knew their customer, and deliberately made the 248 old-fashioned, with plenty of wire bracing (though the B-9 bomber of 1931 was a perfect stressed-skin cantilever). In January 1934 the delightful little Boeing was delivered to the Army Air Corps as the P-26A, becoming famed as 'the Peashooter'. Compared with the Dewoitine it was much smaller; and though it could not easily carry more than two rifle-calibre guns, its small wing limited radius of turn and made the landing rather fast for the small, rough grass airfields of the mid-1930s. Undoubtedly Boeing should have made a bigger P-26 with stressed-skin cantilever wing and retractable landing gear, able to take the much more powerful engines that appeared in the mid-1930s.

In the late 1930s the whole question of just how a fighter should be conceived was far from settled. Most of the squadron pilots, all over the world, were certain it ought to be a biplane, with open cockpit, and their view of future development was simply that more powerful engines would allow them to increase performance and armament. They looked askance at the sleek new monoplanes, with highly loaded wings, fast landing speeds, complicated systems to work landing gear and flaps (which would need armies of ground crew and would probably prove unreliable and vulnerable in combat) and claustrophobic enclosed cockpits which would interfere with the vital requirement of all-round vision. The only point of the new monoplanes was that they could go faster, but that was of no value if biplanes could out-manoeuvre them and shoot them down.

In the Soviet Union a little fighter even more compact than the Boeing Peashooter appeared at the same time, but in those days Russian designers were hardly taken

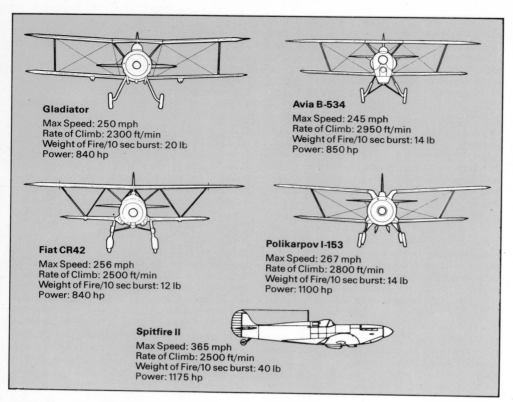

Gladiator
Max Speed: 250 mph
Rate of Climb: 2300 ft/min
Weight of Fire/10 sec burst: 20 lb
Power: 840 hp

Avia B-534
Max Speed: 245 mph
Rate of Climb: 2950 ft/min
Weight of Fire/10 sec burst: 14 lb
Power: 850 hp

Fiat CR42
Max Speed: 256 mph
Rate of Climb: 2500 ft/min
Weight of Fire/10 sec burst: 12 lb
Power: 840 hp

Polikarpov I-153
Max Speed: 267 mph
Rate of Climb: 2800 ft/min
Weight of Fire/10 sec burst: 14 lb
Power: 1100 hp

Spitfire II
Max Speed: 365 mph
Rate of Climb: 2500 ft/min
Weight of Fire/10 sec burst: 40 lb
Power: 1175 hp

seriously. The designer concerned was Nikolai N. Polikarpov, by far the most experienced Soviet designer and already responsible for several important programmes of combat aircraft. In 1927 he had written a classic report on fighter design, pointing out how one could achieve the best compromise between high power, low weight, a low wing loading (for manoeuvrability) and high speed. One of his conclusions was that the air-cooled radial was clearly superior as an engine, as discussed in the next chapter. His basic conclusions led naturally to a new fighter that was unlike anything seen before. His guidelines were: make the whole aircraft as small as possible, but make the wing area large; use a large radial engine, with variable-pitch propeller; use some form of trailing-edge flap; and make the landing gear retract. The result was the TsKB-12, later adopted as a standard fighter as the I-16. This was one of the great warplanes of history, and at least 7000 were built despite the fact that it was obsolescent by the time Germany invaded the Soviet Union in June 1941. It was developed through at least 24 major versions with increasing power and speed. In the Spanish Civil War the I-16 Model 10 showed itself generally superior to the later and much more expensive Bf 109B. Many I-16s operated on skis in winter, and were among the first aircraft to fire the RS-82 rocket against both air and surface targets.

Soviet philosophy tried to match the speedy I-16 with the even more manoeuvrable I-15 biplane from the same design bureau. The idea was that enemy formations would be caught and brought to battle by the monoplane fighter and then, some minutes later, outmanoeuvred and defeated by the slow biplanes that had had time to catch up. In practice this never worked; indeed in the large-scale air fighting over Mongolia in the first half of 1939 the rigid Soviet political doctrine negated the performance of the I-16 and the manoeuvrability of the I-15, letting the Japanese establish almost complete superiority.

Nevertheless the I-15 biplane ran parallel in timing with the I-16, and was succeeded by the I-15bis in 1937. Today we regard this era as one in which the biplane was fast becoming outmoded; the Gladiator, first delivered to the RAF in 1937, had little chance in 1940 even of surviving. Yet the Soviet Union decided to cut back the speedy I-16 and boost output of the biplanes, and in the I-15bis introduced a completely new design. Moreover, in 1938 yet a third generation of biplanes appeared, the I-153 with retractable landing gear.

It is important not to fall into the trap of concluding that the Russians were backward in clinging to biplanes, or (as one Western 'expert' writes) that in June 1941 they were 'even driven to throwing into the battle obsolete biplanes', and no nation conducted more exhaustive tests on the contrasting kinds of aircraft than the Soviet Union. Polikarpov's bureau was by far the most important in the field of fighters, and throughout the first half of the 1930s concentrated on monoplanes, backed up by the extremely competitive I-15 biplane. It looked as if the future lay with the monoplane, provided it had adequate manoeuvrability. On 1 September, 1934, Polikarpov's team watched the first flight of the TsKB-15, the first fighter in the world to have completely stressed-skin construction, completely retracting landing gear, and all the other modern attributes. It had a liquid-cooled engine, but this long and heavy unit made the aircraft less manoeuvrable than the existing I-16. Though development continued, and small numbers of an improved version saw service as the I-17-2, the emphasis swung increasingly in favour of the biplane. The Spanish Civil War and the intermittent fighting with the Japanese on the Mongolian and Chinese frontiers tended to confirm the view that dogfight manoeuvrability counted for more than speed. Even as late as 1941 the biplane I-153 was still in full production. Every possible effort was made to push this battle-proven type of aircraft to the ultimate. The engine power reached 1000 hp, and variable-

pitch propellers were introduced. The landing gear, which could be wheels or skis, was made to retract, and the armament was increased to four of the outstanding ShKAS machine-guns plus bombs, rockets or drop tanks (a new idea pioneered in the Soviet Union).

At the end of the decade new Soviet designers – Mikoyan and Gurevich, Lavochkin (assisted by Gorbunov and Gudkov) and the more experienced Yakovlev – all produced completely new fighters to the cantilever monoplane formula that by then was sweeping the board everywhere. These were to prove the salvation of their country in the grim days after June 1941, partly because the low-powered I-16 and the biplanes were simply outclassed and partly because they were destroyed in their hundreds and thousands in the catastrophic first weeks of Operation *Barbarossa*, as the Germans had planned. But despite the promise of the new and much faster monoplanes the Soviet engineers and air staff were extremely reluctant to give up the apparent dogfighting advantage of the biplane. An important secondary factor was that the highly loaded monoplanes needed long, smooth runways and were almost incompatible with the short-rough fields that served as bases for most Soviet fighter units. The last attempt to get the best of both worlds was one of the most remarkable fighters in history. In 1939 V. V. Nikitin and V. Sevchenko took an I-153 and rebuilt it with a retractable lower wing! There had previously been various research aircraft with wings that could be extended in span or modified in other ways, but nothing like this. There were no interplane struts, and when the pilot took off he first selected 'wheels up' (the main gears folding into the inboard lower wings) and then selected 'lower wing up'. The lower wing hinged at the root and almost half-way to the tip, the inboard section folding into a recess in the side of the fuselage and the outer panel fitting into a recess under the upper wing. The problems are obvious. For example, any recess in the upper wing would cut into the depth of the spars and weaken the whole wing, and the entire scheme was complex, heavy and fraught with mechanical difficulties. Yet, surprisingly, the prototype flew in late 1940 quite successfully. It is doubtful that anyone seriously expected the Nikitin-Sevchenko IS-1 to go into production, but it shows the boldness of Soviet design thinking. Slightly later Britain experimented with a simpler idea: the 'slip-wing' fighter in which an otherwise conventional monoplane could have an extra upper wing for short take-off, the biplane wing then being jettisoned. This was a good idea in that it left the fighter ready for battle unencumbered by any added devices, but denied the fighter any added dogfight manoeuvrability or slow landing capability.

Gloster Gladiator
One of the last fighter biplanes to see operational service, the Gladiator was obsolete even before it flew. It nevertheless fought over Finland, Norway, during the Battle of Britain (over the Orkneys), and distinguished itself over North Africa and the Mediterranean
Span: 32 ft 3 in *Length:* 27 ft 5 in *Engine:* Bristol Mercury IX, 840 hp *Max speed:* 253 mph *Ceiling:* 33,000 ft *Max take-off weight:* 5420 lb *Armament:* 4×0.303-in mg

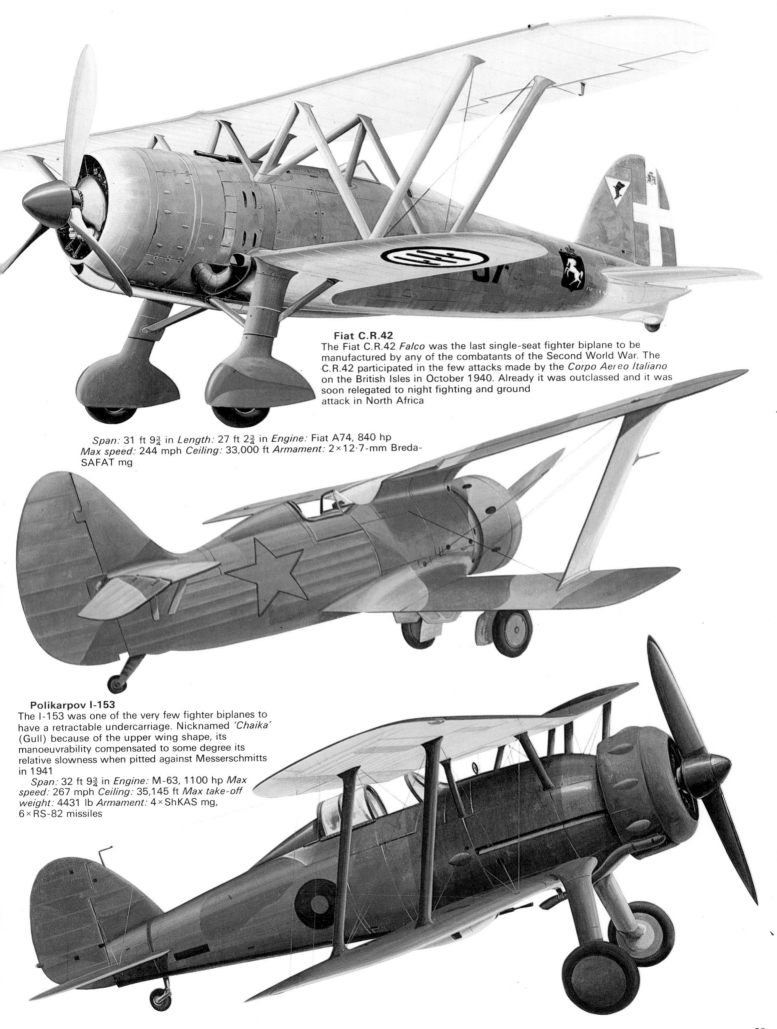

Fiat C.R.42
The Fiat C.R.42 *Falco* was the last single-seat fighter biplane to be manufactured by any of the combatants of the Second World War. The C.R.42 participated in the few attacks made by the *Corpo Aereo Italiano* on the British Isles in October 1940. Already it was outclassed and it was soon relegated to night fighting and ground attack in North Africa

Span: 31 ft 9¾ in *Length:* 27 ft 2¾ in *Engine:* Fiat A74, 840 hp
Max speed: 244 mph *Ceiling:* 33,000 ft *Armament:* 2×12·7-mm Breda-SAFAT mg

Polikarpov I-153
The I-153 was one of the very few fighter biplanes to have a retractable undercarriage. Nicknamed *'Chaika'* (Gull) because of the upper wing shape, its manoeuvrability compensated to some degree its relative slowness when pitted against Messerschmitts in 1941
Span: 32 ft 9¾ in *Engine:* M-63, 1100 hp *Max speed:* 267 mph *Ceiling:* 35,145 ft *Max take-off weight:* 4431 lb *Armament:* 4×ShKAS mg, 6×RS-82 missiles

In Britain, the vital decision had been taken chapter, the vital decision had been taken by 1934 to use not just two machine-guns but a whole battery. Inevitably this demanded a much more powerful fighter, and the first of the new eight-gun monoplanes to go into production was Sydney Camm's Hurricane, by Hawker Aircraft. Partly because of its early start, and derivation from an earlier 'Interceptor Monoplane' with spatted landing year, this was a far from bold design – nothing like as advanced as Messerschmitt's new monoplane that ran parallel in timing in Germany. First flown on 6 November, 1935, the Hurricane was of considerable size, with a span of 40 feet, and it had a thick wing and rather deep and lumpy fuselage. Structure was of traditional Hawker form, with a fuselage based on a girder of tubes held together by multiple bolted fittings and with fabric covering everywhere except the nose and the wing leading-edges. The main advantage of the Hurricane was that it was put into production early and at a high rate, and enough were available to halt the Luftwaffe in its tracks in 1940. As a fighter it was outstanding in being a good steady gun platform, strong and reliable, and easy to repair; and if the pilot flew really boldly it was a fair dogfighter. But by 1940 it was severely handicapped in confrontations with the Bf 109E. which was smaller, faster and had cannon armament.

Partner to the Hurricane, Reginald Mitchell's Spitfire was smaller and of later concept, with stressed-skin construction. It was about as different as it could be from the Supermarine company's seaplanes, also designed by Mitchell, that had won the Schneider Trophy three times in succession. It was a fortunate thing for humanity that this was the case, because the fact that the Spitfire was of modern conception enabled it not only to beat all other fighters in direct combat in 1940 but also made it suitable for progressive development throughout the war. By 1945 the same basic design had double the power, much heavier armament and much higher performance. Its structural basis was a wing with a single spar at 25% chord (one-quarter of the way back from the leading edge) which, together with a thick skin wrapped round the leading edge, formed a D-section 'torsion box' that gave the wing great strength. As everyone knows, the wing was elliptical in plan-form, partly because this is an efficient shape and partly because it gave adequate depth well outboard for the outermost of the eight guns. But for a fighter to be built with minimum effort in huge numbers it was a curious choice.

Another series of fighters with elliptical wings came from the Seversky Aircraft Corporation in the United States. Designer Alexander Kartveli built an experimental two-seat fighter (the SEV-2XP) in early 1935 that established this form of wing as an efficient shape for an all-metal stressed-skin machine, and it was to last right through three generations of fighters of which the last was the famed P-47 Thunderbolt of the Second World War. From the original prototype emerged a rebuild called SEV-1XP with the rear cockpit removed, which led to a succession of attractive fighters called P-35 and 35A by the US Army Air Corps and EP-106 by Sweden. Fitted with landing gear that folded to the rear, projecting under the wing in stream-lined fairings, these shapely machines led to the XP-41 of early 1939 and the turbocharged AP-4 ordered into production in 1939 as the P-43 Lancer, the company having by this time been renamed Republic Aviation.

Chief rival to Kartveli's fighters were the new monoplane pursuits from the drawing board of Don R Berlin at Curtiss-Wright. His Design 75 was ready in May 1935, and was thus one of the first stressed-skin retractable-gear fighters to fly. Though beaten for Army orders by the Seversky P-35, Curtiss kept improving the aircraft, replacing the experimental XR-1670 by a familiar R-1820 Cyclone, and eventually (as did Seversky) finding success with the Pratt & Whitney Twin Wasp. In July 1937 the Army ordered 200 as the P-36, thus launching one of the biggest and most diverse families of fighters in all history. Fractionally larger than the P-35, the P-36 was a better basis for development, and while Republic had to suffer two total redesigns to increase the size, Curtiss kept in production with the same size of fighter until December 1944. A feature of virtually all the 15,000-odd monoplane 'Hawk fighters was that the landing legs rotated as they folded backwards so that the wheels could lie flat inside the wing. An exception was the Hawk 75 export model of 1937 which, following a policy of simplification, had fixed gear. This was sold to China and Thailand and mass-produced in Argentina.

In the second half of the 1930s the French industry, racked by the problems of an enforced nationalisation which still left a vast profusion of separate organisations as well as numerous private firms (which were deliberately deprived of priorities and subjected to many unnecessary delays and pinpricks), contrived to develop no fewer than 31 types of fighter. Of these the only one that came off the assembly line in large numbers before 1940 was the Morane-Saulnier M.S.406, an heir to a famous fighter name but a far from outstanding aircraft. Having only 860 hp and an armament of one 20-mm cannon and two machine guns it was described by one of its pilots as 'too slow to catch the enemy and too poorly armed and armoured to avoid being shot down'. Marcel Bloch, who later changed his name to Dassault (as today's world knows), produced one of the few fighters in history that actually refused to get off the ground. After a year of redesign it took to the air in October 1937 and eventually led to a family of radial-engined fighters greatly superior to the Morane. The late 1930s were marked by chaos and confusion in French defence production, with a liberal sprinkling of sabotage (caused mainly by the political left, despite the fact that the arms were needed for defence against Fascist Germany), and this crippled the Bloch fighters more than most. Not until 1940 were gunsights and propellers available so that pilot training could begin. Another French fighter that was even better, but available in quantity only after February 1940, was the Dewoitine D.520, a beautiful little machine that ought to have been started several years earlier as a natural follow-on to the D.510.

Italy and Japan doggedly clung to the old tradition of supreme manoeuvrability at all costs. Celestino Rosatelli of Fiat created a famous series of biplane fighters which had this quality in full, and they were especially notable for the Warren bracing of their wings (the diagonal struts having a W shape seen from the front). The only concession made to firepower was that the machine guns changed during the 1930s from 7.7-mm (rifle calibre) to 12.7-mm (the same as the US 0.50), and two 12.7-mm remained the armament of the new monoplanes produced by Fiat's other designer, Gabrielli, and the rival companies Macchi, Reggiane and Caproni-Vizzola. The basic

Even with a trousered undercarriage, the Martin-Baker MB.1 of 1934 looks elegant. The size of the tiny fin was increased after the first flight

Prototype Hurricane. The first flight was in November 1935

XP-40, a re-engined P-36 with an Allison in-line

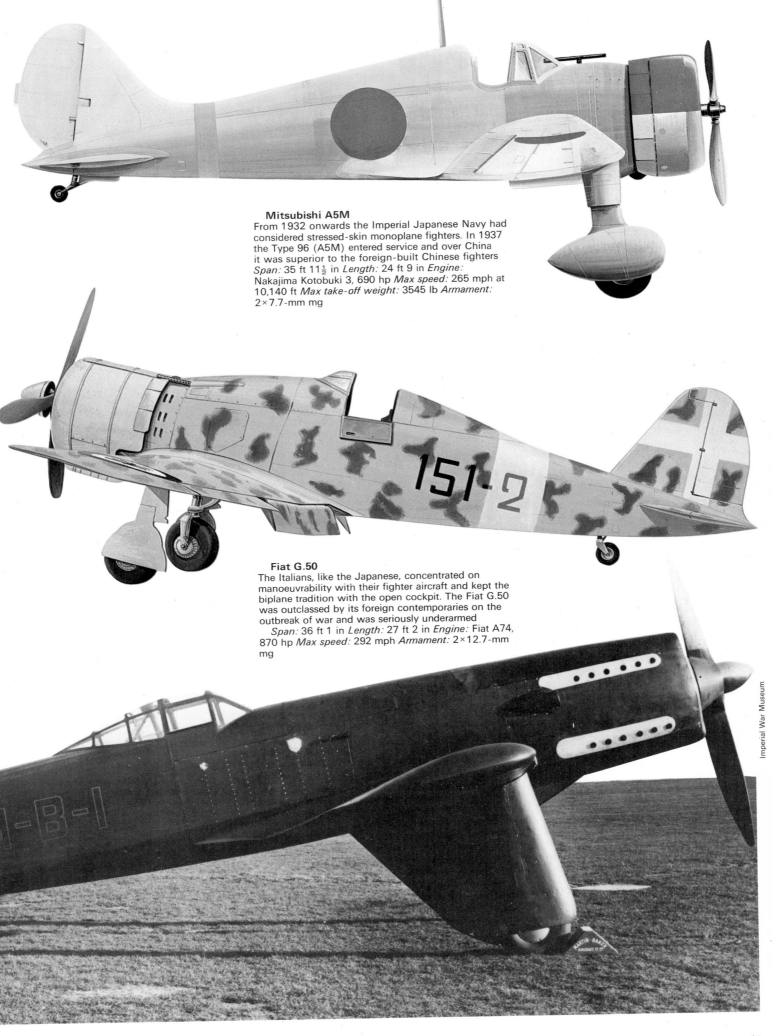

Mitsubishi A5M

From 1932 onwards the Imperial Japanese Navy had considered stressed-skin monoplane fighters. In 1937 the Type 96 (A5M) entered service and over China it was superior to the foreign-built Chinese fighters *Span:* 35 ft 11½ in *Length:* 24 ft 9 in *Engine:* Nakajima Kotobuki 3, 690 hp *Max speed:* 265 mph at 10,140 ft *Max take-off weight:* 3545 lb *Armament:* 2×7.7-mm mg

Fiat G.50

The Italians, like the Japanese, concentrated on manoeuvrability with their fighter aircraft and kept the biplane tradition with the open cockpit. The Fiat G.50 was outclassed by its foreign contemporaries on the outbreak of war and was seriously underarmed
Span: 36 ft 1 in *Length:* 27 ft 2 in *Engine:* Fiat A74, 870 hp *Max speed:* 292 mph *Armament:* 2×12.7-mm mg

Imperial War Museum

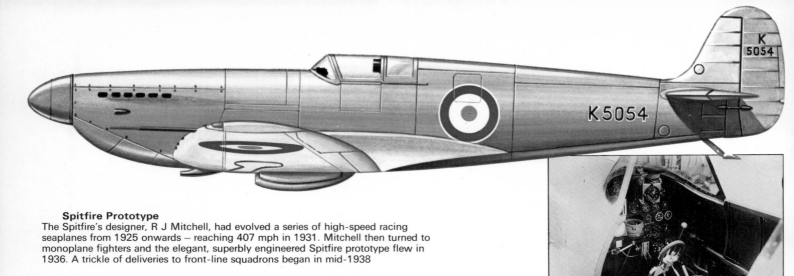

Spitfire Prototype
The Spitfire's designer, R J Mitchell, had evolved a series of high-speed racing seaplanes from 1925 onwards — reaching 407 mph in 1931. Mitchell then turned to monoplane fighters and the elegant, superbly engineered Spitfire prototype flew in 1936. A trickle of deliveries to front-line squadrons began in mid-1938

fault lay in a shortage of high-power engines, which condemned Italy to mediocre performance despite the light armament. In Japan the engine position was slightly better, though the chief fighters of the late 1930s were designed around developments of the Bristol Jupiter rated at a mere 600–700 hp. The Imperial Navy's main fighter was the Mitsubishi A5M, first flown in February 1935; that of the Army was the Nakajima Ki-27, flown in October 1936. Both were low-wing monoplanes with spatted wheels and open cockpits, and armed with a pair of Vickers guns just like a Sopwith Camel. But they were among the most nimble fighters ever made, and the prototype A5M reached 279 mph on only 585 hp, and climbed to 16,400 ft in less than six minutes. The loaded weight of the fully equipped service models was more than 1000 lb less than that of a Gladiator and not much more than half the weight of a Curtiss P-36 or Spitfire I.

These little monoplanes 'danced like a butterfly and stung like a bee', and in countless bitter battles that were hardly even mentioned in Western newspapers achieved dominance over the carefully designed monoplanes and biplanes of the Soviet Union. In the mid-1930s nobody could say with certainty how a fighter ought to be planned. The variables all fight each other. Less armament means less chance of downing the enemy, but more means a sluggish fighter with poor performance and reduced manoeuvrability. There is a fair element of luck in hitting the best basic design, and this certainly attended German Willi Messerschmitt when he bent over his drawing board at the Bayerische Flugzeugwerke in the winter 1934–35 and sketched his company's first military aircraft. Back in 1929 Messerschmitt had had a flaming row with Erhard Milch, the future Nazi Air Minister, in a dispute which bankrupted the company. Back in business in 1933, he got no work from the Nazis, and it was only when he was criticised for building aircraft for export (replying 'then give me a contract') that he was invited to build a prototype to meet the Luftwaffe's requirement for a new fighter. The aircraft flew, with a British Rolls-Royce engine, in September 1935.

Nobody devoted much attention to the Bf 109 at first, and it was regarded as such a rank outsider as to be almost a joke. Even Ernst Udet, the World War I ace who became head of the technical procurement section at the RLM (air ministry), scornfully said, 'That thing will never make a fighter'. It was small, long and rakish, with

a remarkably small wing and extremely severe lines. The cockpit seemed cramped, and had a hinged canopy that enclosed it completely. It looked tricky, unpleasant and utterly unlike the nimble, open-cockpit kind of machine Udet and other pilots hoped for. Trials at Travemünde began in October 1935, and it was very soon evident that the Bf 109 and its closest counterpart the Heinkel He 112 were way ahead of the other prototypes. It was expected that the Heinkel would win, but prolonged comparative testing kept bringing out the fact that the severe 109 could outfly the pretty 112. The narrow-track landing gear did not seem to bother pilots, and the fact the wheels were far forward made it possible to clamp the brakes on without nosing over. Full-span slats on the wings allowed extremely tight turns to be made, and altogether the 109 seemed to have the best chance of being developed with more powerful engines and heavier armament.

Fighter-Bomber
To the amazement of Heinkel and many others, an order for ten Bf 109s was placed in January 1936, and by May 1937 the Bf 109B was in large-scale production with the 635-hp Jumo 210 engine and armament of three machine guns. This sub-type proved extremely formidable in Spain, and the 109C, with four guns (two of them in the wings) was followed by the 109D with the 1000-hp DB 601 engine. Many D models had a 20-mm cannon firing through the propeller hub, and this was also common in the 1100-hp DB 601-engined Bf 109E, the first mass-produced series, which was the standard Luftwaffe fighter from 1938 until 1941. Some E models had two machine guns and no fewer than three cannon, and many also carried bombs weighing up to 551 lb, becoming the first land-based fighter-bombers in history.

The qualification 'land-based' must be added because from the late 1920s the US Navy had devoted great attention to hitting ships and other surface targets with relatively small carrier-based aircraft. While Britain's Fleet Air Arm made do with biplane fighters carrying two Vickers guns, the US Navy bought such advanced monoplanes as the Brewster F2A and Grumman G-36, both of which could carry two 100-lb bombs as well as four 0.50-in guns. Even previous US Navy generation, exemplified by the tubby Grumman F3F biplanes, had been fast and powerful, and able to carry the same bomb load. It was sheer bad luck that in Japan a designer named Jiro Horikoshi at the Mitsubishi company was

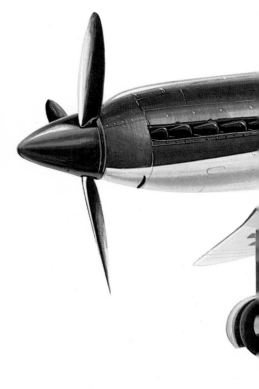

Inside the prototype Spitfire, a long way from the open cockpits of its fixed-undercarriage biplane contemporaries

creating a monoplane that would out-manoeuvre even the land-based fighters, outrange all other fighters, and carry two 20-mm cannon as well as two machine guns.

There remains one other category of fighter that came strongly to the fore after 1935. Whereas the *Multiplace de Combat* was virtually a non-starter, there seemed to be a need for a modern high-speed monoplane with two seats and/or two engines to serve as a bomber escort and to fly other long-range missions. Most countries bought such machines in numbers. France began with the Potez 63 family, the first of which flew in April 1936, so enough were on hand to make a real contribution to defence in May 1940 (and versatile

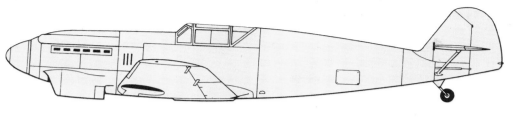

Bf 109VI

Bf 109A

Heinkel He 100

~~E~~xtremely fast but with very poor handling, the 12
~~pr~~oduction He 100D-1s were really high-speed
~~re~~search aircraft. They made excellent propaganda
~~wh~~en repeatedly repainted and photographed, baffling
~~Br~~itish intelligence into beleiving that large numbers of
~~th~~ese 'fighters' existed
~~Sp~~an: 30 ft 10¾ in *Length:* 26 ft 10¼ in *Engine:*
~~DB~~ 601M, 1020 hp *Max speed:* 416 mph at 13,120 ft
~~M~~ax take-off weight: 5512 lb *Armament:* 2×7.92-mm
~~M~~G 17 mg, 1×20-mm MG FF/M cannon

fighter. The Blenheim was also the only RAF night fighter, fitted with the newly invented AI radar, until the arrival of the Beaufighter (first flown in July 1939) which the RAF had never asked for.

Possibly the most successful of the early long-range fighters was the Messerschmitt Bf 110, which proved outstandingly useful in numerous duties until the summer of 1940 when it encountered the formidable and determined single-seaters of the RAF and suddenly proved vulnerable. Earlier the Luftwaffe had tried to buy an all-purpose aircraft with a *'Kampfzerstörer'* specification, but this proved a mistake (the Fw 57, Hs 127 and 124, Bf 162 and Ju 85/88 competed). Even the 110 would have proved a long-term error had it not been just right much later as a basis for a formidable radar-equipped night fighter. In the United States the Bell company chose as its first prototype in 1937 an extraordinary throwback to the concepts of 1916 but translated into modern stressed-skin and near-300-mph speed. The XFM-1 Airacuda had two pusher Allison engines in enormous overwing nacelles, in the front of which were gunners manning 37-mm cannon. But this was just one of many strange fighters. Britain's Hotspur and Defiant ought to have been regarded as freaks, because their entire armament was four machine guns in a power-driven turret behind the pilot; but the Defiant was actually mass-produced (it eventually made a good target tug).

Following a principle first explored by Dunne in 1907, the Westland Pterodactyl V of 1932 was a tailless fighter-bomber with pilot and rear gunner in a stubby nacelle hung under a swept wing with fins on the tips (it flew beautifully). In Holland Koolhoven built the F.K.55 with contra-rotating propellers driven by an engine behind the pilot, while Fokker built the G.1 with twin tail booms and a battery of eight guns in the nose, and the push-pull D.23 with an engine at each end of the central nacelle. To show the Dutch really could not make their minds up, De Schelde built the S.21 with a central nacelle housing one pilot, four machine-guns, a forward-firing 23-mm Madsen cannon and a second big Madsen firing aft through the hub of the pusher propeller driven by a DB 601 engine. This 370-mph machine could have been really formidable, but for some reason that will possibly never be explained was thought in Britain to be a German fighter called 'Focke-Wulf Fw 198'. Needless to say, several RAF pilots reported seeing the 'Fw 198', just as an even larger number reported the 'He 113' which was dreamed up by Goebbels using pictures of the prototypes of the defunct He 100. All fighters, good and bad, were at the mercy of faulty aircraft recognition until long into the era when electronics was supposed to take care of such matters.

enough to be developed for bombing and reconnaissance also). The Breguet 690 family were potentially even better, but suffered from faulty operational techniques that (among other things) made them sitting ducks for the German flak, in their role of attack bomber. The British Whirlwind was simply ill-conceived. Planned as a fighter armed with 20-mm cannon, it had a small wing and useless low-power engines of poor reliability and made only a minor contribution to the war. Likewise the Blenheim IF was a pathetic lash-up, converted from a bomber by fitting four puny machine guns under the belly to try to fill the yawning chasm in the RAF caused by complete absence of a modern long-range

Focke-Wulf 187 *Falke*
While Messerschmitts Bf 110 received full offical backing as the Luftwaffe's *Zerstörer* aircraft, Focke-Wulf developed its own twin-engined two-seat interceptor fighter as a semi-private venture. The few that were flown over Norway in 1940 were warmly praised by their pilots but not by the RLM, the German Air Ministry. The *Zerstörer* idea itself was soon disproved when the Bf 110s suffered a mauling during the Battle of Britain

Span: 50 ft 2⅜ in *Length:* 36 ft 5 in
Engine: 2×Jumo 210G, 700 hp *Max speed:* 326 mph at 13,800 ft *Ceiling:* 32,800 ft *Armament:* 4×7.92-mm MG 17 mg, 2×20-mm MG FF cannon

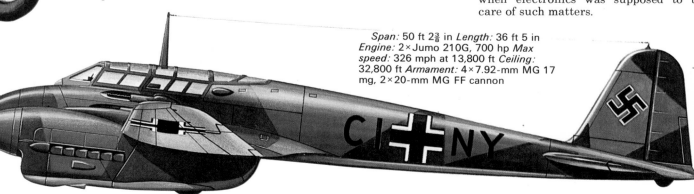

POWER FOR COMBAT

During the First World War the basic choice open to the designer of a fighter was to use either a water-cooled in-line or vee engine, closely related in concept to the engines of automobiles, or a totally different air-cooled rotary. As explained earlier, the rotary was subject to inherent shortcomings which made it gradually fade from the scene, but its place was taken by another engine that owed little to road vehicles. This was the static radial, with its cylinders arranged in the same way as those of the rotary, like spokes of a wheel, all the connecting rods acting on a single crankpin. The first radial in military aircraft was the Swiss-designed Canton-Unné, mass-produced by the Salmson company, and this was cooled by water. Virtually all subsequent radials were cooled by air flowing past the finned cylinders.

Throughout the inter-war period (1918–39) the question of which kind of engine was best for a fighter was the subject of prolonged and heated argument. Until the mid-1920s the water-cooled engines were dominant, partly because they were highly developed whereas the radials were a relatively new species dating from after 1917. But the proven advantages of such engines as the Bristol Jupiter, perfected in 1920–21, and the Pratt & Whitney Wasp, of 1925–26, gradually gave them the dominant share of the market. Really the only factor in favour of the water-cooled in-line was that it looked slimmer and more streamlined than the bluff, flat-fronted radial. This was not too apparent at first, but by 1922 the designers of racers were installing water-cooled engines in a way that seemed almost perfectly streamlined, with a pointed propeller spinner faired into a beautifully smooth engine cowl. Of course, the water cooling radiator spoilt things, but eventually ways were found to use flush cooling radiators in the wings, as had sometimes been done in the First World War.

Those who preferred the radial pointed out that the flush radiator systems of the racers were useless for fighters because they were troublesome, vulnerable to bullets and incapable of working in harsh service conditions. They demonstrated that the simple air-cooled radial, with a short crankshaft with all cylinders working on one crankpin, was lighter, cheaper to make and much easier to maintain. Its finned cylinders, much hotter in relation to the surrounding air than a water radiator, got rid of excess heat perfectly even in the hottest desert climate. Unlike the water-cooled engine, there was nothing to freeze in Arctic winter conditions, and no water circuit to need warming up. Absence of the water circuit and radiator saved weight and drag, while the shorter and more compact engine was especially suited to a fighter because it improved manoeuvrability and handling.

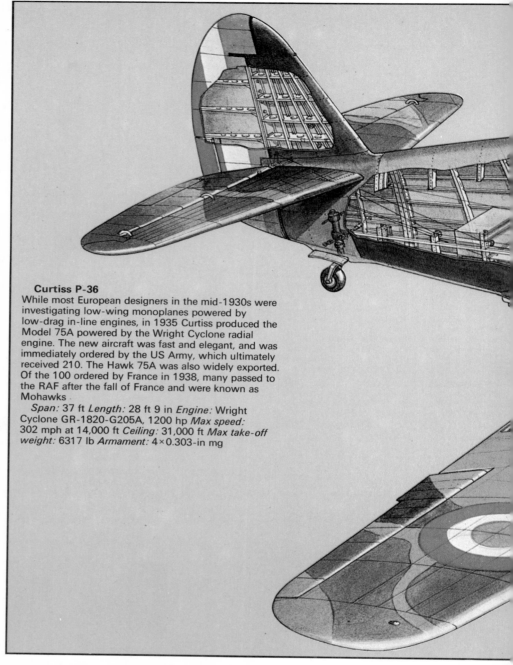

Curtiss P-36
While most European designers in the mid-1930s were investigating low-wing monoplanes powered by low-drag in-line engines, in 1935 Curtiss produced the Model 75A powered by the Wright Cyclone radial engine. The new aircraft was fast and elegant, and was immediately ordered by the US Army, which ultimately received 210. The Hawk 75A was also widely exported. Of the 100 ordered by France in 1938, many passed to the RAF after the fall of France and were known as Mohawks
  Span: 37 ft *Length:* 28 ft 9 in *Engine:* Wright Cyclone GR-1820-G205A, 1200 hp *Max speed:* 302 mph at 14,000 ft *Ceiling:* 31,000 ft *Max take-off weight:* 6317 lb *Armament:* 4 × 0.303-in mg

After extensive comparative trials the US Navy declared in 1928 it would buy no more water-cooled aircraft, and even discarded or re-engined almost new machines with such engines. The US Army kept using Liberty, Packard and, above all, Curtiss water-cooled engines until 1935, though by that time the radial had come to the fore in the Army also. Most air forces used either the radial or a mixture. By 1929 more than 70 per cent of the horsepower delivered for the French air force and navy was comprised of one radial, the Jupiter (built under licence by Gnome-Rhône), and as late as 1939 Bristol radial engines accounted for 52 per cent of the horsepower in the RAF. But behind the squadrons the influence of racing was distorting the picture.

During the 1920s the water-cooled V-engine was especially well suited to out-and-out racing. It could develop higher output from a given cubic capacity (engine cylinder size), was more readily installed in a streamlined way, and so tended to be used almost exclusively for the seaplanes that battled to win the coveted Schneider Trophy. In 1927, 1929 and 1931 British Supermarine

seaplanes powered by special Rolls-Royce racing engines won the trophy three times consecutively, thus bringing the contests to an end with the trophy in British hands for ever. This had the effect of putting a giant spurt behind high-power water-cooled engines and of planting in people's minds the belief that the radial could not compete. This was the situation when, in 1934–35, the future monoplane fighters were designed for the RAF (Hurricane and Spitfire) and Luftwaffe (Bf 109). By 1940 the resulting aircraft were locked in combat, powered by the Merlin and DB 601. The only fighters with radial engines were poor second-class citizens, such as the Curtiss Mohawk, the Polish PZL family and the Italians. The Russian and Japanese fighters were hardly taken seriously. It was a cosy feeling, but unfortunately totally erroneous.

Even today the powerful emotional link between the Schneider Trophy success, the Merlin engine and the Hurricane and Spitfire makes it difficult to accept the true facts. The superiority of such engines as the Merlin lay partly in the intense effort applied to their ancestors in the years of

racing, partly in the fact that they were simply bigger than most radials (and thus more powerful) and, above all, in the fact that it took a long time for designers to learn how to instal a radial in a high-speed aircraft. At first they simply stuck the cylinders out in the airstream. Then they tried to fair the cylinders in with individual 'helmets', or with tapering fairings behind each 'pot'. By 1929 the Townend ring was added, behaving like a slender circular wing helping to pull the aircraft along. In the early 1930s the NACA (US National Advisory Committee for Aeronautics) had developed long-chord cowls that enclosed the whole engine. Bristol then refined this by ducting the exhaust into the leading edge of the cowl and adding controllable flaps around the rear edge to adjust the cooling airflow. Each month, in 1929–39, the power of radial engines went up, the cooling was improved and the drag reduced.

Liquid-cooled engines fought back by switching from plain water to ethylene glycol, which prevented freezing, and allowed the transfer of heat to be greatly speeded up by using a high-pressure system

cooled by a smaller radiator offering less drag to the aircraft. Many fighters flew with no ordinary radiator at all, with steam cooling dissipating heat through surface condensers. The steam-cooled Rolls-Royce Goshawk was much in evidence in fighters in 1931–34 but eventually the steam-cooling philosophy was abandoned. Extremely attractive to the British Air Ministry, it resulted in an engine installation even more complicated and troublesome than ordinary water-cooling, and Rolls-Royce were glad to let it drop.

One of the fighters with a steam-cooled Goshawk was the Westland P.V.4 (F.7/30) of 1934. This reverted to an idea tried in one or two fighters in the First World War, but for different reasons. The heavy engine was placed in the mid-fuselage, between the biplane wings, while the pilot's cockpit and four Vickers guns were put in the nose. This seemed a sensible arrangement in that it gave the pilot a perfect view with an excellent armament installation, and having the engine on the centre of gravity improved manoeuvrability. Others thought so too. Among a crop of mid-engined fighters

emerged the Koolhoven FK.55 with an 860-hp Lorraine Petrel driving two contra-rotating propellers via a long shaft passing through the cockpit, the Italian Piaggio P.119 with a 1700 hp air-cooled radial buried in the centre-fuselage behind the cockpit, and the American Bell XP-39 Airacobra and carrier-based Airabonita. The latter differed in that the Airacobra was even more radical in having a nosewheel-type landing gear, yet it alone was built in large numbers and gave good service in the Second World War. Yet another way of putting the engine on the centre of gravity was to use a pusher propeller and carry the tail on booms, as was done by the De Schelde company with the S.21. An even more radical arrangement was to have no conventional tail at all, as in the Pterodactyl V and the Italian SAI S.S.4, first flown in May 1939, which had such revolutionary features as a steerable nosewheel, canard horizontal controls on the nose, and armament of two 20-mm and one 30-mm cannon. The tail-first idea was to be pursued by several fighter builders during the Second World War.

On balance, posterity must conclude that

the best place for the engine in a single-piston-engined fighter was in the nose, but there remained problems. As engines increased in power, from the 450 hp of the 1920s to 750 hp by 1935, 1000 hp by 1938 and 2000 hp in the prototypes of 1940, so did the area of the propeller blades to absorb the power have to increase. This end could be attained by increasing the number of blades, increasing the chord (width) of each blade or increasing the propeller diameter, but there were drawbacks to each of these choices. Later, all these answers were to be seen in abundant measure, together with the increasing use of the heavy, complex and possibly troublesome contraprop. A great advantage of the contraprop was that it cancelled out the reaction from a single large propeller which tends to rotate the whole aircraft in the opposite direction, whilst surrounding the tail in a powerful slipstream of air rotating in a vicious spiral. During the 1930s fighter pilots for the first time learned (often 'the hard way') to live with powerful engines in small fighters. Opening the throttle on take off caused a violent pull to left or right, depending on the direction of propeller rotation, and the torque (twist) imparted to the fuselage dug one mainwheel into the ground and tended to lift the other off, which in turn caused offset wheel drag during the take off run. The answer was 'a bootful of rudder', possibly accompanied by aileron, which had to be eased off as speed increased and the fighter left the ground. Of course, another and usually unrelated problem was that many fighters tended to 'swing' badly on takeoff, landing or both. A fighter would 'swing' by trying to pirouette round in a sudden half-circle on the ground and proceed tail-first, or sit on its belly amidst portions of smashed landing gear. This became an everyday occurrence in the

Second World War, and the only aircraft usually free from the hazard were the new breed with nosewheels.

More important than mere handling problems – which, authority decreed, competent pilots should learn to cope with – were those associated with maintaining power at high altitude and in turning shaft power into thrust. As outlined earlier, the answer to the need for power at height was the supercharger. At first this was a centrifugal blower, geared up from the crankshaft to rotate at very high speed to pump air into the cylinders. Special clutches were soon found to be necessary to remove shocks from the drive gears, eliminate vibration and, by the late 1930s, allow for a gearbox much like that in a road vehicle to drive the blower at different speeds. Later more complicated superchargers were developed with two blowers in series, the air being rammed in at a forward-facing inlet, compressed in the first blower, cooled in an intercooler to increase its density, and then pumped into the cylinders by a second blower. But in the United States the technically difficult turbo-supercharger had been under development since before the First World War, and during the late 1920s began to come into US Army service in advanced high-altitude biplane fighters. In 1935 a turbocharged Conqueror engine powered the Consolidated P-30 (PB-2A) two-seat monoplane fighter, giving it a speed of almost 250 mph at 25,000 ft and a ceiling of almost 29,000 ft. Turbochargers followed on many American fighters, the advantage being that, whereas the mechanically driven blower took power out of the engine via the gearwheels, the turbocharger merely used some of the power otherwise wasted in the hot exhaust gas.

Turning the power of the engine into thrust had traditionally been done by a

propeller carved from laminations of mahogany or other hardwood. By 1930 metal propellers were becoming common, especially for high-speed aircraft, because they were no longer significantly heavier and in many cases not only lasted longer but could be 'bent straight' after hitting the ground and put back into use. By this time the variable-pitch propeller had been more than ten years under development, and the two-position Hamilton was about to come into use in the USA. This relatively simple variable-pitch propeller could operate either in fine pitch, with the blades set at a small angle to the air, for maximum engine speed and power on takeoff or landing, or in coarse pitch, set at a large angle, for high-speed flight. During the 1930s these propellers came into general use, mainly on airliners and bombers rather than fighters until after 1936, when the absolute need for improved propellers could be seen even by the British (who were slowest off the mark, having been the first to work on the variable pitch propeller in the First World War).

By 1939 virtually every fighter in production in every country had an advanced variable-pitch or constant-speed propeller, the constant-speed type having a governor to adjust pitch automatically to any desired setting for best engine power or efficiency, without input from the pilot. The main French propellers were the Chauvière and Ratier, the Germans used the extremely good VDM and the Americans the pioneer Hamilton and the newer Curtiss electric. The only exceptions were the otherwise excellent Hurricane and Spitfire, which poured off the assembly lines fitted with solid wooden propellers just like those used on a Sopwith Camel. This disgraceful state of affairs was eventually put right by frantic efforts in 1940.

Liberty V12 Engine
The Liberty was designed by a consortium of US car manufacturers with the aid of Allied engineers and was rushed into production to power European and US aircraft. The First World War ended before the Liberty could make its full impact, but the engine remained in service through the 1920s and established the US aero-engine industry
 Power: 400 hp at 1750 rpm

Fitters work on the 110-hp Le Rhône engines of the Nieuport 17s of an American Expeditionary Force training squadron, 1917. The power:weight advantages of the rotary engine kept it in the front line until 1918 the war

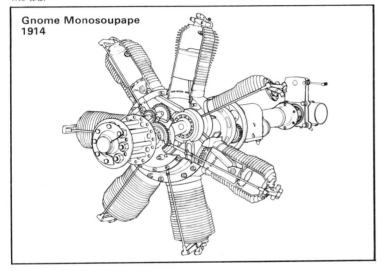

Gnome Monosoupape
1914

Aero-Engine Development 1909-1945

Date	Engine	Type	Power
1909	Anzani	3 cyl semi-radial	25 hp
1909	Gnome	rotary	50 hp
1912	Salmson/Canton-Unné	radial	110-130 hp
1913	Gnome Monosoupape	rotary	100 hp
1915	Oberursel	rotary	100 hp
1915	Rolls-Royce Eagle	V12	225 hp
1915	Benz Bz IV	6 cyl in-line	200 hp
1916	Le Rhone 9J	9 cyl rotary	110 hp
1917	Bentley B.R.2	9 cyl rotary	235 hp
1917	Siemens-Halske Shl	9 cyl geared rotary	110 hp
1917	Liberty	V12	400 hp
1920	Bristol Jupiter	9 cyl radial	480 hp
1923	Curtiss D-12	V12	435 hp
1924	Napier Lion	W12	450 hp
1930	Rolls-Royce Kestrel	V12	575 hp
1934	Pratt & Whitney R-1830 Twin Wasp	9 cyl radial	1200 hp
1935	Rolls-Royce Merlin	V12	990 hp
1936	Nakajima Kotobuki 2-kai-1	9 cyl radial	585 hp
1939	Daimler Benz DB 601A	V12	1100 hp
1940	Hispano-Suiza 12Y-45	V12	910 hp
1940	BMW 801C	14 cyl radial	1600 hp
1940	Nakajima NK1C Sakae 12	14 cyl radial	925 hp
1940	Fiat A-74	14 cyl radial	840 hp
1941	Napier Sabre IIA	H24	2180 hp
1941	Mikulin AM-35A	V12	1350 hp
1941	Daimler Benz DB 605A	V12	1475 hp
1943	Shvetsov M-82FN	14 cyl radial	1700 hp
1944	Junkers Jumo 004B	turbojet	1980 lb
1944	Walter HWK 509	liquid rocket	3750 lb

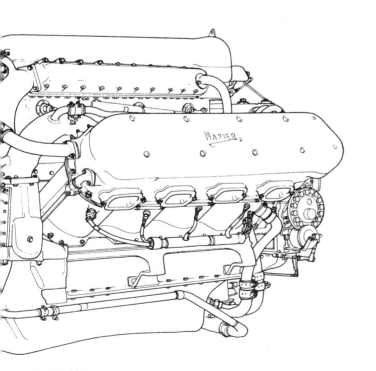

Napier Lion
When the British government issued a specification in 1916 for a 'high-power altitude engine', the Napier Lion with its 'broad arrow' W12 cylinder formation was a brilliant response and the engine was one of the most important of the 1920s undergoing continuous development
Power: (1927 VIIB) 875 hp at 2600 rpm

THE EAGLE ASCENDANT

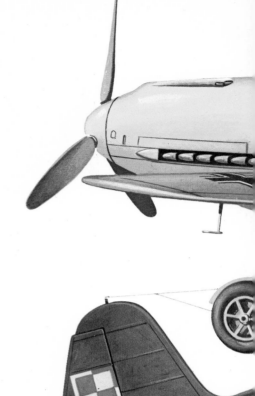

The opening of the Second World War was carefully stage-managed by Hitler after a faked 'incident' on the frontier between Germany and Poland. The start of operations, code-named *Ostmarkflug* in the Luftwaffe's secret orders, was timed for 04.45 on Friday 1 September, 1939, but the Ju 87B dive bombers of *Stuka Geschwader 1* were over-eager, and three of them, led by *Oberst* B Dilley, swooped on the bridge over the Vistula at Dirschau fifteen minutes too early. But this was of small consequence. The Poles had virtually no chance of stemming the German invasion, and the campaign that opened the greatest of all wars was completed in twenty-seven days of fierce action.

Hitler's Generals and Air Fleet Commanders liked to plan their campaigns in detail. Though strategic planning was almost totally absent – and in the long term this was to make a very large contribution to final defeat – in the short term everything possible was done to catch the enemy off-guard, hit him hard and, especially, knock out his fighting power in the shortest time. So on 1 September most of the initial strikes by the Luftwaffe were flown against Polish airfields, and within hours all the known military bases had been reduced to a shambles. More than 70% of the Polish front-line air strength was destroyed or incapacitated on the ground, though some aircraft escaped the initial attack, having been secretly dispersed a few days earlier.

By 3 September fewer than 30 Polish fighters were operating, out of the inventory total of 148, all of the P.11c type. The record of combat losses is confused. One frequently quoted report states that the P.11c squadrons shot down 126 German aircraft for the loss of 114 of their own number. This is erroneous. About 126 Luftwaffe aircraft were almost certainly shot down in air combat in the Polish campaign, but 114 is more than the total of Polish fighters available to be shot down. Almost the whole force of 148 was lost, but the best estimate is that more than 100 of these were written off in attacks on airfields, or in accidents in trying to operate from bombed airstrips.

On the whole the Polish pilots were experienced, and they lacked nothing in courage; but by 1939 the P.11c was obsolescent. The first P.11 had flown in August 1931, and though at that time it was one of the best fighters in the world, eight years later it was not in the same class as the opposition. The P.11c's structure was mixed. The landing gear was fixed, the gull wing externally braced, and the 645-hp Skoda-built Bristol Mercury radial was housed in a simple Townend ring cowl, driving a fixed-pitch wooden screw. Though the later P.11c, first flown in 1933, was able to carry the above-average armament of four 7.7-mm KMWz.33 machine guns, most of the 175

aircraft delivered to the Polish Air Force had only two, and they still had only two in 1939.

The gallant Polish Air Force set the pattern for most of the air forces that were to confront the Luftwaffe in the first year of war. Its strength was inadequate, and its attempts to remedy this had been hampered by late starts, muddles, delays and bad luck.

Compared with the Bf 109E, the P.11c had only one advantage: its radius of turn at speeds around 200 mph was marginally better. In the relatively few air combats that took place over Poland, the well-trained and confident Germans soon learned that even the early models of Bf 109 were excellent dogfighters, while the new E-1 sub-types, delivered in the six weeks prior to the Polish campaign, had two MG FF cannon and could pick off their targets at a distance. Earlier E-1s, and the E-0 and D variants, all of which participated in the Polish invasion, were armed with only four MG 17 machine guns.

The basic Messerschmitt design was an inspired conception by a design team with no previous experience of military aircraft, or even high-speed aircraft. Though at the start of its career it was widely derided, principally by pilots suspicious of any fighter with an enclosed cockpit and highly loaded monoplane wing, the Bf 109 gradually emerged as the most important combat aircraft of the war. It was built in much larger numbers than any other aircraft in history, save the Russian I1-2 armoured ground-attacker, and held its own to the bitter end despite the emergence of seemingly much superior designs and even jet aircraft.

During the Polish campaign the Luftwaffe was still using the Bf 109B, C and D in front-line fighter wings, but all were being replaced as fast as possible by the E. The B and C had modest performance on the Junkers Jumo 210 engine of 720 or 730 hp, the maximum speed falling well short of 300 mph. Armament of the B, which had equipped the *Legion Kondor* in Spain from 1937, was only three 7.92-mm MG17 machine guns, the middle gun lying between the engine cylinder-blocks and giving prolonged trouble from overheating. The C had four MG 17s, two of them in the wings. The D was the first model with the 1000-hp Daimler-Benz DB 600 engine, and the usual armament was one 20-mm MG FF cannon firing through the propeller hub, and two wing-mounted MG 17s. It was an adequate fighter, but the E (*Emil*) was even better, and supplanted the D when only about 200 of the latter had been built. The most important change was the DB 601A engine, which suffered development snags that held back the E until 1939, but in return gave 1175 hp (with promise of a lot more to come) and featured direct injection of fuel into the cylinders. This enabled the *Emil*, and many

PZL P.11

The P.11, based on the P.7, was in its P.11c variant the most numerous Polish fighter to engage the invading German forces in September 1939. The licence-built P.11f version was operated by the Romanian Air Force as late as 1941, but the fall of Poland prevented the introduction of the improved P.11g *Kobuz* variant

Span: 35 ft 2 in *Length:* 24 ft 9½ in *Engine:* PZL-built Bristol Mercury VI S.2, 645 hp *Max speed:* 242 mph at 18,000 ft *Ceiling:* 36,000 ft *Max take-off weight:* 3960 lb *Armament:* 2 or 4×7.7-mm KM Wz.33 mg, 2×27-lb bombs

other Luftwaffe aircraft, to ignore cold weather and outmanoeuvre their opponents. Not least of the *Emil*'s assets was its powerful armament of two 20-mm MG FF cannon in the wings and two synchronised MG 17s.

Admittedly the MG FF was a relatively puny 20-mm weapon, but it was reliable and could destroy opposing fighters with a single good hit. Moreover, it was effective from ranges more than double the effective limit for rifle-calibre weapons, and in some of the Polish fighting this advantage was exploited to the full (it had not been possible in the limited, close dogfighting in Spain to come to any conclusions about the few E-1s that fought there, often with only four MG 17s).

Combat over Poland invariably took place between isolated aircraft, and the fact that it was one-sided prevented the Luftwaffe from learning useful lessons. There was only one aeroplane in Poland that approached the 109 in performance, and even that fell far short. The PZL P.50 *Jastrzab* was started too late and was

68

Messerschmitt Bf 109E-3

The Bf 109E series were the first true mass-production models, and the E-1 was standard equipment when Germany went to war in 1939. The E-3 with a 20-mm cannon mounted to fire through the spinner entered production later that year and by mid-1940 was the main type

Span: 32 ft 4½ in *Length:* 28 ft 4 in *Engine:* Daimler-Benz DB 601A, 1100 hp *Max speed:* 354 mph at 12,300 ft *Ceiling:* 37,500 ft *Max take-off weight:* 5523 lb *Armament:* 2×7.92-mm MG 17 mg, 3×20-mm MG FF cannon

Business end of a Bf 109E-3 with a 20-mm cannon firing through the airscrew hub. (Inset) Professor Willy Messerschmitt, designer of some of Germany's most important wartime aircraft

John Batchelor

69

grossly underpowered (840-hp Mercury) and generally undistinguished; the solitary prototype was mistakenly shot down by Polish anti-aircraft fire.

In the Norwegian campaign the Luftwaffe came up against the RAF. The first RAF unit in Norway was 263 Sqn, equipped with Gladiators, which had flown from HMS *Glorious*, lying off the Norwegian coast, on 24 April 1940. Thereafter they operated from the frozen Lake Lesja.

The Gladiator was the ultimate answer to the RAF's F.7/30 requirement, and in 1930, the year it was drawn up, it would have been outstanding. Although it could have been in service (with a slightly earlier Mercury engine) in 1932, the Gladiator was so delayed by official indecision that it did not fly until 1934, and did not reach the RAF until well into 1937. At first armed with two synchronised Vickers machine guns and two Lewis under the lower wing, the Gladiator was totally obsolete by 1939, even though by then the armament had been changed to four rifle-calibre Brownings. It was a pleasant and manoeuvrable machine, but with a fixed-pitch wooden screw was not in the same class as the 109E; moreover, it lacked any form of armour protection. So, too, did most Bf 109s at this time, but the Gladiator was much more in need of it. The Norwegian Air Force had bought six Gladiator Is and six Mk IIs with three-blade fixed-pitch metal propeller, and these were still on their winter skis when the Luftwaffe arrived.

Nevertheless the Gladiators did extremely well. Nine Norwegian Gladiators had remained in April 1940, and these destroyed considerably more than nine of the enemy. Although all were eventually destroyed, only one was shot down. The same pattern characterised 263 Sqn. The RAF machines had wheels instead of skis, and on the ice were barely controllable. Subjected to daily bombing and strafing, it is a marvel that any survived to the second day, but in fact five were still serviceable three days later. In that time 13 had been destroyed on the ground, but only one in the air. The embattled 263 Sqn claimed 15 aerial victories, including BF 110s, He 111s and He 115s, Ju 52/3m transports, and at least one Bf 109. When fuel ran out on 27 April, the five survivors were burned, and it took three weeks to steam back to Britain and return with fresh aircraft. This time 16 Gladiators operated for two weeks in May–June 1940 from Bardufoss airfield, where there were at least hangars and huts. They claimed a further 26 confirmed victories for the loss of only five in the air and ten on the ground. Sadly, the rest were sunk whilst homeward bound in *Glorious*.

These remarkable results run counter to the assertion that the Gladiator was an obsolete aircraft. The fact that it was so judged is inescapable, and the type played virtually no part in the desperate battles over France or England. Gladiators, and the very similar Sea Gladiator, saw much action in the Mediterranean theatre in 1940–41, but this was simply because they were better than nothing. Although it possessed an adequate turn radius, by 1940 standards the Gladiator was deficient in every aspect of performance and lacked firepower and protection. The Gladiator was an exact parallel to the Italian C.R.42, but its scoreboard was dramatically better, in Norway at least.

In Finland, Gladiators saw fierce action in the 1939–40 war against the Soviet invader. The Finnish Air Force had 30 Gladiators, and these were soon condemned as virtually useless. According to the Finns, the I-16 could always get the better of a Gladiator unless the latter had an exceptional pilot; against the I-15 *bis* and I-153 biplanes a Gladiator had no chance, and 13 were destroyed in air combat. Against Soviet bombers the weak firepower of the British fighter was compounded by its inability to catch either an SB-2 or an Il-4. Yet the volunteer Swedish squadron of J8A Gladiators sent to help the Finns downed six fighters and six bombers for the loss of two Gladiators in the air and one on the ground. The reason lay in the small engine, of only 645 or 840 hp, which by 1940 was unable to carry adequate firepower, armour and equipment and reach a competitive performance.

However, there are always exceptions to most rules. In the early 1930s the French Caudron-Renault company designed a series of outstanding baby racers, chiefly for the Coupe Deutsch de la Meurthe trophy, which were truly remarkable for the performance they obtained on 450-hp Renault engines. These inverted V-12 engines had a frontal area smaller than that of the seated pilot, and unlike other in-line engines were air-cooled and thus needed no plumbing or radiator.

Polikarpov I-16
The I-16 remained the Russians' most important front-line fighter well into 1941 and thousands were destroyed on the ground and in the air during the opening stages of the German attack. During the Winter War skis were standard equipment
Span: 29 ft 6½ in *Length:* 20 ft 1¾ in *Engine:* M-62 radial, 700 hp *Max speed:* 300 mph *Ceiling:* 31,500 ft *Max take-off weight* 4546 lb *Armament:* 4×7.6-mm mg

Gloster Sea Gladiator
The Sea Gladiator, the Fleet Air Arm's last single-seat biplane fighter, differed from its land-based counterpart in having an arrester hook, catapult attachment points and provision for a dinghy beneath the fuselage
Span: 32 ft 3 in *Length:* 27 ft 5 in *Engine:* Bristol Mercury VIIIA, 840 hp *Max speed:* 245 mph at 15,000 ft *Ceiling:* 32,000 ft *Max take-off weight:* 5420 lb *Armament:* 4×0.303-in Browning mg

By 1939 the *Armée de l'Air* had extensively tested several prototypes or racers and ordered 100 C.714 fighters. One Caudron had carried two cannon, but the 714 had just four machine guns. Later the French cancelled the contract, claiming that rate of climb was inadequate (though it was only fractionally worse than for an M.S. 406 or Hurricane I). Eventually, between 50 and 100 were built, a few reaching Finland and the rest equipping GC I/145, an *Armée de l'Air* fighter unit manned by escaped Poles. The slim Caudrons saw brief but violent combat over northern France, and certainly gained a much better than 1:1 kill ratio. In Finland, however, they proved too 'hot' for the short, boggy airstrips.

This neat and significant machine was built of wood, needed only 5000 man-hours to manufacture, and had a gross weight of 3858 lb. Moreover, in January 1940 testing began of the C.R.760, with more powerful engine, metal fuselage, and six guns with the exceptional ammunition capacity of 500 rounds per gun. It proved to be a splendid performer, reaching 334 mph, having outstanding manoeuvrability and being very simple to maintain. In May 1940 the C.R.770, powered by an 800-hp Renault, reached 367 mph. France, and possibly all the Allies, may well have done better to have concentrated on aircraft of this class in the

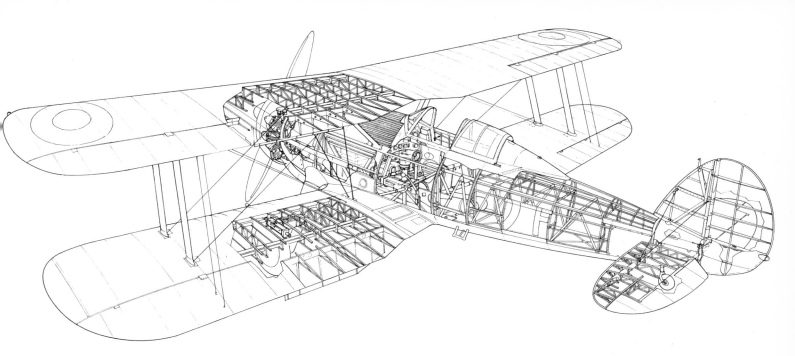

late 1930s rather than on a profusion of much larger and more complex machines which could not be made available in quantity in time.

In almost every respect the French aircraft programme of the late 1930s was a disaster. To some degree the situation resulted from an excess of planning, with the plans continually being changed. The industry had been thrown into chaos by nationalisation under a law of 1936, which grouped most manufacturing capacity into geographical units quite unrelated to their products and left other companies in private hands hamstrung by their inability to get delivery of vital parts (which were reserved for the priority use of the nationalised plants). But the worst problem of all was the multiplicity of different types, and when this was combined with the activities of what must have been a substantial number of saboteurs and troublemakers, the result was that few aircraft reached the *Armée de l'Air*.

The only fighter to reach the *Groupes de Chasse* in reasonable numbers was the Morane-Saulnier M.S.406, and this was a second-rate machine that reflected its early conception. Although developed at the same time as the Bf 109 and Hurricane, the root cause of the aircraft's inadequacy was the mere 860 hp of its Hispano-Suiza 12Y engine. Production began at Bouguenais in June 1938, and by the outbreak of war had reached eleven per day, backed up by a second line at Puteaux. By the Armistice

Fokker D.XXI
First flown in 1936, the D.XXI was licence-built in Finland from 1939 and was immediately involved in the fighting with Russia, becoming responsible for the first Finnish air victory in the Winter War
Span: 36 ft 1 in *Length:* 26 ft 3 in *Engine:* Pratt & Whitney Twin Wasp Junior, 825 hp *Max speed:* 272 mph at 9000 ft *Ceiling:* 32,000 ft *Max take-off weight:* 4820 lb *Armament:* 4 × 7.9-mm mg

of 25 June, 1940, some 1080 Moranes had been delivered, but according to their pilots they were, 'though free from vices and very manoeuvrable, too slow to catch the German bombers and too badly armed to shoot them down. Ill-armoured, our losses were high.'

Second in importance among French fighters was the Bloch 150 series. This had started with a 1936 prototype which refused to fly, but by 1939 the Bloch 151 was in production and could have given the *Armée de l'Air* some much-needed muscle. Bloch had been nationalised as SNCASO, but though this organisation enjoyed priority over such private companies as Breguet, the prevailing muddle and sabotage prevented delivery of more than a trickle of propellers and then halted output of gunsights completely. Eventually, 140 moderately useful 151s, with 920-hp Gnome-Rhône radial and four machine guns, were followed by 488 152s with an improved engine of just over 1000 hp and two 20-mm cannon and two machine guns. Unfortunately they arrived too late, and in many cases the Bloch pilot's first combat mission was also his first flight on the type. But the record of 188 victories for the loss of 86 Bloch pilots dead, wounded or taken prisoner is testimony to a sound combat aircraft, which was extremely strong, excellent to fly, and possessed adequate performance and more than adequate hitting power.

France's third most numerous fighter was the Hawk 75A, bought from Curtiss in the United States. Though only 291 actually reached the *Armée de l'Air* before the Armistice, they did much more fighting than any other type except the Morane for the simple reason that Curtiss (unlike the French industry) delivered ahead of time, and there was plenty of time to get pilots and ground crews trained and squadrons operational. The standard Hawk 75A had a Pratt & Whitney Twin Wasp of 1050 or 1200 hp and armament of four or six FN-built Browning machine guns. Speed was comfortably over 300 mph, most reaching 311-323 mph; structural strength, manoeuvrability, handling qualities and ease of maintenance were all good. The Curtiss equipped five groups – GC I/4, II/4, I/5, II/5 and III/2 – and these were credited with a remarkable 311 victories. In the 1er *Escadrille* (squadron) of I/5 were *Lt* Marin-la-Meslée (20 victories), *Capts* Accart (15) and Vasatko (15), *Sous-Lt* Perina (13) and *Sgt-chef* Morel (12); virtually all these victories were gained between 10 May and 23 June 1940. The Curtiss units had the advantage of proper equipment and thorough training, which in turn resulted in high morale even in the adversity and chaos of the great retreat.

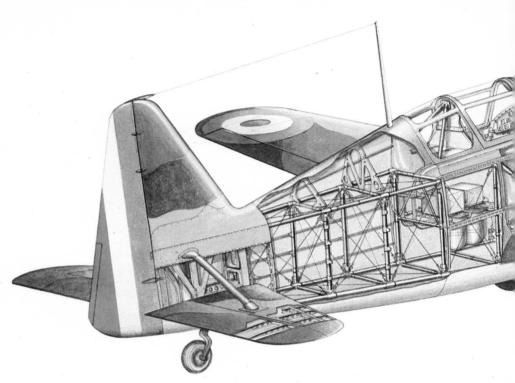

France did possess superior fighters, but these made only a small impact on the battle. The Dewoitine D.520 is generally judged the best of the fighters that saw action, but though the nationalised SNCA du Midi worked production up to an excellent 299 aircraft during June 1–25, no aircraft reached a squadron until March 1940, when GC I/3 began to convert. A neat and extremely manoeuvrable machine, the 520 reached an adequate 329 mph on only 910 hp and carried one Hispano cannon and four machine guns. Though most of the pilots who flew it into action had no experience on the type, they were credited with 147 victories for the loss of 85 aircraft and 44 pilots. Beyond the 520 were many excellent prototypes and projects, such as the Merlin-engined 521, the even more powerful 520Z, and the redesigned 551. Likewise the Bloch 155 was in production in June 1940, followed by the outstanding Bloch 157 which, with a 1700-hp Gnome-Rhône 14R radial, reached 441 mph and easily out-performed all other fighters of the first half of the war.

A list of the remaining French fighters of 1940 seems endless. By far the most important of the twin-engined long-range escort and night fighters was the Potez 631, first flown in 1936 and in production with Hispano-Suiza 640-hp radials the following year. The main production variant had 670-hp Gnome-Rhône engines, reached approximately 280 mph and carried two 20-mm cannon under the slim two-seat fuselage. In February 1940, when just over 200 were in use, six machine guns were added in trays under the outer wings, making the Potez the most heavily armed machine in service. It was an attractive aircraft, and pleasant to fly, but as a combat aircraft simply lacked power. It took nine minutes to climb to 4000 m (13,120 ft) and was much slower even than a Ju 88, let alone a Bf 109. The Potez plant turned increasingly to attack and reconnaissance versions of the 630 family, a novel single-seat fighter, the Potez 230, remaining a one-off.

Breguet's neat 690 family were used mainly in the attack role, and to speed output of these machines the SNCAC Bourges plant dropped the Hanriot NC 600 twin-engined fighter despite the latter's excellent performance (337 mph), heavy armament (three Hispano cannon and two machine guns) and generally good handling.

An even more impressive twin-engined fighter was the S.E.100, first flown on 2 April, 1939. This was a remarkable aircraft, with ailerons forming the wing-tips, a stumpy body, a single nosewheel and three small wheels on the rear tip of the body and under the twin fins. However, there was nothing wrong with the S.E.100's speed (360 mph), handling or armament of four forward-firing Hispano cannon and a fifth firing from the rear cockpit. In 1940 a second S.E.100 was built with six forward-firing cannon, two in a rear dorsal turret and one in a ventral tunnel. To mount nine 20-mm cannon in a 360-mph fighter in the spring of 1940 was an extraordinary accomplishment.

Probably the best of all the French fighters were the Galtier/Vernisse designs at the Arsenal de l'Aéronautique, which reached mass production by the spring of 1940 as the VG 33. This aircraft did the very best it could with an Hispano-Suiza of only 860 hp, and with one cannon and four machine guns reached the excellent speed of 347 mph. It was a fine-looking aircraft, and 160 had taken shape on the assembly line by the Armistice, though only seven reached the squadrons (beginning with GC I/2) and pilot conversion had not started. Prototypes had flown of the 910-hp VG 34, 1100-hp VG 35 and 1280-hp VG 39, which reached 388 mph with one cannon and six machine guns.

The strangest Arsenal fighter was the Delanne 10, which achieved the excellent speed of 342 mph on only 860 hp. Delanne was the pioneer of the tandem-wing aircraft, for which he claimed many advantages in centre of gravity travel, manoeuvrability and safety. The Delanne 10 had slats on the forward wing and a rear wing which could be considered as a large tailplane/elevator combination. At the rear sat the pilot and rear-facing gunner with two machine guns to discourage tail-chasers. Forward-firing armament comprised one cannon and two machine guns, but this had not been fitted when the extraordinary fighter first flew, under German supervision, in October 1941.

There were many other French fighters that never reached the starting line, including the CAO.200 (culmination of the Loire Nieuport 160 and 161 families) and even seaplanes. But one fighter that did get into action was the Dutch Koolhoven F.K.58, ordered for the *Armée de l'Air* in the winter of 1938 to help make up for the lateness of nearly all the French programmes. Fritz Koolhoven's team at Waalhaven, near Rotterdam, had produced many interesting aircraft, including the F.K.55 fighter with contra-props driven by an engine behind the pilot. But the F.K.58 was a straightforward machine, constructed in a mere two months in August–September 1938, which reached 313 mph on its first flight, powered by a 1080-hp Hispano-Suiza radial. Armed with four FN-Browning machine guns, it was merely an adequate aircraft; only 18, delivered to France in the late summer of 1939, reached squadrons (one reason was that later French batches specified Gnome-Rhône engines which were never delivered). But the 18 that reached France were formed into local-defence *Patrouilles de Protection*, manned by escaped Polish pilots.

No F.K.58 reached the LVA (Dutch Air Force), whose principal fighter in May 1940 was the outdated Fokker D.XXI. First flown in 1936, this was a serviceable and workmanlike machine, but too advanced in concept. It had mixed wood/metal construction, with covering of fabric or metal panels, just as in aircraft of the 1920s; though it was a cantilever monoplane with small split flaps, it

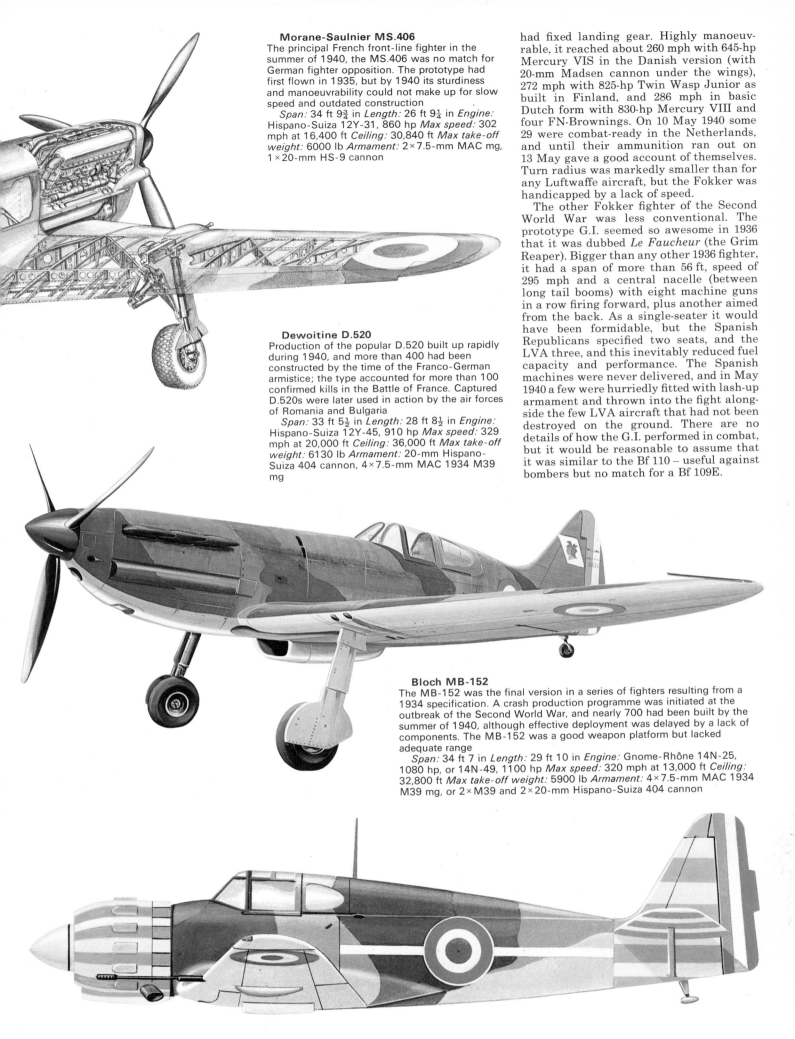

Morane-Saulnier MS.406

The principal French front-line fighter in the summer of 1940, the MS.406 was no match for German fighter opposition. The prototype had first flown in 1935, but by 1940 its sturdiness and manoeuvrability could not make up for slow speed and outdated construction

Span: 34 ft 9¾ in *Length:* 26 ft 9¼ in *Engine:* Hispano-Suiza 12Y-31, 860 hp *Max speed:* 302 mph at 16,400 ft *Ceiling:* 30,840 ft *Max take-off weight:* 6000 lb *Armament:* 2×7.5-mm MAC mg, 1×20-mm HS-9 cannon

Dewoitine D.520

Production of the popular D.520 built up rapidly during 1940, and more than 400 had been constructed by the time of the Franco-German armistice; the type accounted for more than 100 confirmed kills in the Battle of France. Captured D.520s were later used in action by the air forces of Romania and Bulgaria

Span: 33 ft 5½ in *Length:* 28 ft 8½ in *Engine:* Hispano-Suiza 12Y-45, 910 hp *Max speed:* 329 mph at 20,000 ft *Ceiling:* 36,000 ft *Max take-off weight:* 6130 lb *Armament:* 20-mm Hispano-Suiza 404 cannon, 4×7.5-mm MAC 1934 M39 mg

Bloch MB-152

The MB-152 was the final version in a series of fighters resulting from a 1934 specification. A crash production programme was initiated at the outbreak of the Second World War, and nearly 700 had been built by the summer of 1940, although effective deployment was delayed by a lack of components. The MB-152 was a good weapon platform but lacked adequate range

Span: 34 ft 7 in *Length:* 29 ft 10 in *Engine:* Gnome-Rhône 14N-25, 1080 hp, or 14N-49, 1100 hp *Max speed:* 320 mph at 13,000 ft *Ceiling:* 32,800 ft *Max take-off weight:* 5900 lb *Armament:* 4×7.5-mm MAC 1934 M39 mg, or 2×M39 and 2×20-mm Hispano-Suiza 404 cannon

had fixed landing gear. Highly manoeuvrable, it reached about 260 mph with 645-hp Mercury VIS in the Danish version (with 20-mm Madsen cannon under the wings), 272 mph with 825-hp Twin Wasp Junior as built in Finland, and 286 mph in basic Dutch form with 830-hp Mercury VIII and four FN-Brownings. On 10 May 1940 some 29 were combat-ready in the Netherlands, and until their ammunition ran out on 13 May gave a good account of themselves. Turn radius was markedly smaller than for any Luftwaffe aircraft, but the Fokker was handicapped by a lack of speed.

The other Fokker fighter of the Second World War was less conventional. The prototype G.I. seemed so awesome in 1936 that it was dubbed *Le Faucheur* (the Grim Reaper). Bigger than any other 1936 fighter, it had a span of more than 56 ft, speed of 295 mph and a central nacelle (between long tail booms) with eight machine guns in a row firing forward, plus another aimed from the back. As a single-seater it would have been formidable, but the Spanish Republicans specified two seats, and the LVA three, and this inevitably reduced fuel capacity and performance. The Spanish machines were never delivered, and in May 1940 a few were hurriedly fitted with lash-up armament and thrown into the fight alongside the few LVA aircraft that had not been destroyed on the ground. There are no details of how the G.I. performed in combat, but it would be reasonable to assume that it was similar to the Bf 110 – useful against bombers but no match for a Bf 109E.

THE BATTLE OF BRITAIN

The Battle of Britain was one of the truly decisive battles in the history of warfare, and, like Waterloo, was 'a damned close-run thing'. It was not entirely a case of David besting Goliath; aircraft and men on both sides were outstanding, and often the fighting was on equal terms, or even in the favour of the Luftwaffe. Nor was either side 'defeated' in any accepted sense of the word; both air forces were approximately as strong at the end of the daylight battle as at the beginning. But imperfect top-level planning and direction by Germany allowed the desperately hard-pressed RAF a vital breathing-space; and geography restricted the Bf 109 to penetrations hardly extending beyond Kent and Sussex. Moreover, Sir Robert Watson-Watt's early-warning radar chain (combined with the inventions of IFF – Identification Friend or Foe – and VHF voice links with a ground-based fighter controller) made an incalculable difference to the effectiveness of every British fighter.

Over Europe the Bf 109 dominated the skies, though the D.520 had run it close, and sheer pilot skill and courage had often narrowed the gap with the Curtiss and Bloch. From the earliest days of the war the 109E had met the Hurricane I over the so-called Western Front in sporadic and usually individual combats. Ultimately no fewer than twelve Hurricane squadrons had fought in France, and, as few returned, the RAF lost about one-quarter of its front-line strength in trying to delay the German advance. Nearly all these Hurricanes had been of the Mk I type with a 1030-hp Merlin I driving a Watts fixed-pitch wooden propeller; armament comprised eight 0.303-in Browning machine guns in a fabric-covered wing. Their performance was markedly inferior to the Messerschmitt in every respect other than turn radius; and even this advantage was seldom exploited because of pilots' inexperience and timidity. To survive, Hurricane pilots needed a wide-open throttle and a stick boldly placed in the far corners of the cockpit. Even then, the direct-injection Daimler-Benz engine, with its complete indifference to negative-g manoeuvres, gave the 109E a major advantage; but again it was pilot inexperience that often left this advantage unused. In any case, if a 109 stuffed its nose down and dived, it made little difference that the Merlin would cough and stop running if the British pilot tried to follow, because – surprisingly – both the Hurricane and Spitfire could catch a diving 109.

From its inception in 1934, at the same time as the 109, the Hurricane had possessed a great asset in the Merlin engine, which was significantly more powerful than the engines of the Luftwaffe's Continental opponents and made a considerable difference to aircraft performance. At the same time the Hurricane was handicapped by being large and cumbersome, having a primitive structure, a crude propeller and rifle-calibre guns. At first it also lacked protection, as did its adversary, but in 1938–40 the Hurricane progressively received an armoured bulkhead forward of the cockpit, bullet-proof windscreen, constant-speed three-blade propeller, metal stressed-skin wings, and finally, from February 1940, seal-sealing tanks and rear armour. Cannon were also fitted, but these did not enter service until 1941.

The heavy attrition in France, amounting to 386 Hurricanes between 10 May and 20 June, 1940, resulted in the urgent re-issue to Fighter Command of many old Mk I Hurricanes with fabric wings and Watts propeller, and with these a dogfight against an experienced 109E pilot was a tough proposition. Maximum speed of a new Hurricane was around 316 mph, but the much-repaired veterans, burdened now by armour and extra equipment, did not, in Lord Dowding's experience, exceed 305 mph. Yet this did not quite put them in the class of such also-rans as the Morane. Determinedly flown, even a patched-up Mk I could out-manoeuvre a 109 sufficiently well to avoid being shot down. The Mk I was also the best and steadiest gun-platform, an extremely forgiving aircraft (so that a badly wounded pilot could get back on the grass in one piece) and easy to repair. Though ability to take punishment does not of itself win wars, it helps. By contrast the 109 did not absorb punishment so well.

The Spitfire also lacked the ability to take heavy punishment. Though much less important numerically than the Hurricane in

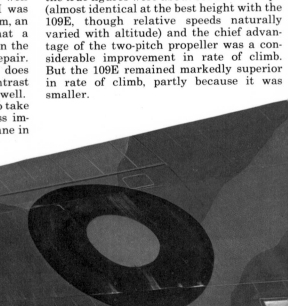

the first year of war, and not used over France (except on occasion over Dunkirk), the Spitfire was the only fighter that could claim to be marginally superior to the 109E – though this remains a matter for argument. It was slightly later in conception, and from the start the structure was unnecessarily complex and difficult to make and repair, remaining so throughout the war until the development of the completely new airframe of the Spiteful in 1944. These manufacturing problems were responsible for delaying production, and the first Spitfire

did not reach the RAF until August 1938. The only propeller was a two-blade wooden monstrosity, but early in production (aircraft No 78) this gave way to a less clumsy product, the American Hamilton two-pitch bracket type for which de Havilland had obtained a licence. In 1938 the published speed of the Spitfire I was 367 mph (387 mph with the new propeller). In fact the true figures were about 355 and 357 mph (almost identical at the best height with the 109E, though relative speeds naturally varied with altitude) and the chief advantage of the two-pitch propeller was a considerable improvement in rate of climb. But the 109E remained markedly superior in rate of climb, partly because it was smaller.

Hawker Hurricane Mk I

The Hurricane was numerically the most important RAF fighter during the Battle of Britain, the first squadron having become operational in January 1938; more than 500 were in service on the outbreak of war. The decision to pull the Hurricane squadrons back from the debacle in France was crucial when the battle over southern England began

Span: 40 ft *Length:* 31 ft 4 in *Engine:* Rolls-Royce Merlin II, 979 hp *Max speed:* 316 mph at 17,750 ft *Ceiling:* 33,750 ft *Max take-off weight:* 6040 lb *Armament:* 8 × .303-in Browning mg

Hurricane squadron scramble. The wooden two-blade propellers were progressively replaced by constant-speed airscrews during the heat of battle. The faster Spitfires had priority, but the Hurricane I remained the most important RAF fighter numerically throughout the summer and autumn of 1940

Bf 109 pilots relax on a Luftwaffe Channel airfield

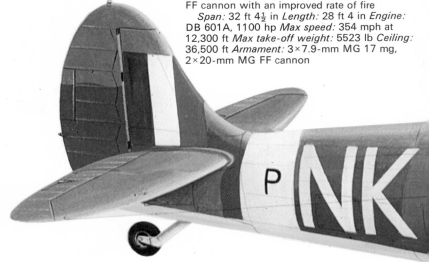

Messerschmitt Bf 109E-4
By mid 1940 the lessons of the French campaign
were being incorporated in the Bf 109E. The E-4
replaced the troublesome engine mounted MG
FF/M cannon with two wing mounted MG
FF cannon with an improved rate of fire
  Span: 32 ft 4½ in *Length:* 28 ft 4 in *Engine:*
DB 601A, 1100 hp *Max speed:* 354 mph at
12,300 ft *Max take-off weight:* 5523 lb *Ceiling:*
36,500 ft *Armament:* 3×7.9-mm MG 17 mg,
2×20-mm MG FF cannon

Spitfire IIa
During the battle a new version of the Spitfire, incorporating the first
results of operational experience, began to reach front-line squadrons. The
Spitfire II, with the Merlin XII engine driving a three-blade constant-speed
airscrew, had increased armour protection and improved speed and ceiling.
The type joined the battle in its closing stages and began the first
offensive sweeps into occupied Europe
  Span: 36 ft 10 in *Length:* 29 ft 9 in *Engine:* Rolls-Royce Merlin XII,
1236 hp *Max speed:* 354 mph at 17,550 ft *Ceiling:* 37,600 ft *Max take-off
weight:* 6172 lb *Armament:* 8×.303-in Browning mg

Possibly Messerschmitt's team placed too much emphasis on compactness. Reginald Mitchell made the Spitfire's cockpit larger and more comfortable, and in planning for the expected ultimate armament of eight machine guns (only four were fitted to begin with) was forced to give the wing generous area, with considerable chord well outboard to accommodate the Nos 1 and 8 guns. This resulted in the characteristic elliptical plan-form. Gross wing area was thus 242 sq ft, compared with only 174 sq ft for the Bf 109E. This enabled the Spitfire to easily out-turn the German fighter at all altitudes. Although this was a tremendous advantage, large numbers of Spitfires, and even Hurricanes, were shot down simply because their pilots failed to fly to the limit. Tests with a captured Bf 109E-3 showed that, when the British fighter (either type) was on the tail of the German, it had no difficulty in keeping the 109 in its sights, with plenty of turn radius in hand. When the positions were reversed, the 109 could invariably get the British fighter in its sights because the RAF pilot was not pulling maximum g. Even the motivation of self-preservation was often not enough to make Spitfire and Hurricane pilots boldly haul back with all their might and use their tight-turn advantage.

The 109 did possess a distinct advantage in that it could climb at full power so steeply that the slats opened and the aircraft was close to the stall. A determined Spitfire or Hurricane pilot could hold this for a while, but it was very hard indeed to bring the reflector sight to bear on the 109, even for a moment. Curiously, this manoeuvre was seldom practised by 109 pilots. It was common, however, for a 109 to dive away, and as airspeed built up the German fighter became almost unmanageable. With the Hurricane there was plenty of control at all speeds, though the speeds were generally slightly lower than for its rivals. The Spitfire tightened up considerably more, and the ailerons in particular were very heavy at speeds around 400 mph (these comments do not apply to the much faster later marks of Spitfire). But at around 400 mph the 109 could hardly manoeuvre at all. The ailerons

Hurricanes receive simultaneous refuelling from a bowser

were almost immovable, and in the narrow cockpit the pilot had no room to apply his full force to the stick except in the fore/aft direction. There was a further 109 deficiency that made combat an exhausting business. The 109 had no rudder trimmer and, as speed was increased, the pilot had to apply an increasing amount of left rudder, until at over 300 mph substantial force was needed. This became exhausting after a few minutes, and made gun sighting more difficult. Moreover, the slats snatched open and shut in tight turns, causing asymmetric drag and throwing the pilot off his aim.

It was remarkable that with so many deep-seated deficiencies the 109 remained in production until the end of the war. With a larger wing and improved high-speed lateral control it would have been a far more dangerous opponent, but the small 173–176-sq-ft wing remained unchanged. As a result the 109 was never far from the stall when pulling g, and though the stall was gentle in early versions, it could mean that a fight would be lost rather than won.

Armourers work frantically on a Spitfire Ia at Duxford, October 1940. The eight .303-in Brownings were fed from 300-round belts

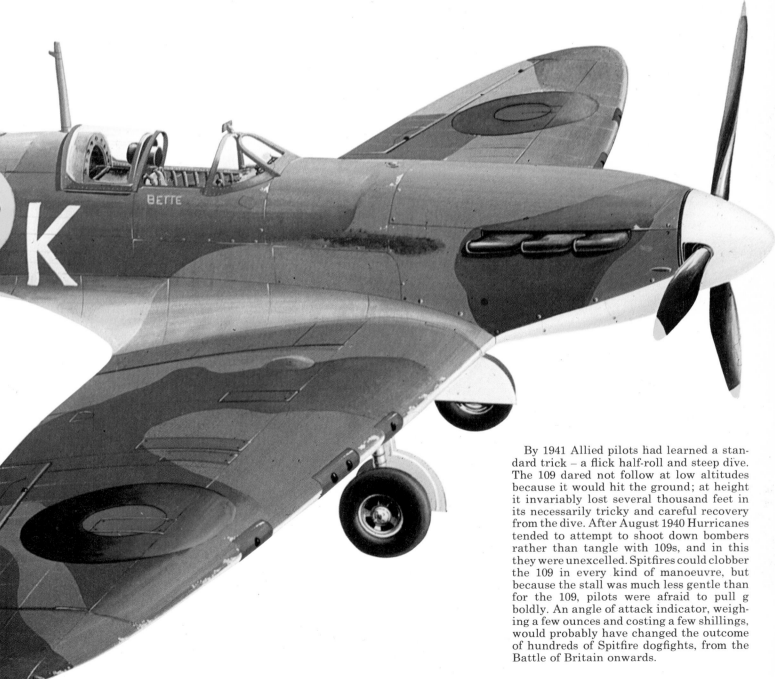

By 1941 Allied pilots had learned a standard trick – a flick half-roll and steep dive. The 109 dared not follow at low altitudes because it would hit the ground; at height it invariably lost several thousand feet in its necessarily tricky and careful recovery from the dive. After August 1940 Hurricanes tended to attempt to shoot down bombers rather than tangle with 109s, and in this they were unexcelled. Spitfires could clobber the 109 in every kind of manoeuvre, but because the stall was much less gentle than for the 109, pilots were afraid to pull g boldly. An angle of attack indicator, weighing a few ounces and costing a few shillings, would probably have changed the outcome of hundreds of Spitfire dogfights, from the Battle of Britain onwards.

Little need be said of the other Battle of Britain fighters. The Boulton Paul Defiant had a wing smaller than a Hurricane yet a weight considerably greater, mainly because it carried a gunner in a 680-lb power-driven turret with four rifle-calibre Brownings. Admittedly one could subtract from this the weight of the guns and ammunition, but the bare turret still weighed 361 lb and the gunner might add another 180, and such figures were important in 1940. The Defiant was a poor fighter in terms of speed, climb and turn radius, and though in May–June 1940 it had one or two moments of startling success, it was soon judged useless except by night.

The Blenheim fighter was also useful only at night. It was not a vicious machine, had a crew of two or three, and good endurance. But it was unable to catch even a Ju 88, and the hitting power of its four Brownings was totally inadequate.

By 1940 the fighter business had grown more serious. Bullet-proof windscreens, armour and self-sealing tanks were fast becoming universal, and the rifle-calibre gun was equally rapidly becoming inadequate. The 860-hp Hispano-Suiza, and similar engines of this power class, were no longer sufficient; even the 1000-hp Merlin and DB 601 had to be worked frantically to yield increased power at ever-greater heights. The beautifully tractable Fiat C.R.42 biplane fighters which accompanied

the *Corpo Aereo Italiano's* Fiat B.R. 20 bombers over Britain in October and November 1940 were totally ineffective. Though they had the manoeuvrability to get out of harm's way, they could neither protect the bombers nor shoot down British fighters, and their value was no greater than the proposed last-ditch defence armed versions of British light aircraft, such as the Mew Gull and Tiger Moth, of July 1940.

Finally, mention must be made of a fighter that never reached the squadrons, although it was designed, built and flown in 65 days, and in some respects was better than the contemporary Hurricane and Spitfire. F G Miles had schemed the M.20/1 fighter in 1939, and in 1940 asked the British aircraft-production minister, Lord Beaverbrook, for permission to build a fighter to help defend the nation. The resulting M.20/2, designed by Walter Capley, was outstanding in many respects. A typical Miles wooden aircraft, with thick wing, it featured a Merlin XX 'power egg' of the form later standardised on the Lancaster and other aircraft, standard parts from Master trainers, eight Brownings with space for another four plus 5000 rounds, and 154 gallons of fuel. Even with fixed landing gear it reached 333 mph with full armament installed. Handling was excellent, the teardrop canopy years ahead of its time, and both ammunition and fuel capacity approximately double that of existing

RAF fighters. It needed longer take-off and landing runs because it had a higher wing loading, although a production version might well have incorporated a hydraulic system, and thus had larger flaps and retractable landing gear. If the M.20 had been built in 1939, there would probably have been thousands; but in 1939 permission to build it would have been unlikely. Thus this excellent basis for development was rejected, as were the equally outstanding fighters by Martin-Baker Aircraft which appeared at intervals up to 1944.

Spitfire Cockpit
The firing button for the eight Brownings is incorporated in the joystick handle. The seat accommodates the parachute and the gunsight base is fitted with a crash-pad

Boulton Paul Defiant Mk I
The tactical concept of the turret fighter (originally as a bomber destroyer) was a disastrous failure in day fighting, although the Defiant had some success early in the battle when mistaken for a single-seater. The type soldiered on as night-fighter and target tug
Span: 39 ft 3 in *Length:* 34 ft 7 in *Engine:* Rolls-Royce Merlin III, 1440 hp *Max speed:* 312 mph at 10,000 ft *Ceiling:* 28, 100 ft *Max take-off weight:* 7510 lb *Armament:* 4×.303-in Browning mg

The Miles M.20, the wooden 'utility' fighter which could outperform the Hurricane and carry twice as much fuel and ammunition as a Spitfire. It never entered production

Imperial War Museum

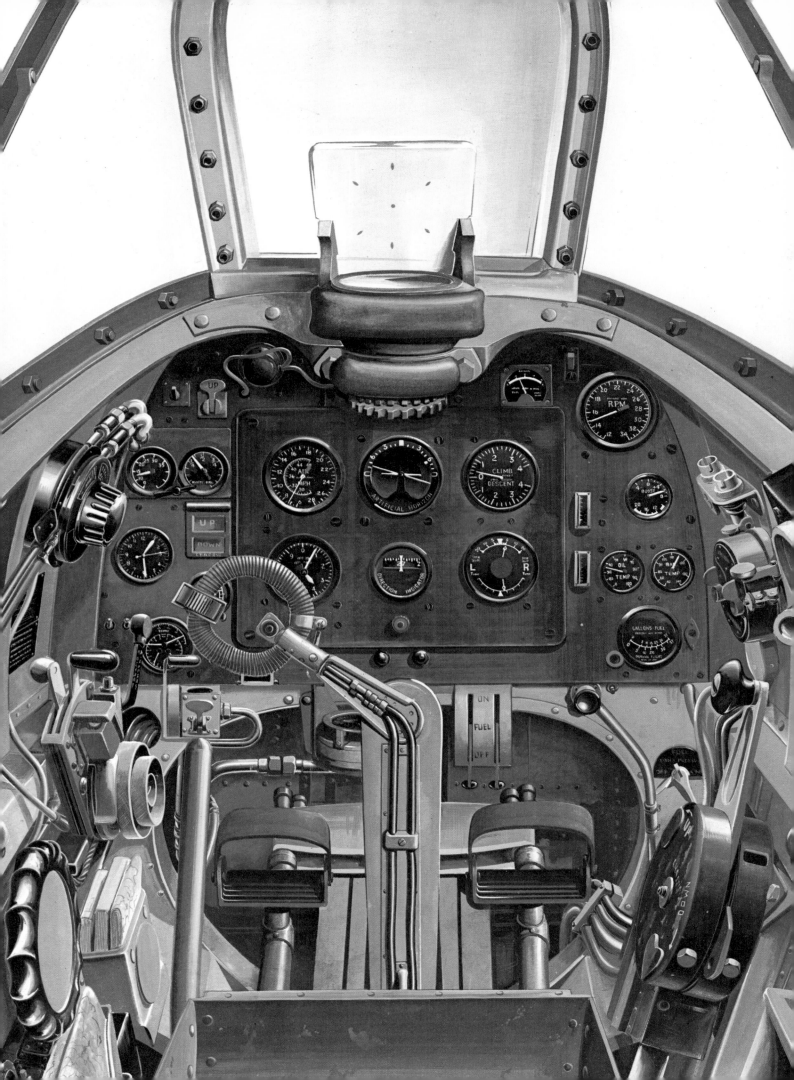

THE SPREADING WAR

Adlertag (Eagle Day), the date of Göring's promised air offensive against Britain, happened as planned on 13 August, 1940. But the date planned for Operation *Seelöwe* (Sealion), the invasion of southern England, was held back because RAF Fighter Command had not been eliminated. But the invasion never came to pass. Though the Luftwaffe's near-total switch to the night-bombing 'Blitz' reduced its losses over England to vanishing point, it meant that, for the first time, it had failed completely in its objective. For the moment Britain was clearly not going to be defeated. Although Hitler promised to return in 1941, to finish off the obstinate islanders, he was forced to look for fresh fields to conquer.

The obvious direction was south through the Balkans to help his faltering ally, Italy, which could not even subdue the island of Malta, let alone conquer the Greeks or drive the British from North Africa. Rumania joined the German/Italian Axis on 23 November 1940, with Bulgaria following on 1 March, 1941. But the Greeks were pushing back the Italians, and the Yugoslavs overthrew their leaders and repudiated the Axis Pact. On 6 April, 1941, the Wehrmacht rolled into both countries.

The principal opposition to the Luftwaffe's Bf 109E was provided by the latest Yugoslav fighters, ironically Bf 109Es. They were valiantly flown, but were soon overcome. However, a few Yugoslav aircraft managed to escape to Greece and later Egypt, including two Do 17 bombers loaded with gold bullion. Yugoslavia also had a few Hurricanes, Hawker Fury biplanes and a handful of home-produced fighters. The parasol-winged Ikarus IK-2 was obsolescent, having been conceived in 1934, but the six or eight still in use saw intensive action and shot down several Luftwaffe aircraft, besides being heavily committed to ground-attack missions. The Rogozarski IK-3 was a later concept, first flying in 1938, and though it looked undistinguished, it proved to be remarkably manoeuvrable. On a 920-hp Czech-built Hispano engine it reached 327 mph, had the same armament of one cannon and two machine guns as the IK-2, and proved to be able to turn inside the Yugoslav Hurricanes. Pilots evaluated the IK-3 against both the Hurricane, which was being built under licence, and the Bf 109E-3, rating it distinctly preferable to either. By 1941 an IK-3 had demonstrated even better performance with a German DB 601 engine, but only six Hispano-powered machines were ready in April 1941, operated by the 52nd Squadron at Zemun. Estimates suggest that they destroyed more than 14 Luftwaffe aircraft before being overcome.

Operations against Greece had been started by Italy in 1940, but that unhappy nation soon found itself in deep trouble in Greece. In sharp contrast to the impressive and flamboyant spectacles of Italian air-power in the 1930s, the performance of the *Regia Aeronautica* was invariably undistinguished. Until mid-1941 Italian fighter philosophy adhered tenaciously to the tradition of seeking the greatest possible manoeuvrability at the expense of performance, firepower and protection. This in turn removed from the brilliant engineers in the famous engine companies – Fiat, Alfa Romeo, Isotta-Fraschini and Piaggio – the fierce pressure for more power that should have spurred them ahead. As in Japan, Italian fighters tended to opt for engines of 1000 hp or less, with armament of two 0.5-in machine guns and speed barely in excess of 300 mph. Though Italian pilots lacked little in the way of courage or skill, this outdated design philosophy hardly gave them a chance until, under German tuition, they received fighters with abundant horse-power and firepower in 1943. By then their will to fight, never strong, had almost vanished.

Best of the Italian fighter families were those that stemmed from the prototype Macchi C.200 flown in December 1937. C stood for designer Mario Castoldi, who had earlier planned the company's racing seaplanes; but the C.200 had to fit the requirements and was a lumpy machine, with only 840 hp, that could not even catch a Hurricane I, despite its light weight and small size. With just two heavy machine guns, its only favourable attributes were its short field lengths, rapid and steep climb, excellent manoeuvrability and extremely pleasant flying qualities. These qualities were not lost in the subsequent M.C.202, flown in August 1940 with the German DB 601A engine, and M.C.205, flown in April 1942 with the powerful DB 605, which by then was the standard engine of the Bf 109. Unlike the German fighter, the

Macchis were to the end extremely likeable flying machines, and their armament crept up to an eventual standard of three 20-mm Mauser MG 151 cannon and two 0.5-in machine guns. But by this time, in late 1943, about half the M.C.205s had come over to the Allies.

Fiat's biplane fighters ought not to be dismissed as of no consequence in the air fighting of the Second World War; although they were obsolescent, they were so manoeuvrable that RAF fighters found it difficult to shoot them down. At the start of 1940 the most numerous fighter in the *Regia Aeronautica* was still the C.R.32, but it was fast being supplanted by the C.R.42. One of the last C.R.42 was fitted with a DB 601, and its speed of 323 mph may possibly have made it the fastest biplane ever (certainly much faster than the McGregor FDB-1 popularly reported as such). It is a telling reflection on Italian lack of determination and efficiency that the number of C.R.42s

Avia B-534
One of the last of the fighter biplanes, the B-534 constituted the Czech Air Force's front line when the Germans marched in during 1939. Three squadrons fought briefly with the Slovak Air Force on the Kiev Front in 1941
· *Span:* 30 ft 10 in *Length:* 26 ft 7 in *Engine:* Hispano-Suiza HS 17Ycrs, 850 hp *Max speed:* 245 mph at 14,435 ft *Ceiling:* 38, 875 ft *Max take-off weight:* 4365 lb *Armament:* 4×7.7-mm mg

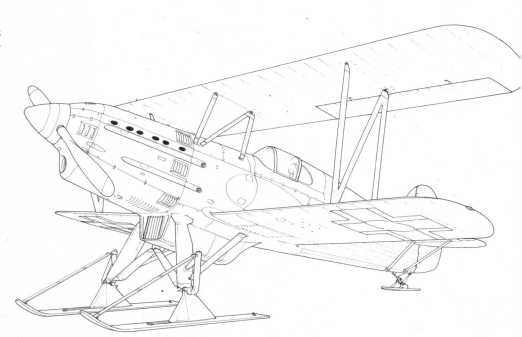

Macchi C202 Folgore
The availability of German liquid-cooled engines
brought Italian fighter design up to world
standard with the C202, an adaptation of the
highly manoeuvrable radial-engined Macchi MC
200. Problems of engine supply kept deliveries of
this most successful of Italian fighters to limited
numbers, however
Span: 38 ft 8½ in *Length:* 29 ft 0½ in *Engine:*
Daimler-Benz DB 601A, 1150 hp *Max speed:*
360 mph at 20,000 ft *Ceiling:* 34, 490 ft *Max
take-off weight:* 6400 lb *Armament:* 2×12.7-mm
mg, 2×7.7-mm mg

Reggiane Re 2000 Falco I
Loser in a fighter competition with the MC 200,
the Re 2000 was exported to Sweden, licence-
built in Hungary and flown by the Italian Navy
Span: 36 ft 1 in *Length:* 26 ft 2½ in *Engine:*
Piaggio P XI(*bis*), 1025 hp *Max speed:* 329 mph
at 16,400 ft *Ceiling:* 36, 745 ft *Max take-off
weight:* 5722 lb *Armament:* 2×12.7-mm Breda-
SAFAT mg

built, a mere 1781, was markedly greater than the total for any other Second World War Italian type. The fact that the C.R.42 was a biplane was immaterial; like the Royal Navy's Swordfish, this helped it continue in useful front-line service while later and faster machines faltered. By early 1942 all the *Regia Aeronautica*'s specialised ground-attack aircraft had failed, but the old C.R.42 filled the gap admirably, and remained in production until well into 1943, flying close-support and attack missions alongside the *Stormi* equipped with the German-built Ju 87.

The C.R.42's major defect was its limited engine power of 840 hp. Though well matched to the aircraft when it was designed, by 1942 this was almost useless. The lesson was learned by American designers in 1940 in time for the mass-produced US fighters of 1942–45 to have 2000 hp under their bonnets. But though the Italians had engines in this class under development, they progressed slowly and played virtually no part in the war. When Fiat planned a monoplane fighter in 1936, the blinkered vision of both the company and customer resulted in the engine being the same as that of the C.R.42, rated at 840 hp. The aircraft was the G.50, the first major design by Giuseppe Gabrielli, and it was uninspired and pedestrian. Fitted with the standard pair of synchronised heavy machine guns, its only advantages were manoeuvrability, durability and fair reliability, and it made little impact on the war. Another Fiat design, the last major effort by Rosatelli, was even less successful. The C.R.25, first flown in 1939, was a large twin-engined fighter for use in the 'Italian colonies', with long range and the ability to fly reconnaissance missions. Though its two engines were the same as those fitted to other Fiat fighters, it was slow and pathetically ill-armed, finishing its career as a transport, surely the ultimate indignity for any fighter!

Of Italy's many other fighters only the Reggiane series deserves mention. The Re.2000 of 1937 had excellent performance, and was widely used by Sweden and Hungary. The first model used by the *Regia Aeronautica* was the Re.2001 with a German DB 601 engine; the 252 built included versions capable of carrying a 1410-lb bomb or a torpedo. The most important variant was the 2001CN night fighter, with its synchronised heavy machine guns supplemented by two hard-hitting MG 151/20 cannon under the wings. Reggiane, a Caproni company, also developed the Re.2002 close-support fighter, with radial engine, heavy bomb load and armour. However, no more than 50 were built. The output of other Italian fighters did not reach double figures: the Caproni Ca 331B three-seat twin-engined night fighter, with up to six 20-mm cannon firing ahead; the Caproni Vizzola F.4 (DB 601), F.5 (Fiat A74 radial) and F.6 (licensed DB 605); IMAM Meridionali Ro 57 and 58 twin-engined fighters (the former with forward-firing armament of two machine guns and the latter with five cannon); the Piaggio P.119, with very advanced features and 1700-hp radial engine behind the pilot; the outstanding light fighters of SAI (Ambrosini), beginning with the tail-first S.S.4 and finishing with the SAI.403 *Dardo*, which achieved 403 mph on a mere 750 hp while carrying two cannon and two heavy machine-guns; and the extremely interesting and promising Savoia-Marchetti

Bristol Centaurus-powered Hawker Tornado prototype

The cockpit of the prototype Hawker Tempest V, powered by the Napier Sabre II, first flown in September 1942

S.M.91 and 92 with two DB 605 engines at the front of long tail booms, the 91 having a central nacelle and the 92 having the tandem-seat cockpit in the left boom. These little-known machines would have been formidable, had more than one of each been built.

Like France in 1935–40, the potentially important Italian industry frittered away its strength in badly managed programmes. By 1942 its only hope lay in advanced developments of existing conventional fighters redesigned with German engines. The standard engine was the DB 605, and the normal armament three MG 151 cannon and two heavy machine guns. It is remark-

able that Macchi, Fiat and Reggiane were able to fit almost double the horsepower and many times the armament into their fighters with only very slight increase in weight. Comparing such machines as the Macchi 205N, Fiat G.55 and Reggiane Re.2005 with the far more important Bf 109G series is very instructive. While the German fighter had about 174 sq ft of wing, all the Italian aircraft had considerably more than 200 sq ft, yet on the whole were comparable in weight. All three were evaluated against the 109G and proved to have dramatically better manoeuvrability, and at least equal performance. But by late 1942 Italy's production had fallen away sharply, and none of these three excellent machines made any significant contribution to the war. In no case did deliveries to the *Regia Aeronautica* reach 100 aircraft.

At first the Allied fighters in the Mediterranean were an old and motley collection, but by late 1940 some Mk I Hurricanes were made available, backed up by Fulmar squadrons of the Royal Navy. The Fulmar was a tandem-seat carrier fighter based on a pre-war light bomber somewhat smaller than the Battle. Though a pedestrian machine, as was inevitable with 342 sq ft of wing, a gross weight exceeding 10,000 lb and a mere 1080 hp, the Fulmar met all the requirements and was quickly put into use. The prototype flew on 4 January, 1940, yet by August 806 Sqn was fully equipped and combat-ready aboard *Illustrious* in the Mediterranean. Altogether 600 of these useful machines were built, the last 350 having 1300 hp and consequently a speed raised from 244 to 272 mph, which almost kept it abreast of typical Italian aircraft. A much more formidable carrier fighter was the Grumman G.36, first ordered by the French *Aéronavale* in 1939 but transferred to Britain on France's capitulation. As the

Martlet it went into use with 804 Sqn of the Royal Navy in October 1940. On Christmas Day 1940 two Martlets destroyed a Ju 88 near Scapa Flow. Variously powered by the Wright R-1820 Cyclone or Pratt & Whitney R-1830 Twin Wasp, both of 1200 hp, the Martlet had a squarish wing of 260 sq ft. As it could comfortably exceed 300 mph and carry four 0.5-in guns (later six) it was extremely welcome in the Mediterranean and in many other battle areas.

In 1941 there were numerous important developments in Britain, which included both new marks and new types. The evergreen Hurricane grew versatile wings containing 12 Browning 0.303-in, four 20-mm British Hispano cannon or two 0.303-in (for sighting) and two underslung 40-mm Rolls-Royce or Vickers anti-tank guns, with racks for 250-lb (later 500-lb) bombs, rocket projectiles, small-bomb containers, drop tanks or smoke generators. The Merlins for Hurricanes rose in power to 1260, 1460 and finally 1635 hp, in each case the engine being low-blown for peak performance at low altitude. Following the 'Hooked Hurricanes' came a navalised Sea Hurricane which still lacked folding wings but gave vitally needed defence aboard escort carriers and merchant ships equipped with catapults in 1942. The CAM (Catapult – Armed Merchantman) enabled fighter cover to be provided for convoys without a

carrier, at the cost of the pilot having to bale out or ditch after every sortie, with loss of the fighter. A scheme was studied for a Hurricane carried on a pylon above a Liberator, for release upon hostile aircraft sighted possibly 1500 miles from the nearest RAF airfield, but the scheme remained only a study by Short Brothers. A related idea was the Hillson 'slip wing' Hurricane, with a jettisonable upper wing to help overload takeoffs.

Hawker's completely new generation of fighters began with the prototype Tornado, built to specification F.18/37 and flown on 6 October 1939. The forward-looking specification called for 2000 hp, and the chosen armament was 12 machine guns. The work was eventually directed towards two fighters, the R-type with the Vulture engine and the N-type with the Sabre. Two more unfortunate engines could hardly have been selected, but after long and painful development the N-type reached the RAF as the Typhoon IB in September 1941. Though powerful, it had a disappointing climb and altitude performance, and was also unable to turn as tightly as a Bf 109F or Fw 190A. Coupled with persistent engine failure and structural weakness of the rear fuselage, the Typhoon almost failed to make it. However, by 1944 it was the RAF's top low-level tactical attack aircraft, with rockets, 1000-lb bombs and four cannon.

Hurricane IIC

Powered by the Merlin XX with two-speed supercharger, the Hurricane II had much improved performance at altitude. The IIB had twelve wing machine-guns and the IIC four 20-mm cannon and provision for bombs. 'Hurribombers' first went into action over Europe and the desert in late 1941

Span: 40 ft *Length:* 32 ft 3 in *Engine:* Rolls-Royce Merlin XX, 1460 hp
Max speed: 330 mph at 20,800 ft *Ceiling:* 35,900 ft *Max take-off weight:* 7397 lb *Armament:* 4×20-mm cannon

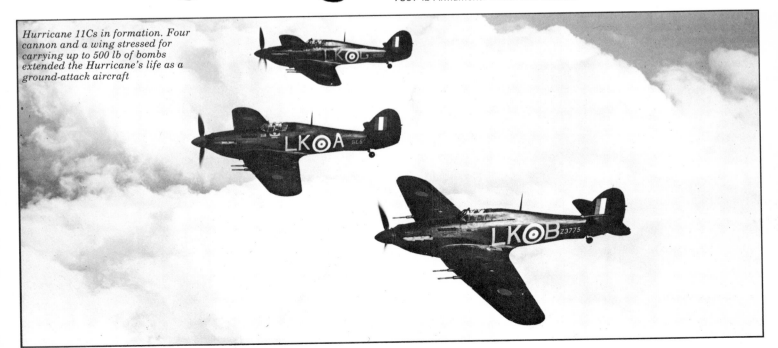

Hurricane 11Cs in formation. Four cannon and a wing stressed for carrying up to 500 lb of bombs extended the Hurricane's life as a ground-attack aircraft

When the might of the Luftwaffe was launched against the Soviet Union in Operation *Barbarossa* on 22 June, 1941, the objective was to kill or capture as much as possible of the Red Army in the shortest possible time. More than half the Soviet combat aircraft in the West were put out of action within the first week, mainly by attacks on airfields. Soviet losses of all kinds were grievous; yet the Russians were not to be entirely discounted in the air, as the German planning had tended to do. Though the invaders penetrated to the suburbs of Moscow before winter set in, the campaign was not over in six or eight weeks as had been hoped. By October 1941 the Soviet aircraft industry was being evacuated more than 1000 miles to the East, beyond the Urals, in an operation without parallel. At a cost of some five weeks' output, the whole manufacturing operation was re-started in completely new factories which proved, in the event, to be beyond the reach of the invaders. Whilst this was done, the types in production changed completely to the new designs which were first delivered in 1940–41.

Numerically by far the most important fighters in 1941 were still those from the Polikarpov bureau. These were of basic types dating from the 1930s when it seemed impossible to decide whether to build biplanes or monoplanes. The I-15 biplane and I-16 monoplane were in production side-by-side for years, and both proved to be fast, highly manoeuvrable, reliable and fitted with possibly the best machine gun of the day. Numerically the I-16 family was predominant, output exceeding 7000 in all. These were outstanding performers on primitive technology, and though extremely stubby and prone to poor longitudinal stability and tail-heaviness, they were fast, good at altitude and capable of very tight turns. They could absorb severe punishment, and were easy to maintain. By 1941 the most common fighter versions had the 1000-hp M-62 engine and two 20-mm cannon in place of the wing machine guns. Racks were standard for various external loads including six of the new RS-82 rockets for use chiefly against armour. The 50-kg (110-lb) PTAB hollow-charge anti-tank bomb was another common store.

These under-wing weapons were also carried by the biplane fighters which began with the I-15 of 1933. By 1941 most of these 700-hp four-gun machines had been replaced by the slightly faster and more capable I-15*bis*, with upper wing carried clear of the fuselage, and the 1000-hp I-153 with retractable landing gear. All were extremely manoeuvrable, and carried the same attack loads as later I-16 monoplanes, but faded fairly swiftly during 1942. In the course of this year the new monoplanes became available in gigantic numbers. Ilyushin's Shturmovik was not a fighter, though it often had to act like one. The final Polikarpov fighter, the I-17, was outstandingly advanced for 1934 but was withdrawn in 1941 (the last of these 860-hp stressed-skin machines departed in 1942). First of the really important new fighters was the LaGG-1, flown as the I-22 in March 1939. Built almost entirely of wood, this new product of an untried team was startlingly good. It was light, immensely strong and very serviceable, though manoeuvrability would have been better with a larger wing. With 1100 hp, it carried adequate armament (such as a 20-mm cannon and two heavy

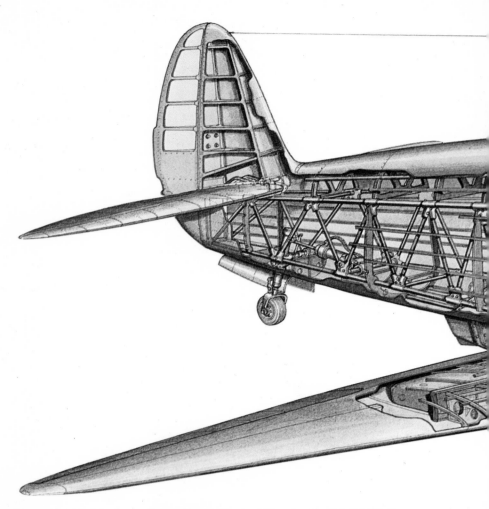

machine guns) and had excellent all-round performance, and the slightly modified LaGG-3 version was built in large numbers in 1941-42. In November 1941 an LaGG-3 flew with the much more powerful (1600-hp) M-82A radial engine, and this so greatly improved the fighter that it at once replaced the more vulnerable liquid-cooled machine, with designation La-5. Until the end of the Second World War the La-5 and its successors were numerically the second most important of all Allied fighters, output exceeding 26,000. Nearly all could exceed 400 mph, and around the cowling were the blast tubes of two or three 20-mm cannon. Metal construction gradually replaced wood, pilot view was improved by cutting down the rear fuselage, and altogether the La-5FN of 1942 and La-7 of 1943 were equal in a close dogfight to the best Bf 109 or Fw 190.

Though today a household name, 'MiG' got off to a mediocre start with the MiG-1, first flown as the I-61 in March 1940. The 1200-hp engine conferred an excellent 390 mph, but armament was only two machine guns and handling was very poor. The MiG-3 of 1941 was even more powerful and reached 407 mph, but as a fighter it was not much of an improvement. Fortunately for the Soviet Union Alexander Yakovlev had flown his I-26 in the summer of 1940, and this entered service in the spring of 1941 as the Yak-1. To meet demands for reduced usage of light alloy it had a wooden wing and steel-tube and ply fuselage, but weight penalties were no worse than for the rival all-wood or mixed-construction fighters, and the

Mikoyan-Gurevich MiG-3
The MiG-3, developed from the MiG-1 and carrying more fuel for the uprated engine, was introduced towards the end of 1941. Several thousand were built, but the type was less manoeuvrable than its opponents and was replaced by fighters from the rival Yakovlev bureau. The MiG-3 then flew reconnaissance missions but was soon withdrawn from front-line service

Span: 33 ft 9½ in *Length:* 26 ft 9 in *Engine:* Mikulin AM-35A, 1350 hp *Max speed:* 407 mph at 23,000 ft *Ceiling:* 39,400 ft *Max take-off weight:* 7700 lb *Armament:* 2×7.62-mm ShKAS mg, 12.7-mm Beresin BS mg, 6×RS-82 rocket projectiles or 2×110-lb bombs or 2×220-lb bombs or two chemical containers (VAP-6M or ZAP-6)

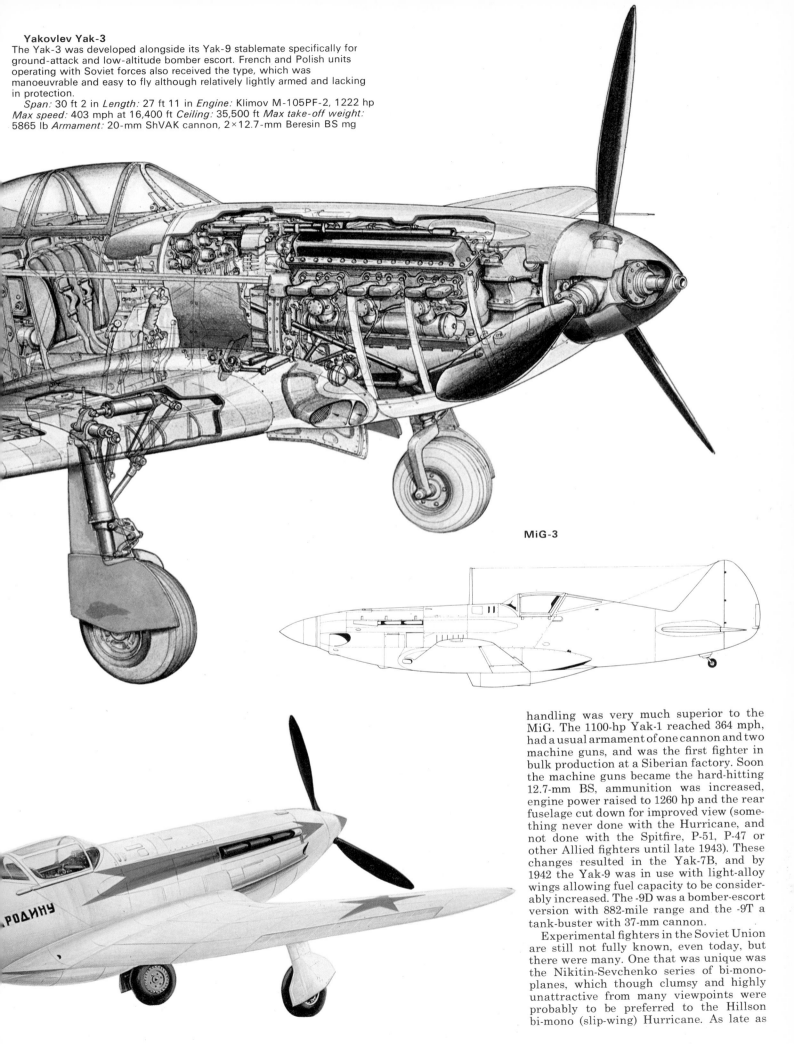

Yakovlev Yak-3
The Yak-3 was developed alongside its Yak-9 stablemate specifically for ground-attack and low-altitude bomber escort. French and Polish units operating with Soviet forces also received the type, which was manoeuvrable and easy to fly although relatively lightly armed and lacking in protection.
Span: 30 ft 2 in *Length:* 27 ft 11 in *Engine:* Klimov M-105PF-2, 1222 hp *Max speed:* 403 mph at 16,400 ft *Ceiling:* 35,500 ft *Max take-off weight:* 5865 lb *Armament:* 20-mm ShVAK cannon, 2×12.7-mm Beresin BS mg

MiG-3

handling was very much superior to the MiG. The 1100-hp Yak-1 reached 364 mph, had a usual armament of one cannon and two machine guns, and was the first fighter in bulk production at a Siberian factory. Soon the machine guns became the hard-hitting 12.7-mm BS, ammunition was increased, engine power raised to 1260 hp and the rear fuselage cut down for improved view (something never done with the Hurricane, and not done with the Spitfire, P-51, P-47 or other Allied fighters until late 1943). These changes resulted in the Yak-7B, and by 1942 the Yak-9 was in use with light-alloy wings allowing fuel capacity to be considerably increased. The -9D was a bomber-escort version with 882-mile range and the -9T a tank-buster with 37-mm cannon.

Experimental fighters in the Soviet Union are still not fully known, even today, but there were many. One that was unique was the Nikitin-Sevchenko series of bi-monoplanes, which though clumsy and highly unattractive from many viewpoints were probably to be preferred to the Hillson bi-mono (slip-wing) Hurricane. As late as

1939 Soviet opinion hovered between monoplanes and biplanes. On the face of the argument, there is no point in having an aircraft that can behave as both, because this is bound to be complex, heavy and possibly potentially dangerous. There might be a case for it if biplane qualities were needed only at one time in each flight (such as take-off or landing) and monoplane speed at another; this is the reasoning behind the 'swing-wing' today. But in fact biplane qualities are needed all the time. Though the monoplane may go faster, the biplane will invariably climb higher and have a smaller radius of turn, so at what point does the pilot convert to a monoplane? Be that as it may, the two Soviet designers, V V Nikitin and V Sevchenko, designed a fighter designated IS-1 (or NS-1) which flew in 1940. It was based on an I-153 but had landing gear folding inwards into the inner panels of the cantilever lower wing, which then folded into the sides of the fuselage and upper wing! A later prototype was designated IS-2 (NS-2) and flown in the same year. According to reports the trials were successful; probably this was one of those bright ideas which one knows all along will never go into general use no matter how successful the trials may be.

Rocket Research

Another aircraft demonstrating the breadth of Soviet research, and its exceedingly advanced nature, was the BI-1 target-defence interceptor produced extremely quickly by A Ya Bereznyak and A M Isayev, under guidance of V F Bolkhovitinov. In 1933 the Soviet Union had set up the RNII, the world's first major rocket research establishment, and by 1941 this was producing reliable engines that flew in many combat types, including the La-7 fighter. The D-1A-1100, apparently rated at 660-lb thrust on nitric acid and kerosene, was fitted into an extremely small and simple fighter of mainly wooden construction, with two 20-mm cannon. The first BI-1 was flown by Capt G Ya Bakhchivandzhi on 15 May 1942, having previously undertaken trials as a glider. No details of performance were disclosed, but the decision to stick to traditional fighters was dictated not by any faults in the BI-1 but by the inability of the short-endurance interceptor to fight a fluid war of movement over enormous distances.

Backing up these Soviet fighters were large numbers of Western types, of which the Bell P-39 Airacobra was one of the most important (4924 supplied). This unconventional machine was the first major product of the new Bell team, and at first it had a struggle. When 601 Sqn of the RAF equipped with it in July 1941 various factors combined to damn the aircraft, to which could be

added some official resistance to the unusual layout. Bell put the 1150-hp Allison engine behind the pilot, to enable a battery of guns to be installed in the nose, to improve pilot view and improve manoeuvrability by putting the engine on the centre of gravity. In practice the P-39 proved a disappointment, and an uphill struggle for Bell in trying to make it a competitive fighter. It never did make a dogfighter, but 9584 were built and used with fair success in low-level attack missions, the 37-mm cannon especially appealing to the Russians.

An even more numerous and far more varied family were the P-40 series by Curtiss, which began with the airframe of the P-36 (Hawk 75A) fitted with the liquid-cooled Allison engine. The RAF used the French-ordered Hawk 81A under the name Tomahawk I, IA and IB, though they were devoid of all protection and lacked most operational gear. The Tomahawk II and USAAF P-40B did have some armour and self-sealing tanks, and reached about 350 mph carrying two synchronized 0.5-in and two rifle-calibre guns. The Tomahawk IIB had six 0.303-in, and served in various sub-types with 17 RAF squadrons in Britain (with the Army Co-operation Command, formed in late 1941) and many parts of Africa. From it were developed the P-40D to P-40M

Warhawk family, called Kittyhawk by British Commonwealth air forces. Fitted with a revised type of Allison engine which shortened the nose and raised the thrust line, the Warhawks were much more formidable with speeds exceeding 360 mph and armament of six 0.5-in in the wings. Just over 2000, with designations P-40F and L, had Packard-built Merlin engines. Strong and reliable, these later P-40 models were very widely used as low-level ground-attack

North American A-36A
The early Mustangs with Allison engines were used almost exclusively for low-altitude reconnaissance and ground attack. Five hundred A-36As (with the USAAF's Attack prefix) were delivered in 1943 equipped as dive-bombers and one (illustrated) was supplied to the RAF in March 1943 for experimental purposes
Span: 37 ft *Length:* 31 ft 11 in *Engine:* Allison V-1710-87, 1325 hp *Max Speed:* 356 mph *Ceiling:* 30,000 ft *Max take-off weight:* 10,700 lb *Armament:* 2×.5-in mg, 4×.3-in mg, 1000 lb bombs

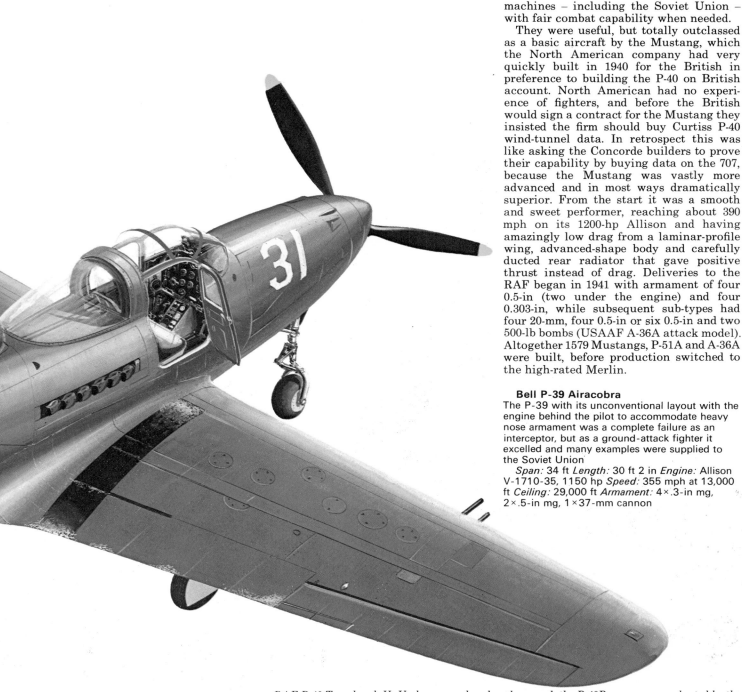

machines – including the Soviet Union – with fair combat capability when needed.

They were useful, but totally outclassed as a basic aircraft by the Mustang, which the North American company had very quickly built in 1940 for the British in preference to building the P-40 on British account. North American had no experience of fighters, and before the British would sign a contract for the Mustang they insisted the firm should buy Curtiss P-40 wind-tunnel data. In retrospect this was like asking the Concorde builders to prove their capability by buying data on the 707, because the Mustang was vastly more advanced and in most ways dramatically superior. From the start it was a smooth and sweet performer, reaching about 390 mph on its 1200-hp Allison and having amazingly low drag from a laminar-profile wing, advanced-shape body and carefully ducted rear radiator that gave positive thrust instead of drag. Deliveries to the RAF began in 1941 with armament of four 0.5-in (two under the engine) and four 0.303-in, while subsequent sub-types had four 20-mm, four 0.5-in or six 0.5-in and two 500-lb bombs (USAAF A-36A attack model). Altogether 1579 Mustangs, P-51A and A-36A were built, before production switched to the high-rated Merlin.

Bell P-39 Airacobra
The P-39 with its unconventional layout with the engine behind the pilot to accommodate heavy nose armament was a complete failure as an interceptor, but as a ground-attack fighter it excelled and many examples were supplied to the Soviet Union

Span: 34 ft *Length:* 30 ft 2 in *Engine:* Allison V-1710-35, 1150 hp *Speed:* 355 mph at 13,000 ft *Ceiling:* 29,000 ft *Armament:* 4×.3-in mg, 2×.5-in mg, 1×37-mm cannon

RAF P-40 Tomahawk II. Underpowered and underarmed, the P-40B was soon supplanted by the E-series with considerably more horsepower

Cockpit, Fw 190A-8: Key

1 Volume control and FT (communications) -ZF homing switch
2 Frequency selector (FuG 16 ZY)
3 Elevator trim switch
4 Throttle friction knob
5 Undercarriage and flap actuation buttons
6 Elevator trim 6 position indicator
7 Undercarriage position indicators (L & R) Flap position (centre)
8 Emergency circuit-breaker
9 Flap degree indicator
10 Throttle
11 Instrument panel dimmer control
12 Engine starter brushes withdrawal button
13 IFF camera unit (FuG 25a)
14 Fuel tank selector lever
15 Undercarriage manual extension handle
16 Cockpit ventilation knob
17 Rudder pedal with integral braking
18 Bomb fuzing selector unit
19 Disposable load indicator lights
20 21-cm rocket control unit
21 Altimeter
22 Pitot tube heater light
23 Air speed indicator
24 Fuel and oil pressure gauge
25 MG 131 'Armed' lights
26 Oil temperature gauge
27 Windscreen washer lever
28 Engine ventilation flap positioning lever
29 Artificial horizon
30 Armament switch and round counter control unit (SZK 4)
31 Rate-of-climb indicator
32 Fuel contents gauge
33 Gun sight unit
34 Repeater compass
35 AFN 2 Homing indicator (FuG 16 ZY)
36 Propeller pitch indicator
37 Supercharger pressure gauge
38 Ultra-violet cockpit light
39 Fuel low-level indicator light and rear tank switchover light
40 Tachometer
41 Fuel gauge selector switch
42 Flare pistol holder
43 Canopy operation wheel
44 Oxygen flow indicator
45 Oxygen pressure gauge
46 Oxygen flow valve
47 Canopy jettison lever
48 Clock
49 Flare box cover
50 Operation data card
51 Starter switch
52 Fuel pump circuit breakers
53 Flare box cover plate release button
54 Compass deviation card
55 Armament circuit breakers
56 Seat
57 Map slot
58 Control column
59 Machine-gun firing button
60 Bomb release button

Focke-Wulf Fw 190A-8

The A-8 variant was introduced at the end of 1943 with increased internal fuel tankage. Sub types of the series included the A-8/R-1 with four 20-mm MG 151 cannon and the A-8/R3 ground support variant with wing-mounted MK 103 cannon.

Span: 34 ft 5½ in *Length:* 29 ft *Engine:* BMW 801D-2 1700 hp *Max speed:* 408 mph *Ceiling:* 37,400 ft *Armament:* 2 × 13-mm MG 151 mg, 4 × 20-mm MG 131 cannon

Opposition from the Luftwaffe intensified sharply during 1941, that year's crop of new fighters being among the best of the whole war as far as handling was concerned. By far the biggest, and least pleasant, Luftwaffe revelation was the Focke-Wulf Fw 190. The prototype of this totally new fighter had flown on 1 June, 1939, but the event escaped the notice of the Allies so that, when in the summer of 1941 RAF pilots reported radial-engined fighters, they were described officially as 'Mohawks captured from the French'. The RAF were soon disabused of this cosy notion, and in June 1942 an Fw 190A-3 landed by mistake in England. The lessons learnt in a technical inspection of it put a bomb under the RAF procurement machine. It taught the officials that a fighter can have an air-cooled radial and be dramatically faster than a pointed-nose liquid-cooled machine (this was obvious from the US Navy's Corsair, flown at over 400 mph in 1940, but this made no impact in Britain). It also taught that aircraft can be small and compact and still carry heavy armament and heavy external loads. Truly the 190 was an outstanding piece of engineering, and unlike the later Bf 109 models had no evident shortcomings.

Though the prototype had had the BMW 139 engine, initially with a ducted spinner that made the machine look like a jet, the production engine was the BMW 801, rated at 1600 hp. The big 18-cylinder radial was beautifully cowled, with a fast-revving cooling fan just behind the spinner and multi-stack ejector exhaust around the cooling exit slits. Above the engine were two 7.92-mm MG 17, replaced in many later models by 13-mm MG 131. Inboard in the wing were two of the hard-hitting MG 151 cannon, previously unknown in Britain, while early models had two 20-mm MG FF cannon outboard. Speed began at 389 mph, but soon the BMW 801D-2 engine with MW50 boost giving 2100-hp raised emergency speed to 416 mph, and armament schemes began to proliferate. The A-4 carried a 551-lb bomb and then a 1102-lb bomb and two drop tanks. The A-5/U3 carried a 2205-lb bomb load, and the A-5/U15 a torpedo. The A-8/R1 had six MG 151 cannon, while the A-10 was the first to carry the 3968-lb SC1800 heavy bomb. This bomb load, four times that of a Blenheim, was impressive for the smallest combat aircraft in the west with a span of 34 ft. In combat the 190 proved fast, small, elusive and unbreakable. Features included a beautiful clear-vision hood and very wide-track landing gear, and handling was well-nigh perfect. Even to sit in the cockpit without the chance to get airborne – as the author did in 1942 – was tremendously exciting.

Fw 190A-5/U3 Trop, with special filters for desert operations and racks for up to 2200 lb of bombs for Jabo (fighter-bomber) operations

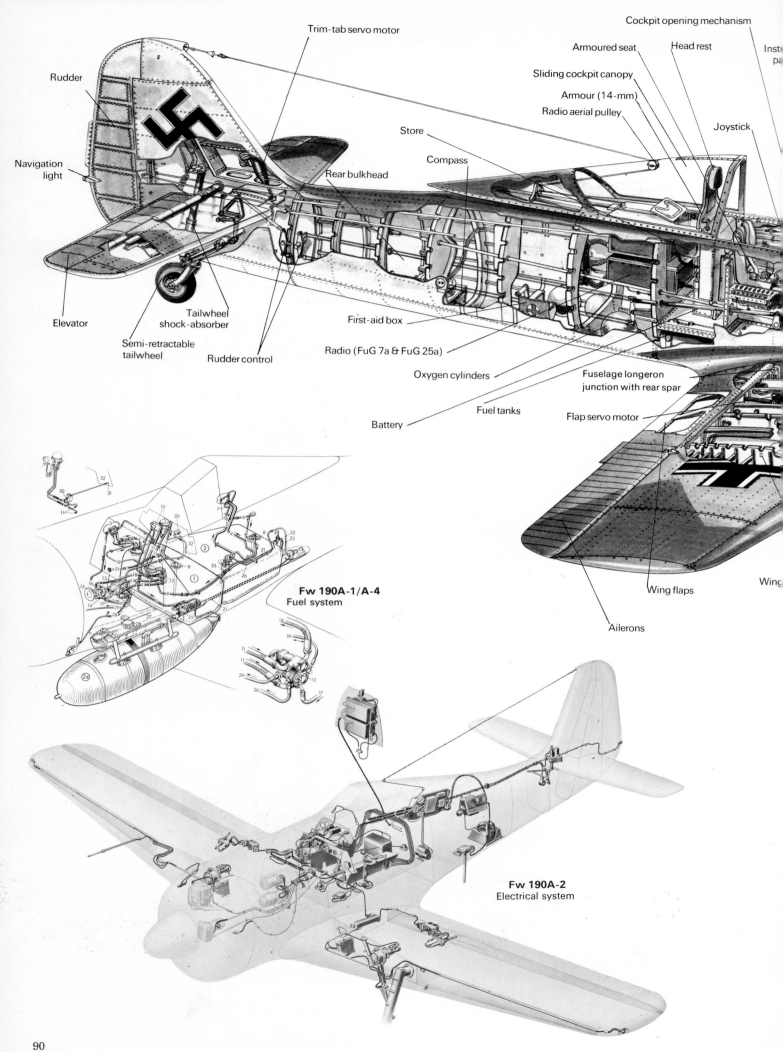

Rudder

Navigation light

Elevator

Trim-tab servo motor

Tailwheel shock-absorber

Semi-retractable tailwheel

Rudder control

Rear bulkhead

Store

Compass

First-aid box

Radio (FuG 7a & FuG 25a)

Oxygen cylinders

Battery

Fuel tanks

Cockpit opening mechanism

Armoured seat

Head rest

Sliding cockpit canopy

Armour (14-mm)

Radio aerial pulley

Joystick

Inst... pa...

Fuselage longeron junction with rear spar

Flap servo motor

Wing flaps

Wing

Ailerons

Fw 190A-1/A-4
Fuel system

Fw 190A-2
Electrical system

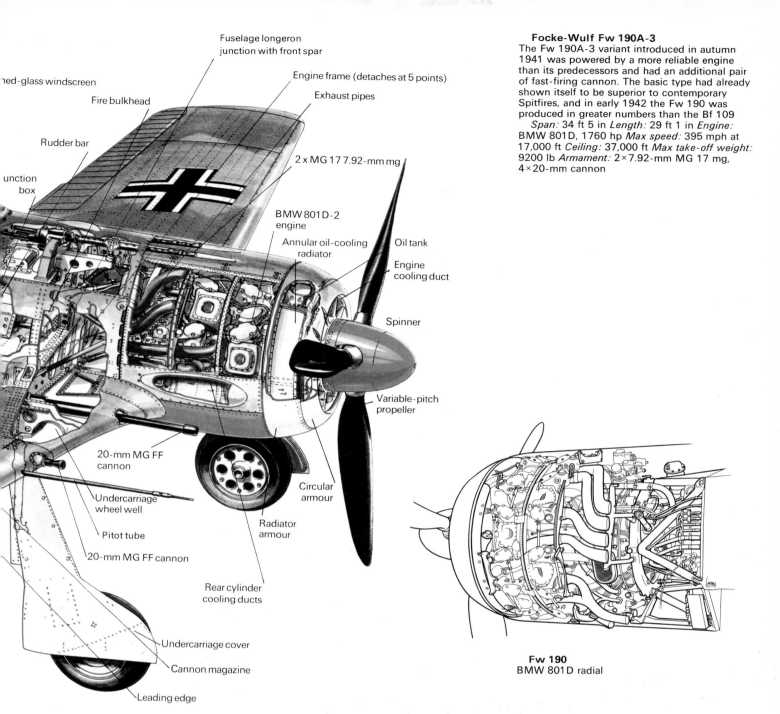

Fuselage longeron
junction with front spar

hed-glass windscreen

Engine frame (detaches at 5 points)

Fire bulkhead

Exhaust pipes

Rudder bar

2 x MG 17 7.92-mm mg

unction
box

BMW 801D-2
engine

Annular oil-cooling
radiator

Oil tank

Engine
cooling duct

Spinner

Variable-pitch
propeller

20-mm MG FF
cannon

Undercarriage
wheel well

Circular
armour

Pitot tube

20-mm MG FF cannon

Radiator
armour

Rear cylinder
cooling ducts

Undercarriage cover

Cannon magazine

Leading edge

Focke-Wulf Fw 190A-3

The Fw 190A-3 variant introduced in autumn
1941 was powered by a more reliable engine
than its predecessors and had an additional pair
of fast-firing cannon. The basic type had already
shown itself to be superior to contemporary
Spitfires, and in early 1942 the Fw 190 was
produced in greater numbers than the Bf 109
Span: 34 ft 5 in *Length:* 29 ft 1 in *Engine:*
BMW 801D, 1760 hp *Max speed:* 395 mph at
17,000 ft *Ceiling:* 37,000 ft *Max take-off weight:*
9200 lb *Armament:* 2×7.92-mm MG 17 mg,
4×20-mm cannon

Fw 190
BMW 801D radial

*Fw 190A-1, part of the initial production batch of 100 aircraft tested
under operational conditions by Luftwaffe fighter units*

John Batchelor

In contrast Messerschmitt went one step forward with the Bf 109 and later took two steps back. In late 1940 the first evaluation models of Bf 109F were coming off the line, and these are generally judged the nicest 109 sub-types ever built. They had the 1300-hp DB 601E in a redesigned and more streamlined cowling, with a fat-spinner propeller of reduced diameter, and cooled by shallow redesigned wing radiators. Control surfaces, flaps and other aerodynamics were altered, the tailplane was restressed so that the bracing strut could be eliminated and the tailwheel was made retractable. Most obvious of all, the wingtips were rounded, though span and area remained almost unchanged. Altogether the result was a substantial reduction in drag and improvement in control. Most F models were lightly armed, with a single engine-mounted cannon (MG FF, then MG 151/15 and finally MG 151/20) and two synchronized machine guns; yet it was to remain the preferred type of several of the top-scoring aces of the Luftwaffe. It was a superior dogfighter, and effective in the hands of an expert pilot. From January 1941 it gave all Allied fighters a hard time, and when the Fw 190 appeared alongside it there was a marked qualitative superiority on the side of the Luftwaffe.

In fact, as described later, the F was soon to give way to the G, and though this far outnumbered all other 109s and all other Luftwaffe fighters (unless all Fw 190s are grouped as one type) it was a thoroughly retrograde step that replaced the F's virtues by vices, all for the sake of piling on additional guns and equipment. All was not well on the twin-engined front, either. Though by 1940 the Bf 110C series were well-proven and reliable, they received such a mauling at the hands of Hurricanes and Spitfires

that they were themselves escorted by Bf 109s, and soon withdrawn entirely from the British theatre. There followed a major rethink of the once-proud *Zerstörer* (destroyer) wings, which Göring had regarded as the lead elements of the entire Luftwaffe, ranging across the breadth of Europe and clearing a path for the bombers. It was clear by October 1940 that the concept worked only in the absence of top-quality opposition. Many ZG *(Zerstörergeschwader)* were reassigned in the tactical attack role, and, though the Bf 110 gave good service in the Balkans, North Africa and on the Eastern Front, flying many kinds of mission, it was never again effective.

Barbettes

In 1940–41 the poor showing of the 110 over Britain was not judged important because production was already running down and in 1941 was scheduled to terminate in favour of the completely new Me 210. The latter seemed an ideal successor, with 1395-hp DB 601F engines, an internal bomb bay, remotely controlled MG 131 barbettes covering the entire rear hemisphere and various arrangements of forward-firing armament. But no fighter ever suffered from more deep-seated faults than the Me 210, and though production deliveries did begin in early 1941 the result was a series of disasters. In April 1942, after countless faults and accidents, production was stopped, while the Bf 110 remained in increasing production. Eventually Messerschmitt developed the 210 into the DB 603-powered Me 410 for use as a day and night fighter, bomber, anti-tank machine, reconnaissance aircraft and anti-ship fighter, but it was never a success and only just over 1100 were built. Meanwhile, the old 110 strove to fill a widening gap.

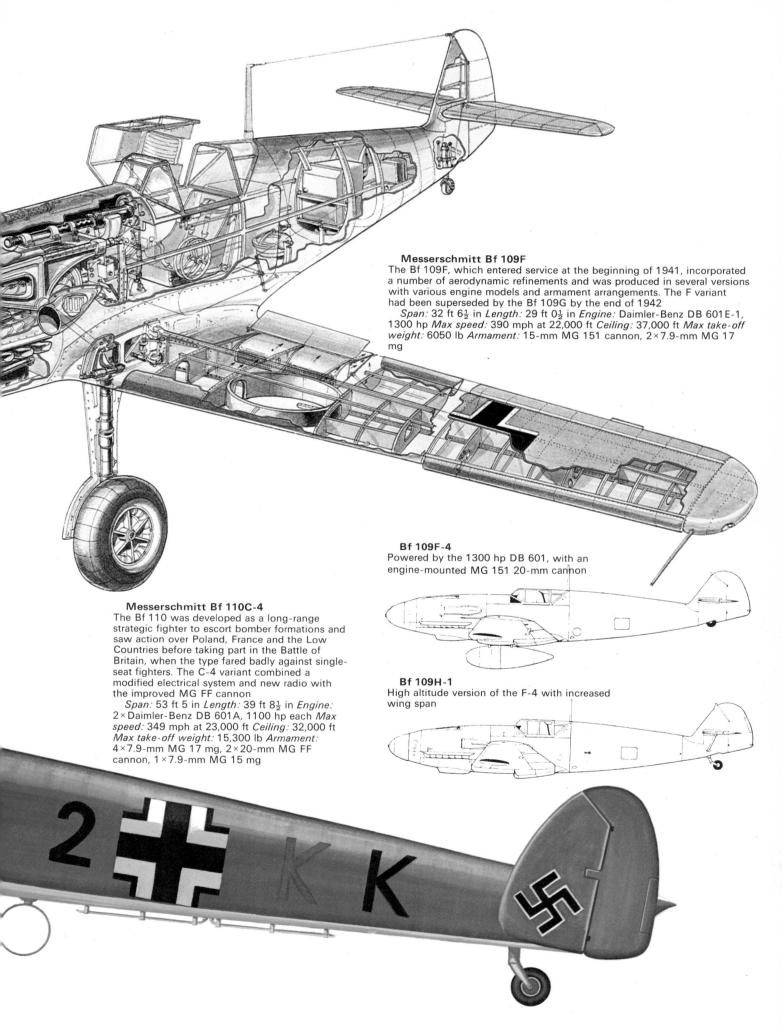

Messerschmitt Bf 109F

The Bf 109F, which entered service at the beginning of 1941, incorporated a number of aerodynamic refinements and was produced in several versions with various engine models and armament arrangements. The F variant had been superseded by the Bf 109G by the end of 1942

Span: 32 ft 6½ in *Length:* 29 ft 0½ in *Engine:* Daimler-Benz DB 601E-1, 1300 hp *Max speed:* 390 mph at 22,000 ft *Ceiling:* 37,000 ft *Max take-off weight:* 6050 lb *Armament:* 15-mm MG 151 cannon, 2×7.9-mm MG 17 mg

Bf 109F-4
Powered by the 1300 hp DB 601, with an engine-mounted MG 151 20-mm cannon

Bf 109H-1
High altitude version of the F-4 with increased wing span

Messerschmitt Bf 110C-4

The Bf 110 was developed as a long-range strategic fighter to escort bomber formations and saw action over Poland, France and the Low Countries before taking part in the Battle of Britain, when the type fared badly against single-seat fighters. The C-4 variant combined a modified electrical system and new radio with the improved MG FF cannon

Span: 53 ft 5 in *Length:* 39 ft 8½ in *Engine:* 2×Daimler-Benz DB 601A, 1100 hp each *Max speed:* 349 mph at 23,000 ft *Ceiling:* 32,000 ft *Max take-off weight:* 15,300 lb *Armament:* 4×7.9-mm MG 17 mg, 2×20-mm MG FF cannon, 1×7.9-mm MG 15 mg

THE RISING SUN

In August 1940, at the height of the Battle of Britain, Chinese and Japanese fighters were locked in combat over the city of Chungking. Japan and China had been at war since 1937, and during that time there had been severe fighting in the air. However, in August 1940, in a dogfight 27,000 ft over Chungking, a swarm of Japanese fighters massacred the Chinese defenders. All the accounts of the engagement record that every one of the Chinese fighters was shot down. The few surviving pilots could suggest only that the Japanese aircraft appeared to be of a new type.

General Claire Chennault of the US Army Air Corps, leader of the American Volunteer Group (Flying Tigers), immediately sent urgent signals to Washington, warning of the new fighter. However, it appears that these signals were ignored, for on 7 December, 1941, the 'Zero' burst on the astonished defenders at Pearl Harbor. One early testimony to the Zero's quality is provided by the fact that during the 18 months between the dogfight over Chungking and the attack on Pearl Harbor not a single piece of one Zero fell into Allied hands, although the new fighter had been heavily engaged in battle over China almost daily.

The A6M *Zero-Sen*, designed by Jiro Horikoshi, chief designer of Mitsubishi, became a symbol to the Japanese of their air power. The aircraft's initial successes were so spectacular that it gained an aura of invincibility. However, just as with Hitler's Luftwaffe, belief in this myth proved disastrous. Though it was greatly developed over the years, the A6M remained in production to the end of the war, by which time it was outclassed. Its successor was started late and never saw front-line service. Meanwhile the ageing A6M remained in production, total output reaching at least 10,937, far outstripping all other Japanese aircraft before or since.

In the 1930s Japanese fighter philosophy had been based on attaining the greatest possible manoeuvrability. This had resulted in the two mass-produced fighters that dominated the Chinese war, the A5M of the Imperial Navy and the Army Ki-27. Both were stressed-skin monoplanes with open cockpits, powered by 710-hp Nakajima radial engines derived from the Bristol Jupiter; standard armament was two synchronised machine guns based on the Vickers. Their turn radius was outstanding, and with a time to 4000 m (16,400 ft) of $5\frac{1}{4}$ minutes, and speed at that height of around 280 mph, they were among the greatest performers of the 1936–40 era.

With this tradition of clean monoplane design and extremely lightweight construction, the next stage was predictable. Nakajima followed the Ki-27 with the Ki-43 *Hayabusa* (Peregrine Falcon) for the Army, while Horikoshi created the A6M. Both proved successful. The Ki-43 was slightly compromised by its small size and limited capability, but the A6M was just sufficiently endowed with horsepower to carry reasonable armament from the outset —two machine guns above the engine and two 20-mm Type 99 cannon in the wings immediately outboard of the tall landing gear. From the start provision was also made for two bombs of up to 60 kg (132 lb) each. After delivering sixty-four of the A6M2 Model 11 type, which immediately went to China in January 1940, Mitsubishi began volume production on the A6M2 Model 21 with folding wing-tips for carrier operation. These were the first aircraft to explore long-range flights on an operational basis, as distinct from special long-range flights formed for record-breaking purposes. With a small engine, clean design and drop-tank, the range was exceptional from the start, and pilots had no difficulty flying missions considerably longer than 2500 km (1553 miles). By the summer of 1940 careful cruise techniques had stretched the limit to almost 2000 miles, 1940 miles being the usual published figure.

This allowed the Model 21s in service at the time of Pearl Harbor – there were approximately 420 – to cover vast areas of the Pacific, China and SE Asia, often appearing at places where the presence of Japanese fighters had been thought impossible. During the crucial period after Pearl Harbor the entire Japanese ascendancy in the air rested on the achievements of the A6M. On countless occasions these lightweight fighters appeared several hundred miles from the nearest Japanese carrier or airstrip, inflicting crushing defeats on Allied pilots flying such machines as the Brewster Buffalo or P-40 near to their own bases. Though the stern dogfighting that ensued showed that the Zero could in fact be shot down, its marked ascendancy over the motley and obsolescent array of Allied fighters gave the Allies a respect for Japanese fighters that was perhaps greater than the latter deserved, until the winter 1942–43. By this time there were many new A6M versions, including the A6M2-N float seaplane (code-named 'Rufe') for use where land or carriers were not available, the A6M3 with clipped wings, and the A6M2-K tandem trainer.

Surprisingly, Mitsubishi's next Navy fighter was a complete about-face. The J2M *Raiden* (Thunderbolt) sacrificed manoeuvrability, and even good handling, in order to attain higher speeds and rates of climb. Fitted with an engine much larger than the A6M (the 1820-hp 14-cylinder *Kasei*) it had a much smaller wing, and at first even had a shallow cockpit with a curved, almost horizontal, windscreen like a racer. Pilot view was totally unsatisfactory, and when this was combined with poor manoeuvrability and unforgiving handling the result was not promising. The J2M entered service at the end of 1943 after an extremely troublesome period of development, receiving the Allied code-name 'Jack'. Subsequent variants had heavier armament, such as four 20-mm cannon of a modified type, and a much better canopy with proper forward view. Gradually the handling was improved, and late models captured in 1944–45 were judged to be excellent by Allied test

pilots. Like so many Japanese combat aircraft, the J2M suffered such troubled development that only small numbers reached the squadrons, and these were mainly inadequate, undeveloped versions.

The design of the principal fighters of the Imperial Army also followed the philosophy of manoeuvrability. Parallel with the Navy A6M came the Nakajima Ki-43, which adhered more closely to earlier concepts; it was small, and even lighter than the Zero, and was armed with only two machine guns. The overriding need for less weight and better manoeuvrability resulted, in the early development in 1939, in much discussion about replacing the retractable landing gear by a fixed type.

Deliveries of this beautiful little fighter, the *Hayabusa*, code-named 'Oscar' by the Allies, began in 1941. It was always a sweet performer, with outstanding manoeuvrability. Most of the Army aces gained nearly all their victories on it, but they had an increasingly difficult task. Though the calibre of the two guns soon went up to 12-mm, this was insufficient to destroy the increasingly tough Allied machines, while the Ki-43 itself was poorly protected. It was by far the most important Army fighter, with 5878 delivered. However, it represented out of date technology for which no replacement was forthcoming in anything like comparable numbers.

Nevertheless, Nakajima did build later fighters. Like the Navy J2M, the Ji-44 discarded all the old goals in favour of more speed and climb, and the first Army pilots to receive it, in 1942, considered this a step backwards. Code-named 'Tojo' by the Allies, the Ki-44 had a more successful career than the J2M; eventually about 1223 were delivered, later models having heavier armament including two low-velocity 40-mm cannon.

After this quite effective machine came a new design that is generally rated the best Japanese fighter of the entire war,

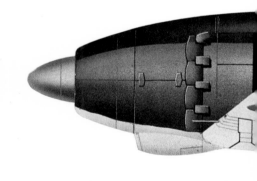

with the possible exception of the Ki-100. The Ki-84 *Hayate* (Gale), called 'Frank' by the Allies, was a thoroughly superior aircraft. No longer was the accent on any specific attribute; instead Nakajima's design team, under T Toyama, strove to produce an aircraft that was outstanding in all respects. Powered by the complex and troublesome *Homare* radial of 1900 hp, the Ki-84 was larger and heavier than earlier Japanese fighters, with an extremely strong structure (though the main legs were prone to snap from faulty heat-treatment of the steel). Eventually, after great efforts, no fewer than 3413 of these superb machines were built, armed with various mixes of 12.7-, 20- and 30-mm guns. Late variants included redesigned versions made of wood to conserve light alloys.

Another manufacturer, Kawanishi, flew a powerful float seaplane fighter in August 1942; from this they derived the N1K1-J *Shiden* (Violet Lightning) landplane. Had

Mitsubishi A6M assembled by Americans from captured aircraft and flown in mock dog-fights against US types

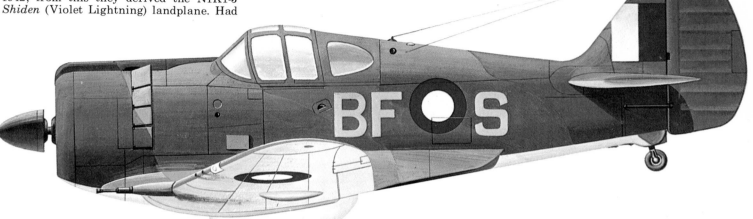

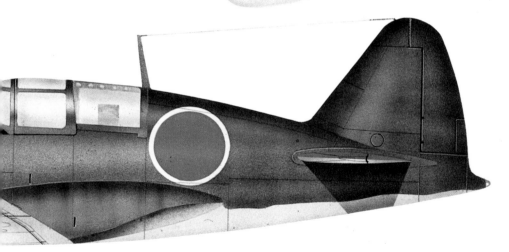

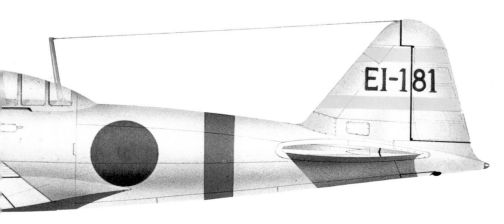

Commonwealth CA-12 Boomerang
The Boomerang, using many components of the Wirraway trainer, was developed to counter Japanese forces in the Pacific and saw extensive action over New Guinea. The type was outclassed by its Japanese contemporaries but operated effectively as a bomber destroyer, on reconnaissance missions and in co-operation with ground forces
Span: 36 ft 3 in *Length:* 25 ft 6 in *Engine:* Pratt & Whitney R-1830-S3C4G Twin Wasp, 1200 hp *Max speed:* 296 mph at 7600 ft *Ceiling:* 29,000 ft *Max take-off weight:* 7600 lb *Armament:* 2×20-mm Hispano cannon, 4×.303-in Browning mg, 1×500-lb bomb

Mitsubishi J2M3 Raiden
The Raiden (Thunderbolt) was the Japanese Army Air Force's first specialist intercepter, with emphasis placed on climb rate and speed rather than pure manoeuvrability. The J2M3 was the first variant with the armament doubled to four cannon and the fuselage-mounted machine-guns deleted
Span: 35 ft 5 in *Length:* 32 ft 7½ in *Engine:* Mitsubishi MK4R-A Kasei 23a, 1820 hp *Max speed:* 371 mph at 20,000 ft *Ceiling:* 38,400 ft *Max take-off weight:* 8700 lb *Armament:* 2×20-mm Type 99-I cannon, 2×20-mm Type 99-II cannon, 2×66-lb or 132-lb bombs

Mitsubishi A6M2 Zero-Sen
The A6M2 was the first operational version of the Japanese Naval Air Force's Type 0 carrier fighter (hence Zero-Sen). The aircraft was blooded over Chungking in August 1940 and later variants were equally devastating in the Pacific war, although the Japanese policy of sacrificing protection for speed and firepower led to many Zeros being lost in combat
Span: 39 ft 4½ in *Length:* 29 ft 9 in *Engine:* Nakajima Sakae 12, 925 hp *Max speed:* 336 mph at 20,000 ft *Ceiling:* 33,800 ft *Max take-off weight:* 5310 lb *Armament:* 2×7.7-mm Type 97 mg, 2×20-mm Type 99 cannon, 2×66-lb or 132-lb bombs (all figures for A6M2 Type 21)

this fighter, called 'George' by the Allies, been designed as a landplane from the start, it might have been as good as the Army Ki-84. As it was, its ancestry left it with a complicated structure, mid wing, poor view and long landing gear which caused much trouble. The 1990-hp *Homare* gave excellent performance, even when carrying four cannon and two machine guns, but was hampered by its poor reliability and complexity. Just over 1000 were built, followed by 428 of the M1K2-J type in which the structure was redesigned to eliminate 23,000 parts and give shorter and better landing gear, improved view and even more outstanding combat performance. According to Imperial Navy records, an N1K2-J flown by Warrant Officer Muto once engaged 12 Hellcats and destroyed four, escaping almost unscathed.

Alone among Japanese fighters in having a liquid-cooled engine, the Army Kawasaki Ki-61 *Hien* ('Tony') was built in large numbers (2654) and served on all fronts. Superior to a P-40 or Bf 109E, it was at first powered by a refined Japanese version of the 1175-hp DB 601 and armed with various mixes of 12.7-mm heavy machine guns, 20-mm cannon (the German MG 151 or Japanese Ho-5) or 30-mm. Though possessed of fair performance and well protected, the Ki-61 suffered from engine and other troubles which were exacerbated by the introduction of the 1500-hp Ha-140 engine. However, the Ki-61 suddenly sprang into the limelight when a radial engine was fitted as a matter of necessity.

Nakajima Ki-84 Hayate

The Hayate (Gale) represented a departure from normal Japanese fighter design methods, being much sturdier than its predecessors. Although marginally slower than its adversaries — Thunderbolts and Mustangs — the Ki-84 could outmanoeuvre and climb faster than its rivals. The strong construction also well suited the dive-bombing and close-support roles

Span: 36 ft 10 in *Length:* 32 ft 6½ in *Engine:* Nakajima Ha.45/11 Type 4, 1900 hp *Max speed:* 388 mph at 20,000 ft *Ceiling:* 34,500 ft *Max take-off weight:* 9200 lb *Armament:* 2×12.7-mm Type 103 mg, 2×20-mm Type 5 cannon, up to 1100 lb of bombs

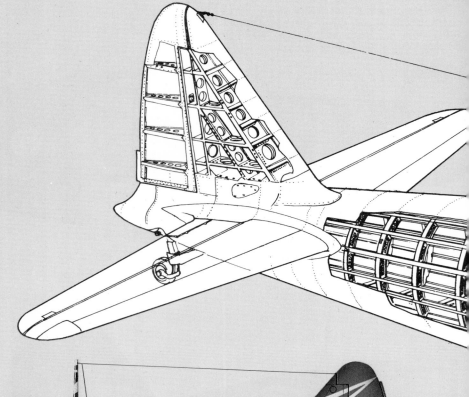

Kawasaki Ki-61 Hien

The Hien (Swallow) entered service with the Japanese Army Air Force in the spring of 1943 and was at first mistakenly thought by the Allies to be a derivative of the Bf 109. The fighter did use a development of the Daimler-Benz DB 601A, however, and was the only Japanese fighter with a liquid-cooled engine to see service in the Second World War. The Ki-61 remained operational until the end of the war, serving in every Pacific theatre

Span: 39 ft 4 in *Length:* 29 ft 4 in *Engine:* Kawasaki Ha.40 Type 2, 1175 hp *Max speed:* 348 mph at 16,400 ft *Ceiling:* 32,800 ft *Max take-off weight:* 7650 lb *Armament:* 2×12.7-mm mg, 2×20-mm Ho-5 cannon, 2×550-lb bombs (all figures for Ki-61-Ic)

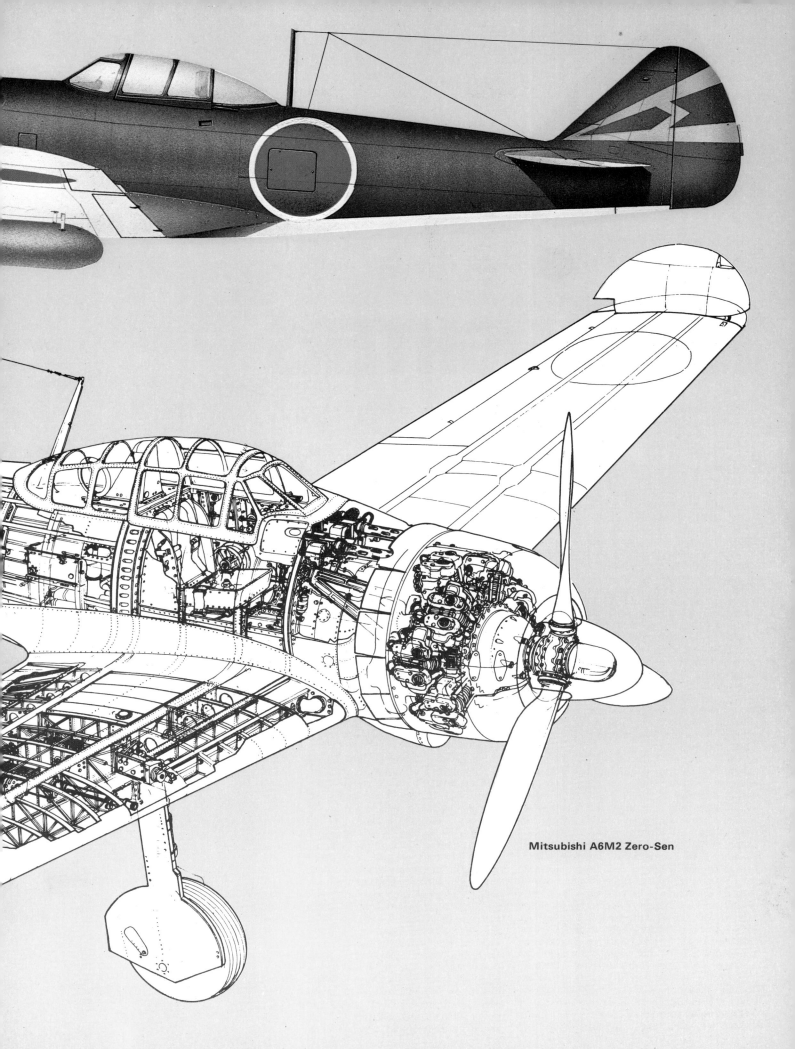

Mitsubishi A6M2 Zero-Sen

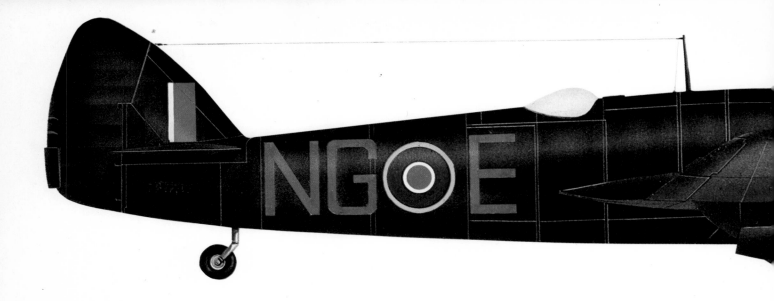

NIGHT FIGHTERS

Until 1939 night fighters were usually merely day fighters equipped with cockpit lighting, flares to light up the airfield for landing, and similar minor additions. But by July 1939 an extremely difficult process of technical development in Britain had resulted in a primitive, though practical AI (airborne interception) radar set. The original 'Radio Direction Finding' equipment, built around Britain's coasts from 1936 onwards, was too large to fit into a fighter. It took completely new technology, greatly reduced operating wavelength, and the solution of problems of a kind never previously encountered, before the first Blenheims could be fitted with AI Mk III in the final weeks of peace. The early set was hopelessly erratic in operation, and even with a skilled operator (a crew-member assigned to watch the flickering cathode-ray tube and advise the pilot which way to steer) results were invariably most discouraging. In theory the AI radar gave pictorial indications on the CRT, like a dim television screen, from which the observer could work out the position and range of a hostile target. In practice, the targets tended not to be there, or merely to vanish into thin air.

GCI, Ground Control of Interception, played a vital part in the night battles over Britain, which began in earnest in the early summer of 1940. With the clearer VHF (very high frequency) voice communications, the controller could inform the patrolling night fighter of the location and approximate height of the nearest hostile bomber. The controller's objective was to guide the night fighter to a position astern of the enemy, where the marauder would betray its presence by casting a 'blip' as a small spike of light on the bearing and elevation CRTs in the fighter. On the nose or wing of the fighter were two sets of transmitter aerials forming a device resembling a double-headed harpoon. This sent out intense pulses of radio energy, a minute fraction of which would be reflected back by the enemy. A rapid rotary switch fed the the CRT displays with the reflected signals picked up by four sets of receiver aerials in turn: left and right azimuth (bearing)

aerials, looking like pairs of vertical wires on the sides of the fuselage or wing leading-edge; and upper and lower elevation aerials, like another harpoon projecting above and below the left wing. The signals picked up by these four combinations of receiver gave four sets of illuminated 'blips' on the CRTs, and skilled observers were taught to translate the lengths and positions of these faint traces into clear instructions to the pilot. The climax of the chase was meant to be closure of the range until the enemy suddenly appeared as a recognisable shape in front, even blacker than the night sky, where it could be shot down.

Blenheims had few successes, and their poor performance and armament did not help. Throughout 1940 they could not match ordinary Hurricanes and Spitfires flown by experienced pilots who had the same GCI to a position somewhere a mile or two behind the enemy but thereafter were on their own. Another successful night fighter was the Defiant, which had the advantage that, backing up the pilot, the observer in his turret could search constantly all over the upper hemisphere and sometimes could shoot down bombers from abeam or directly below.

By far the greatest night fighter of the early part of the war was the Bristol Beaufighter, first flown as a company private venture in July 1939 to make up for the glaring omission in the RAF's fighter inventory: a long-range twin. Powered by two Bristol Hercules 14-cylinder sleeve-valve radials, the early Beaufighters could reach about 320 mph despite their great weight and bulk. The somewhat fat body was oddly arranged, with the pilot in the nose and the radar observer well aft under a separate cupola which in some later versions was fitted with a flexible machine gun. Under the floor was the extremely welcome armament of four 20-mm Hispano cannon, and by 1941 there were also six machine guns in the wings, two on the left and four on the right. Through official stupidity the cannon had to be fed with 60-round drums by the observer despite the fact that a continuous belt feed had been offered by Bristol from the start. Eventually, in September 1941, a

Bristol Beaufighter Mk IIF
The Mk IIF version of the Beaufighter, fitted with Mk IV AI (Airborne Interception) radar, succeeded Blenheims in the night-fighting role in 1941 and bore the brunt of bringing night interception techniques to the fine pitch achieved with later marks of AI. The observer was responsible for changing ammunition drums as well as operating the radar.
Span: 57 ft 10 in *Length:* 41 ft 8 in *Engine:* 2 × Bristol Hercules, 1460 hp each at 6250 ft *Max speed:* 301 mph at 20,200 ft *Ceiling:* 26,500 ft *Max take-off weight:* 19,190 lb *Armament:* 4 × 20-mm cannon, 6 × 0.303-in mg

Junkers Ju 88G-6
The ever adaptable Ju 88 airframe was extensively redesigned to accept specialised night-fighter equipment, and the result was a potent and successful aircraft. The three seater G-series entered service in mid-1944 equipped with sophisticated interception radar
Span: 65 ft 10½ in *Length:* 54 ft 1½ in *Engines:* 2 × Jumo 213A, 1750 hp each *Max speed:* 344 mph at 19,700 ft *Ceiling:* 32, 800 ft

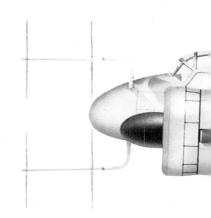

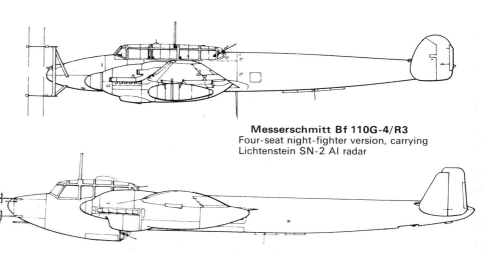

Messerschmitt Bf 110G-4/R3
Four-seat night-fighter version, carrying
Lichtenstein SN-2 AI radar

Dornier Do 217N-1
Night-fighter version of the Do 217 bomber. The
Do 217N-1/U3 variant carried four 20-mm
cannon in a *Shräge Musik* installation

belt feed identical to the Bristol pattern
was adopted from the 401st aircraft. Thus,
during the night Blitz over Britain in
September 1940 to May 1941, the 'Beau' had
to make do with the drum-fed guns. Moreover, it also lacked AI radar until November.
By this time the AI. MkIV set was available,
still rudimentary by later standards but
much better than the Mk III.

The first Beaufighter kill was a Ju 88 on
11 November, 1940. As more aircraft, with
more proficient crews, came into service
kills mounted. There were 22 in March
1941, 48 in April, and 96 in the final 11 days
ending on 11 May. Subsequently many
marks of 'Beau' served in many roles on
many fronts. Several hundred formed the
backbone of the Allied night fighter force
in the Mediterranean and Italy, being flown
by all Allied air forces including the
USAAF. Tough, highly manoeuvrable and
with devastating firepower, the Beaufighter
also performed an increasingly useful role
against ground targets.

The only reason one cannot describe the

USAF

*A USAAF Liberator is literally chopped in half by anti-aircraft
fire. The American massed daylight raids were severely mauled
by fighters until the arrival of the Mustang long-range escorts,
leaving the night raids to the unescorted RAF heavies and the
waiting night fighters*

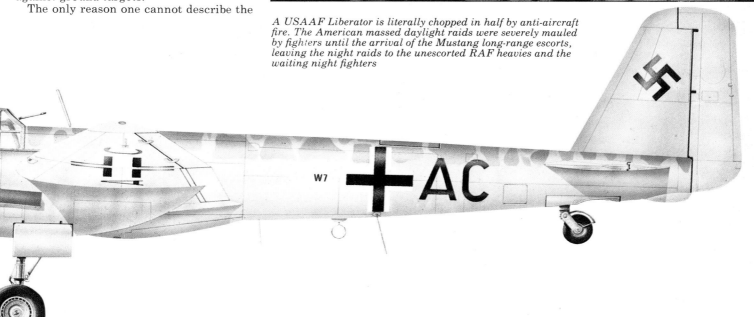

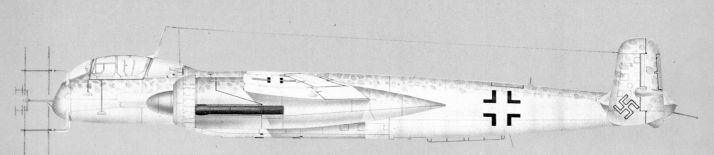

Heinkel He 219 Uhu

The *Uhu* (Owl) was designed as a night fighter, and in this role it was extremely successful. Converted prototypes were claimed to have destroyed 20 British bombers, including six Mosquitoes, in their first six missions during the summer of 1943. Many He 219s were fitted with upward-pointing 'Schräge Musik' cannon, but fewer than 300 entered service

Span: 60 ft 8 in *Length:* 60 ft *Engine:* 2 × Daimler-Benz DB 603G, 1900 hp each *Max speed:* 416 mph at 23,000 ft *Ceiling:* 41,600 ft *Max take-off weight:* 33,700 lb *Armament:* 4 × 30-mm MK 108 cannon, 2 × 30-mm MK 103 cannon, 2 × 20-mm MK 151 cannon

Four .303-in Brownings blast a hail of fire from the rear turret of a Lancaster bomber. A night fighter equipped with Schräge Musik could attack from below – the bomber's blind spot

Popperfoto

Schräge Musik
Radar-equipped Luftwaffe night-fighters
were deadly opponents for RAF Bomber
Command. Equipped with *Schräge Musik*
('Slanting Music' – Jazz) a night-fighter
could attack from below and rake the
unprotected belly of a bomber with 20-mm
cannon fire

The extraordinary Northrop P-61 was an enormous aircraft of some 28,500 lb gross weight, yet with excellent handling and landing characteristics. The shiny all-black finish, designed to conceal the aircraft even in a searchlight beam, earned the P-61 its sinister name

'Beau' as the leading Allied night fighter is because de Havilland's 1938 proposal for an unarmed wooden bomber – contemptuously rejected by the officials – finally led not only to the Mosquito bomber but also to a fighter and many other versions. The first NF.II night fighter 'Mossie' flew on 15 May 1941, with AI.IV radar (fitted later), four 20-mm Hispano under the floor, four Brownings in the nose, a side crew door and flat bullet-proof windscreen. Though unnecessary effort was wasted on such fitments as a four-gun dorsal turret and a Turbinlite searchlight in the nose, the basic NF.II was a superb aircraft; 466 were built in 1941–42. Capable of over 370 mph with full equipment at medium altitudes, the Mosquito was the first aircraft to combine AI radar, heavy armament and fighter-like performance. The robust Beaufighter had come close, but the 'Mossie' was almost 50 mph faster, and could be flung round the sky with its fighter-type stick in a way that made it a dangerous opponent even in a day-time dogfight.

The NF.II was followed by many more powerful versions. Some of these were day multi-role fighter/attack machines (notably the mass-produced FB.VI) while others exchanged the nose machine guns for AI radar of the new centimetric kind. The first sets had worked on wavelengths of about one metre, but by 1942 another British breakthrough in technology, the Magnetron valve, had opened the way for new families of radars with wavelengths that began at about 10 cm. The new sets had transmitting and receiving aerials combined into a single unit, backed by a parabolic 'dish' reflector which could be aimed to search the sky ahead in a spiral fashion. The first of the new sets, AI.VII, was flown in November 1941 in Beaufighter X7579, the first aircraft to carry the excrescence today familiar as a radome. In this case the dome was on the nose, and described as of thimble shape. In

1942 the AI.VIII, with minor improvements, was fitted to the Mosquito II, the result being called NF.XII (197 were later converted). The Mk VIII radar could be used at low level, because its screen was less prone to obliteration by the reflection from the ground, which had hampered the old radars. Range was increased, and there were other improvements, but the arc of sky scanned was considerably reduced.

By 1943 hundreds of NF Mosquitoes had been committed to production, including the II, XII, XIII (new build with AI.VIII and underwing tanks), XVII (II converted with American SCR-720 radar) and XIX (with universal 'bull nose' able to enclose any centimetric radar). They ranged far and wide, though centimetric-equipped marks were forbidden to cross enemy coasts until D-Day on 6 June, 1944.

With little to do over Britain, the Mosquitoes were used increasingly as long-range intruders, ranging all over Europe and often making bomb and rocket attacks on enemy airfields. Other Mosquito night fighters served with 100 Group as counter-measures and special-electronic aircraft. The final wartime mark was the NF.30 powered by a high-altitude Merlin 72 or 76 with new flame-damped exhausts and paddle-blade propellers.

In 1940 the RAF had produced a remarkably good night fighter and intruder by converting the Douglas DB-7 (Boston) light bomber. Operations began in early 1941 with a version called Havoc I, with glazed bombardier nose carrying four Brownings and internal bomb load of 2400 lb. They reached about 295 mph on 1200-hp Twin Wasp engines, and once crews had got used to the tricycle landing gear and the unfamiliarity of an American aircraft, they became very popular. The Havoc II was powered by 1600-hp 14-cylinder Cyclones, reaching about 330 mph. Though a considerable number were wasted in experiments

with the Turbinlite and LAM, many had a 12-gun nose. The LAM stood for Long Aerial Mine, a scheme for trailing or releasing explosive charges with long cables intended to catch the wings of hostile bombers. The Turbinlite was even more hare-brained; a searchlight aircraft was required to complete an interception and then, having lined up on the target, switch on a searchlight so that other aircraft (usually Hurricanes) could somehow get past the searchlight carrier and despatch the enemy. The chief result was a high wastage rate in Havocs and Hurricanes.

In 1940 British scientists and engineers visited the United States and handed over details of centimetric radar. At once an American development was started, with British engineers (the leader of the team was Australian) giving advice. While this produced the excellent SCR-720 radar in fairly quick time, the aircraft planned to carry it, the Northrop P-61 Black Widow, took over three years to develop and almost missed the war. The first purpose-designed radar-equipped night fighter, the Black Widow was powered by two 2000-hp Double Wasp engines; it was a large and extremely complex machine with a broad wing with advanced high-lift features, twin tail booms and a nacelle accommodating a pilot, radar observer (above and behind) and rear observer/gunner. In the nose was the SCR-720, under the floor were four 20-mm M-2 cannon, and on top (in some versions) was a remarkable remote-sighted electric turret mounting four 0.5-in guns, aimed by either the front or rear observer, or slewed to fire ahead with the cannon. The P-6IA finally became operational with the USAAF in May 1944 in the Pacific, and in June in Europe. Until then the USAAF had used the Beaufighter and, to a lesser extent, the Douglas P-70 Havoc in various versions with radar and belly cannon, or without radar and with nose guns.

Northrop P-61
The twin-boom layout of the P-61 Black Widow grouped all the specialised functions of the night-fighter in the central nacelle, housing AI radar, pilot, radar operator and rear gunner with his own four-gun barbette
Span: 66 ft *Length:* 40 ft 11 in *Engine:* 2× Pratt & Whitney R-2800-10 Double Wasp, 2000 hp *Max speed:* 362 mph at 20,000 ft *Max take-off weight:* 28,500 ft *Armament:* 4×.5-in mg, 4×20-mm cannon

In the US Navy, development was boldly aimed at an AI radar operating on the short wavelength of 3 cm, and in 1943 this materialised as the APS-4 and APS-6. The set was small enough to fit a single-seater, and first went into action with the F6F-3 Hellcat. Subsequently it equipped the F4U-4 Corsair.

In the Luftwaffe two aircraft designed for other purposes came to dominate the night sky: the Ju 88 and Bf 110. The first Ju 88 fighter prototype flew in September 1938, and in 1940 some of the first NJG (night-fighter wings) were equipped with converted A-1 bombers designated C-2. There followed many night fighters in the C series, as well as day fighters in the R series, with Jumo 211 or BMW 801 engines and heavy nose armament. From 1942 some C models, starting with the C-6b, had been fitted with AI radar of the FuG 212 Lichtenstein type, operating on a wavelength of around a half-metre and notable for a large array of dipole aerials on nose and wings. Though a conversion, as was the Blenheim, the Ju 88 was destined to be one of the greatest warplanes in history.

During 1943 work began on a version tailored from the start for night fighting. Burdened by extra equipment and weapons, the earlier models had placed heavy demands on pilots who – operating under extreme stress caused by fear of the omnipresent Mosquito – suffered high attrition through accidents. In the Ju 88G there was

a complete revision of systems and equipment, and handling was improved by fitting the large tail of the Ju 188. From 1944 almost all Ju 88 output was of the G-6 or G-7 series, powered by the Jumo 213 or BMW 801, and with various radars and devastating armament in ventral blister or *Schräge Musik* installations. The latter, meaning Slanting Music (Jazz), comprised cannon mounted at about 70°–80°, allowing the pilot to formate under the bomber, where the RAF crew could not even see or fire on their enemy. Skilled pilots could aim precisely at the wing spars between the engine, well clear of the bomb bay, and then avoid the stricken monster as it tumbled downwards. Five or six kills a night became common, interceptions being made childishly simple by the Naxos radar, which homed on the bomber's H_2S mapping radar, and the Flensburg, which homed on the bomber's Monica tail-warning radar. Monica had been added to protect the RAF heavies, but in practice it gave so many warnings of other bombers that its indications were often ignored, and it served merely as an aerial lighthouse to guide the Luftwaffe night fighters.

The other important NJG aircraft was the old Bf 110, much more restricted than the Ju 88 but docile and pleasant and, in Bf 110G and H forms, specially planned for night fighting with DB 605 engines. The Luftwaffe's lack of forward planning is well demonstrated by the fact that the 110 was intended to be withdrawn from production in 1941, but in the absence of anything else its output was tripled in 1942–43 and held at the same level in 1944, virtually all being night fighters.

Other German night fighters included special versions of Bf 109G and Fw 190, used chiefly in the free-lance *Wilde Sau* (Wild Boar) role, searching visually for RAF bombers illuminated by searchlights, ground fires or flares. They enjoyed much

greater success than RAF night fighters in 1940, partly because there was more illumination and far greater intensity of bombers.

One of the finest combat aircraft of the entire war was the Heinkel He 219 *Uhu* (Owl), which combined powerful armament and good sensors with outstanding performance and handling. However, only small numbers of this aircraft were built. Night fighter versions of the Do 335 and Me 262 were flying at the end of the war, but these few leaders of the Luftwaffe's last fighter generation appeared too late.

Though Japanese airborne interception radar seldom got into action before the final weeks of the war, the chief twin-engined fighters all served in the vital night role. The Kawasaki Ki-45 *Toryu* (Dragon Killer), code-named 'Nick' by the Allies, served the Imperial Army well but, like the Bf 110, was obsolescent. Many combinations of 12.7-, 20-, 30-, 37-, and even 75-mm guns were fitted; night fighters had an oblique pair of 12.7- or 20-mm weapons and on several occasions managed to shoot down the B-29, which many single-seaters could not even reach. The main Navy twin-engined fighter was Nakajima's JINI, flown in May 1941 as a long-range escort with remotely controlled rear barbettes. There were several subsequent versions, called 'Irving' by the Allies, of which the most important was the JINI-S *Gekko* (Moonlight) night fighter, with oblique pairs of 20-mm cannon firing above and below, and often with nose searchlight or radar. Though successful against the B-17 and B-24, the JINI lacked the performance to reach the B-29. Best of all the Japanese night fighters was probably the Kawanishi PIY2-S *Kyokko* (Aurora), derived from a Yokosuka attack bomber in the class of the Ju 88. Powered by two 1850-hp *Kasei* engines, the *Kyokko* carried AI radar and three cannon (four if a twin-20-mm dorsal turret was fitted), but arrived too late to make an impact on the war.

FIGHTERS' WAR

In the dark winter of 1941–42, dozens of Allied fighter types battled against enemy machines that were generally superior. In the Far East and SW Pacific the A6M and Ki-43 found little difficulty in mastering the early marks of Curtiss P-40, the Dutch Curtiss-Wright CW-21B (1000-hp Cyclone and four machine guns), the Brewster Buffalo (1100-hp Cyclone and four guns) and a collection of other mediocre types.

The CW-21B was nimble but unprotected. The Buffalo was nimble at the start of its career, in 1938, but by 1941 it had been loaded with armour, self-sealing tanks, extra equipment and four 0.5-in guns. The result was a sluggish performance—it took almost half an hour to reach 21,000 ft, and manoeuvrability was pathetic. Often guns were removed, or replaced by small 0.303-in Brownings, in an attempt to restore some performance. In these circumstances the Boomerang, designed and flown in fourteen weeks by Commonwealth Aircraft in Melbourne, was of great value. The only engine

available was the 1200-hp Twin Wasp, yet the Australians created a tough and 'operable' tactical machine with two cannon and four 0.303-in, plus 500-lb bomb, which remained outstanding in the close-support role until the end of the Pacific war.

An identical armament had been adopted in 1940 for the so-called 'B' wing of the Spitfire. In early 1941 this went into production as the Spitfire V, with a strengthened fuselage and more powerful Merlin 45 or 50-series engine. The VB was the standard front-line fighter in 1941–42, flown by all Allied air forces in all theatres. Many had clipped wings, bomb racks, tropical filter under the engine or other changes, and Air Service Training fitted arrester hooks to produce the deck-landing Seafire IB. Large numbers were fitted with the 'C' wing, which could carry four 20-mm Hispanos (but usually did not), and this Spitfire VC in turn led to the Seafire IIC with catapult spools and stronger landing gear. In 1942 a way was found to make the wing fold,

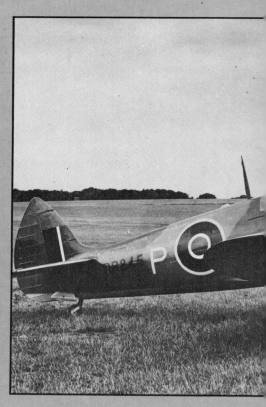

The development of the Spitfire from the first prototype in 1936 right until the end of the war was continuous, making it one of the most 'stretched' aircraft designs in history. The Griffon-engined Mk IV of 1941 was renumbered the Mk XX to avoid confusion with the reconnaissance PR IV

Imperial War Museum

resulting in the excellent Seafire III of 1943; but by this time more performance was needed. While leading-edge tankage and many other changes led to long-range unarmed PR (photo-reconnaissance) Spitfires, the great pressure on Rolls-Royce to deliver more power at greater height resulted in the Merlin 60-series. Supermarine, helped by the Royal Aircraft Establishment, devised a pressure cabin, and in 1941 flew the Mk VI as an interim high-altitude machine with Merlin 47 and extended wingtips. Design went ahead on the definitive high-altitude fighter, the VII, and the all-round version, the VIII.

Meanwhile, Merlin 60-series engines went into production in 1942 and a quick lash-up conversion of the VC went into production as the IX. This had the two-stage engine, twin radiators and four-blade Rotol propeller, but was otherwise unchanged. Possibly a limit should have been placed on the numbers built. However, it stayed in production, and to the end of the war was by far the most numerous Spitfire, 5664 being built. There were LF, F and HF versions, depending on the low, medium or high altitude rating of the engine, often accompanied by clipped, normal or extended tips. A closely related model was the XVI powered by the Packard-built engine; by

1944 the 'E' wing moved the cannon outboard and added 0.5-in guns inboard, the LF.XVI often having clipped wings and later a cut-down rear fuselage and teardrop hood. Other changes included broader, pointed rudder and rear-fuselage fuel tanks. Only modest numbers were made of the pressurized HF.VII and so-called 'definitive' Mk VIII, which had many refinements, including retractable tailwheel, and had been meant to replace the IX. The standard photo-reconnaissance machine became the XI, with unpressurized cockpit but greatly augmented fuel capacity, and numerous other changes, including shiny Cerulean Blue finish and plain red/blue roundels.

Heavily-armed P-47D Thunderbolts prepare for a strike mission over France just prior to D-Day

Republic P-47D Thunderbolt

Heavy, ungainly and with a massive deep fuselage to accommodate supercharger and ducting, the P-47 nevertheless made up in brute power and at altitude its performance was exceptional. Later models had a teardrop hood and the late-model R-2800 Double Wasp, giving no less than 2550 hp emergency power

Span: 40 ft 9½ in *Length:* 36 ft 1¾ in *Engine:* Pratt & Whitney R-2800-59 Double Wasp, 2300 hp *Max speed:* 429 mph at 30,000 ft *Ceiling:* 42,000 ft *Max take-off weight:* 17,500 lb *Armament:* 8×.5-in mg, 1500 lb bombs/rockets

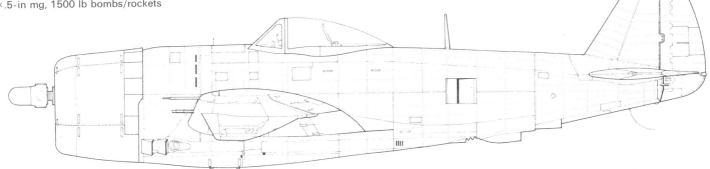

In 1940 Rolls-Royce discussed installation of the Griffon engine, which had a capacity of more than 36 litres compared with the Merlin's 27. A few were fitted in early airframes, and in 1942 production was urgently started on the Spitfire XII, with 1735-hp low-blown Griffon giving a speed at low altitude of around 370 mph, an increase of some 50 mph and fast enough to catch the Luftwaffe's Fw 190 and Bf 109 fighter-bombers making sneak raids on English coastal towns. The Griffon resulted in a bigger nose, with fairings over the projecting cylinder blocks, together with a four-blade propeller and large spinner. In 1943 the more refined Mk XIV entered production with the two-stage Griffon 65, deep twin radiators and five-blade propeller married to an airframe based on the Mk VIII retractable tailwheel and broad rudder. This was a superb combat machine that saw much action in 1944 and restored ascendancy of the Spitfire over the best Luftwaffe machines. It caught flying bombs with ease, reaching over 400 mph near the ground and almost 450 mph at 26,000 ft, and was an impressive dogfighter. The final batches were fitted with the teardrop hood, and small numbers of the long-range Mk XVIII and ultra-long-range PR.XIX were also built. Many of the Spitfires built from 1942 were of the FR (fighter-reconnaissance) type with one or more oblique cameras as well as full armament. Unfortunately, little was done to improve armament, and the RAF ended the war with the same guns, of 1916 design, which it had used in 1939.

Hawker followed the Hurricane through its design office with a totally new fighter, boldly begun in 1937–38, to carry 12 machine guns or four cannon on 2000 hp. After many difficulties and false starts, Gloster Aircraft got into limited production in 1941 with a version called the Typhoon IB, with 2200-hp Napier Sabre engine and four cannon. Though basically extremely strong, this machine at first had a tendency to shed its tail. Coupled with the extreme unreliability of the complex engine and disappointing performance at altitude, this led to the otherwise impressive Typhoon being written off as virtually useless. However, the Typhoon gradually demonstrated its tremendous value as a low-level tactical machine. It was able to catch any Luftwaffe fighter-bomber at low level, and after D-Day wrought havoc among Panzer divisions with cannon, bombs and rockets. Eventually 3330 were built, the majority of them having the odd car-type doors and clumsy canopy replaced by a neat teardrop sliding

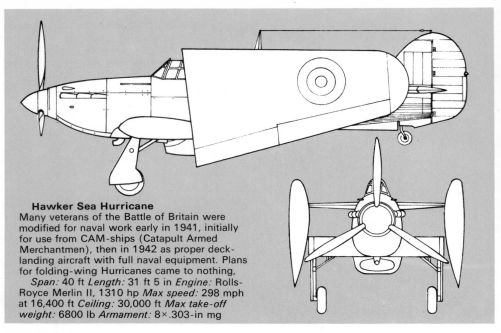

Hawker Sea Hurricane
Many veterans of the Battle of Britain were modified for naval work early in 1941, initially for use from CAM-ships (Catapult Armed Merchantmen), then in 1942 as proper deck-landing aircraft with full naval equipment. Plans for folding-wing Hurricanes came to nothing, *Span:* 40 ft *Length:* 31 ft 5 in *Engine:* Rolls-Royce Merlin II, 1310 hp *Max speed:* 298 mph at 16,400 ft *Ceiling:* 30,000 ft *Max take-off weight:* 6800 lb *Armament:* 8×.303-in mg

hood. Early in Typhoon development buffeting was traced to transonic airflow around the thick wing. A proposed thin-wing Typhoon led to the Tempest, with thin elliptical wing and longer fuselage housing fuel previously carried in the thick wing. Armed with four short-barrel Mk V cannon, the Tempest V went into production in the summer of 1943, proving approximately 40 mph faster than the Typhoon at most altitudes. In the summer of 1944 it destroyed more flying bombs than any other fighter. Later versions, with more powerful Sabre and Bristol Centaurus engines, entered service after the war.

Though they were never adopted, for reasons unconnected with the aircraft, the Martin-Baker M.B.3 and M.B.5 were outstanding fighters, in many ways superior to those used by the RAF. The M.B.3, powered by the Sabre, had six cannon with belt feeds, and features that promised exceptionally easy maintenance. Sadly, the prototype crashed as a result of engine-failure. The Griffon-engined M.B.5 is widely judged the best piston-engined fighter ever built. The official report described the general design as 'infinitely better, from the engineering and maintenance aspects, than any other similar type of aircraft'. Had a positive decision been taken in time, the M.B.5 could have seen war service.

Other British fighters built only as prototypes included the high-altitude Mosquito XV and Vickers 432, the former

having four machine guns and the latter six cannon. The official high-altitude choice fell on the long-span Westland Welkin, powered like its two rivals by two high-blown Merlins and with a wing of no less than 70-ft span. Though 67 were built, including a two-seat night fighter, none reached a squadron.

Hawker Typhoon 1B
The Thyphoon was not suited to its original role as an intercepter but proved to be a devastating ground-attack fighter. The Mk 1B variant carried cannon in place of the earlier machine-guns, but the most effective armament was the rocket projectile. Rocket-firing Typhoons destroyed large numbers of German tanks in the weeks following D-Day

The Martin-Baker MB5, last of a series of remarkable fighter prototypes from this small company

Span: 41 ft 7 in *Length:* 31 ft 10 in *Engine:* Napier Sabre IIA, 2180 hp *Max speed:* 405 mph at 18,000 ft *Ceiling:* 34,000 ft *Max take-off weight:* 11,400 lb *Armament:* 4×20-mm Hispano cannon, 2×1000-lb bombs or 8×60-lb rockets

Imperial War Museum

Testing the Browning machine-guns in the nose of a Mosquito FB.VI, the fighter-bomber sub-type produced in larger quantities than any other variant of this remarkable wooden warplane

With four 20-mm cannon and 1000-lb bombs, Typhoon IBs of No 181 Squadron prepare for an offensive sweep into occupied Europe, mid-1943

John Batchelor

In the United States, Curtiss relentlessly pursued the P-40 design through 15 basic variants; most variants had the advanced Allison engines, but a few were powered by the Packard V-1650 Merlin. Nearly all carried six 0.5-in machine-guns in the wing, giving reliable service as tactical support and fighter-bomber aircraft in many theatres. Handicapped by the fact that even at the most effective altitude the speed seldom reached 350 mph, the P-40 Warhawk/Kittyhawk family took the total of P-40 production to 13,738. None of the shoal of other Curtiss prototypes reached the production stage, though the XP-55 Ascender (Arse-ender), XP-60 family, giant XP-62 with up to eight cannon, and shipboard XF14C were technically of intense interest.

Although the extremely unconventional P-39 Airacobra had been rejected by the RAF, Bell fought to get the aircraft into wide service, eventually succeeding to the tune of 9558 aircraft. Of these just over half went to the Soviet Union, where the effective armament in the ground-attack role and ability to absorb heavy punishment brought the Airacobra a good reputation. Bell also built 3303 P-63 Kingcobras, which looked similar (apart from the tail) but were actually a complete redesign. Armed with the same 37-mm cannon and four 0.5-in as most P-39s, the P-63 saw action almost entirely on the Russian front; 332 P-63s were converted by the USAAF into armoured target aircraft to be shot at by

frangible (easily shattered) practise bullets.

Lockheed's first fighter, the Model 22, was a masterpiece of originality. It was designer Hall L. Hibberd's answer to a challenging Army Air Corps requirement for a speed of 360 mph and endurance at full throttle of one hour. The prototype flew in January 1939, startling observers by its size, twin liquid-cooled Allison engines, twin tail booms and remarkably slim design. By 1941 deliveries began to the RAF, with the turbochangers and handed propellers (rotating in opposite directions) removed. As predicted by Lockheed, these aircraft were poor performers, and the RAF never used the Lightning, as it was named. But the US Army P-38 went from strength to strength, and eventually 9923 were delivered, most having nose armament of one 20-mm and four 0.5-in, with an exceptional amount of ammunition. Most had a combat setting of 8° flap to improve manoeuvrability, and later models also had an extra electrically driven dive-flap under each wing to counter strong nose-down pitch at very high speeds. Comfortable on long missions, and flown by a wheel instead of a stick, the popular P-38 served as an escort and ground-attack fighter. At the end of the war the radar-equipped P-38M night fighter saw action, and many were converted as two-seat 'droop snoot' lead ships for accurate level bombing. The monster XP-58, with 3000-hp double engines, was built only as a prototype.

In the Pacific war two US Navy fighters of

North American P-51B Mustang
The P-51's airframe had proved itself an outstanding and advanced design, and with the decision to mass-produce the Merlin engine in the United States the two were married to produce a completely revitalised fighter of outstanding quality. The introduction of the long range P-51B at the end of 1943 gave tremendous impetus to the US daylight bombing offensive over Europe

Span: 37 ft *Length:* 32 ft 3 in *Engine:* Packard Merlin V-1650-3, 1450 hp *Max speed:* 445 mph at 30,000 ft *Ceiling:* 41,800 ft *Max take-off weight:* 9800 lb

North American P-51D Mustang
Teardrop canopy and a fin fillet to compensate for the reduced side area were the main changes in the D-model. With engines rated for low altitude and equipped with rockets, Mustangs made many successful marauding raids into Europe

Span: 37 ft *Length:* 32 ft $3\frac{5}{16}$ in *Engine:* Packard-Merlin V-1650-7, 1790 hp *Max speed:* 443 mph at 25,000 ft *Ceiling:* 41,900 ft *Max take-off weight:* 10,100 lb *Armament:* 6×.5-in mg, 1000 lb bombs/rockets

Seafire XV comes in to land aboard the escort carrier Pretoria Castle

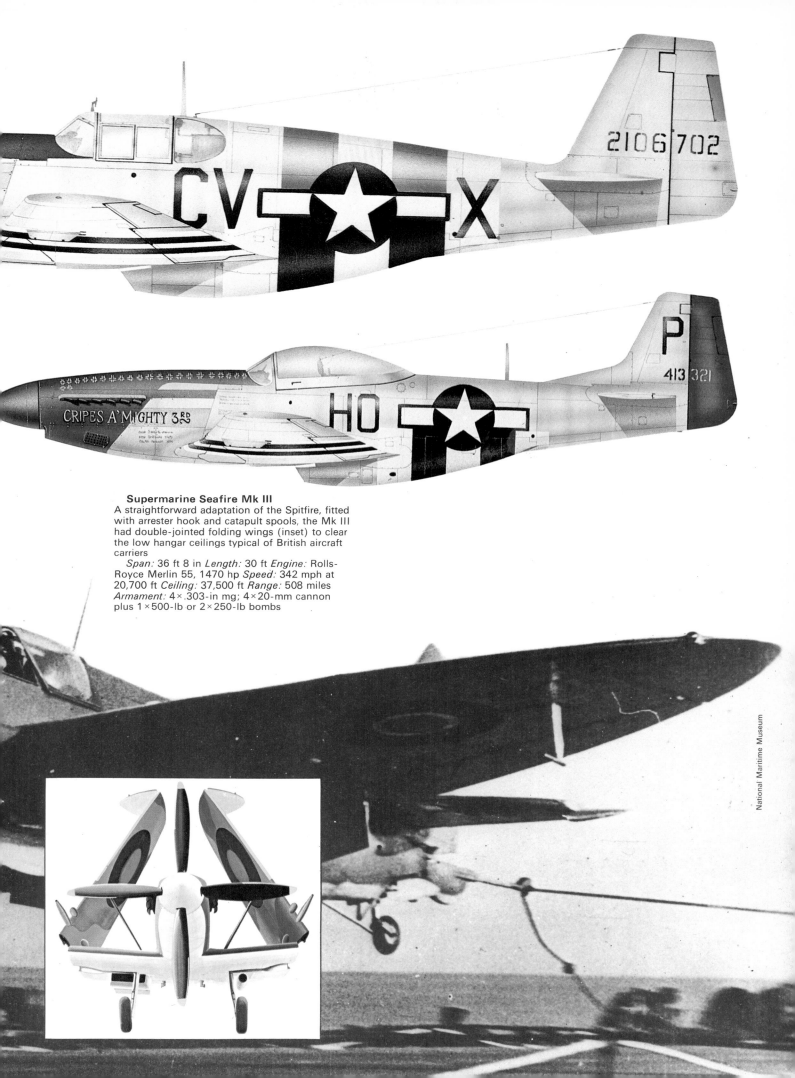

Supermarine Seafire Mk III
A straightforward adaptation of the Spitfire, fitted
with arrester hook and catapult spools, the Mk III
had double-jointed folding wings (inset) to clear
the low hangar ceilings typical of British aircraft
carriers
    Span: 36 ft 8 in *Length:* 30 ft *Engine:* Rolls-
Royce Merlin 55, 1470 hp *Speed:* 342 mph at
20,700 ft *Ceiling:* 37,500 ft *Range:* 508 miles
Armament: 4×.303-in mg; 4×20-mm cannon
plus 1×500-lb or 2×250-lb bombs

CRIPES A'MIGHTY 3ᴿᴰ

similar design and power came into service in 1942–43 and at once turned the tables on the previously victorious Japanese. First to be designed was Chance Vought's F4U Corsair, planned in 1938. At that time there was not the mass of information which was later gleaned from warfare in Europe, and American fighters tended to have 1000 hp. Rex Beisel and his team boldly selected the monster R-2800 Double Wasp aircooled radial, then experimentally giving 1850 hp, and as a result laid the basis for an aircraft many consider the best fighter of the Second World War. In October 1940 the prototype became the first American aircraft to exceed 400 mph, but development was protracted. Fuel was added to the fuselage. moving the pilot aft where his view was poor. The Navy insisted that the F4U could not be used from carriers, but Corsairs of the British Fleet Air Arm, with wings clipped to fit below-decks, successfully operated from small escort carriers from mid-1943 onwards. After a considerable number of engineering changes the F4U-1 was built in large numbers, 4102 by Vought, 3808 by Goodyear (FG-1) and 735 by Brewster (F3A). The F4U-2 interim night fighter was in service in early 1943, followed by the F4U-4E and 4N, all of which had the APS-4 or -6 radar with the aerial in a pod on the right wing. Most Corsairs had six 0.5-in guns and up to 2000 lb of bombs or rockets; some versions had four 20-mm cannon. By 1945 there were further versions, some having the 3000-hp R-4360 Wasp Major; the last F4U was completed when No. 12,571 came off the line in December 1952.

The Grumman F6F Hellcat, partner and rival to the Corsair in defeating the Japanese, was designed in 1941–42, flown in 1942 with two types of engine, and then built with great rapidity after extremely quick development. Like the F4U it was a very large fighter, with an even bigger wing of 334 sq ft housing the same armament of six 0.5-in (in some sub-types, two 20-mm and four 0.5-in). By 1945 no fewer than 12,274 Hellcats had been produced, and their capability is underlined by the fact that, of 6477 enemy aircraft credited to US Navy carrier-based fighters, 4947 were gained by the Hellcat. Again several versions were night fighters, with the aerial system in a pod on the right wing, and most versions could carry two 1000-lb bombs or rockets. Just over 1200 were supplied to the Fleet Air Arm (which originally considered the name Gannet) and there were also high-altitude reconnaissance versions. Though few Hellcats could reach 400 mph, they combined so many attributes that from 1943 onwards the Allies dominated the Pacific skies.

In the Soviet Union the Yakovlev fighters, powered by liquid-cooled M-105 engines, continued to be built in huge numbers, reaching approximately 37,000 by 1945. The mass-produced Yak-7B was replaced on the Urals assembly line in late 1942 by the Yak-9, in which metal wing spars allowed a considerable increase in fuel capacity. Total output of all versions of Yak-9 reached approximately 20,000; despite their light armament of one engine-mounted cannon and one or two machine guns, their all-round performance and manoeuvrability were so good that they were at least equal to Bf 109G or Fw 190 fighters flown by pilots of similar experience to the Russians.

There were many sub-types, with different marks of engine, the gun being 20-, 37- or even 75-mm; the -9D was a long-range model. The trim Yak-3 of 1944 was very similar but had a smaller wing for low-level duties, which increased speed from about 365 to 405 mph. The Yak-9U, a total redesign with all-metal structure, came too late to see action.

The rival Lavochkin bureau achieved great success by switching to the M-82A radial engine, the resulting La-5 going into production in 1942. By the end of that year the -5FN was in production with a more powerful 1640-hp engine and cut-down rear fuselage giving all-round vision. Further development led to increasing use of metal construction, and during 1943 to the La-7 with a third ShVAK cannon on the left side supplementing the original two above the fuselage. Most -7s also had an engine boosted to 1775 hp, and with an aerodynamic clean-up their speed rose considerably above 400 mph. Despite their small wings, which were fully slatted, the Lavochkin fighters were excellent in close combat and were flown by most of the leading Soviet aces, including Ivan Kozhedub (62 victories) and Alexander Pokryshin (59). Total production amounted to about 26,000, the completely new La-9 with all-metal airframe of different shape and four fuselage cannon not entering service until near the end of the European war.

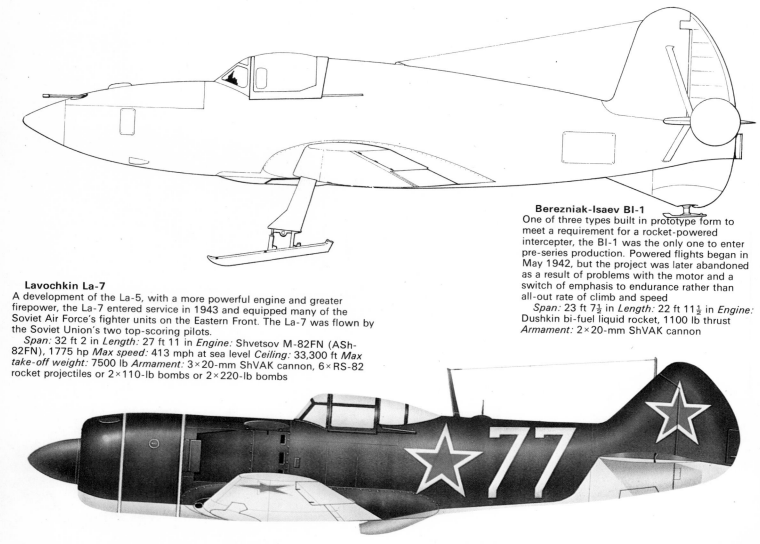

Bereezniak-Isaev BI-1
One of three types built in prototype form to meet a requirement for a rocket-powered intercepter, the BI-1 was the only one to enter pre-series production. Powered flights began in May 1942, but the project was later abandoned as a result of problems with the motor and a switch of emphasis to endurance rather than all-out rate of climb and speed
Span: 23 ft 7½ in *Length:* 22 ft 11½ in *Engine:* Dushkin bi-fuel liquid rocket, 1100 lb thrust *Armament:* 2×20-mm ShVAK cannon

Lavochkin La-7
A development of the La-5, with a more powerful engine and greater firepower, the La-7 entered service in 1943 and equipped many of the Soviet Air Force's fighter units on the Eastern Front. The La-7 was flown by the Soviet Union's two top-scoring pilots.
Span: 32 ft 2 in *Length:* 27 ft 11 in *Engine:* Shvetsov M-82FN (ASh-82FN), 1775 hp *Max speed:* 413 mph at sea level *Ceiling:* 33,300 ft *Max take-off weight:* 7500 lb *Armament:* 3×20-mm ShVAK cannon, 6×RS-82 rocket projectiles or 2×110-lb bombs or 2×220-lb bombs

THE FALLEN EAGLE

John Batchelor

Like the Spitfire, the Fw 190 underwent continuous development. The long-nosed 190D series were powered by the liquid-cooled Jumo 213 and not a radial engine as the annular radiator suggests

Despite having an excellent engineering capability, and at the lower and medium levels good management, the essentially flawed nature of the RLM *(Reichsluftministerium)* procurement machine ensured that, right up to the final defeat in May 1945, the Luftwaffe was equipped in the main with modified versions of the aircraft in service before the war.

Fighters were no exception – the newest type in widespread service was the Fw 190, first flown in June 1939. Though a superb combat aircraft, and technically more advanced than almost all contemporary machines, the 190 was increasingly hard-pressed by the later Spitfires, Mustangs and Tempests; nor did it have things all its own way on the Eastern front. The Fw 190F and G were offshoots from the mainstream of development, intended for various close-support and attack roles and built in large numbers. Heavily armed and armoured, they could carry bombs of up to 3968 lb (1800 kg), the heaviest weapon load of any comparable aircraft until almost 20 years later. Some indication of what had been done to the 190 – dimensionally a small fighter – can be deduced from the fact that the loaded weight of the first prototype was 3968 lb, compared with 12,900 lb in some F and G models.

In 1942 several high-altitude prototype 190s were built with turbochargers under the rear fuselage, some of these being powered by DB 603 liquid-cooled engines. Though not built in quantity, these led to a completely new 190, the D, with a 1776-hp Jumo 213 boosted by MW50 injection to 2240-hp.

By early 1944 the D-9, called Dora 9 by the Luftwaffe and the long-nosed 190 by the RAF, was proving itself faster than radial-engined versions, though carrying fewer guns in most instances (often only two MG 151 and two MG 131). The D-12, however, had a 30-mm MK 108 on the centreline and a useful bomb load, yet in clean condition could reach 453 mph at height with MW50 injection. The RLM rewarded designer Kurt Tank by allowing future aircraft from his team to have the prefix 'Ta', and the Fw 190D series thus became the Ta 152. By late 1944 the effort was becoming dissipated into numerous prototypes, but the formidable Ta 152C and H did reach production, the former having a 2100-hp DB 603L and heavy armament (usually one 30-mm MK 108 and four 20-mm MG 151) and the latter being a high-altitude version with Jumo 213E, long-span wing and lighter armament (e.g. MK 108 and two MG 151). All were great performers. Tank himself simply opened the throttle when bounced by a flight of Mustangs on a test-flight, leaving the straining American aircraft, the fastest Allied fighters in the high-level sky, at a relative speed of about 30 mph, the 152H being capable of about 472 mph. The shortage of both fuel and pilots meant that only very few saw service.

The final mark of Bf 109 also saw only limited combat, though production until 1945 was on an unprecedented scale, 14,212 being delivered in 1944, despite Allied bombing. All the 109G series were powered by various types of DB 605, rated at 1475–1550-hp. This was insufficient to compensate for the increase in weight, and the all-round performance was unimpressive. Many of the inherent virtues of the 109 became

submerged, while the shortcomings of terrible discomfort, limited endurance, and flight controls that seized almost solid at high speeds, persisted or worsened. Despite the wealth of outstanding guns and rocket missiles fitted, the 109G was steadily outclassed even over Germany itself; this process was exacerbated by the failure of the training schools to replace experienced fighter pilots. By mid-1944 the shortage of pilots and fuel was critical, and the task of Allied pilots – notably those flying the P-47 and P-51 – became much easier. The final Bf 109 versions introduced an improved canopy, often called the 'Galland' hood after the Luftwaffe General of Fighters, and a wooden tail of improved shape. These features were seen on many late sub-types of both the G and the K, the latter tending to replace the G in December 1944 with small structural changes. The high-altitude 109H had a long-span centre section but was abandoned, as was the completely new and radical Me 155, which was passed to Blohm und Voss, becoming the Bv 155. The 155 gradually ceased to resemble the 109, and with a wing of various spans from 61 to 69 feet carrying enormous radiators, was intended to fight at up to 56,000 ft.

Messerschmitt's greatest achievements were the Me 163 and Me 262. The former had a history extending back to a 1938 DFS project for a rocket test aircraft. Professor Alex Lippisch made the DFS 194 tailless, and flight tests in 1940 encouraged the RLM to sanction a high-speed aircraft designated Me 163. Glider champion Heini Dittmar reached 570 mph in this in August 1941, and on 2 October, 1941, was towed to 13,000 ft. He cast off, ignited the Walter

Messerschmitt Bf 109G-6

The G-6 version of this famous fighter, which remained in production in one form or another throughout the Second World War, was the first to have a pair of 20-mm cannon mounted beneath the wings. The G series was being built at the rate of 725 a month by mid-1943 but, despite having the more powerful DB 605 engine, was in some ways considered inferior to its Bf 109F predecessor

Span: 32 ft 6½ in *Length:* 29 ft 8 in *Engine:* Daimler-Benz DB 605A-1, 1475 hp *Max speed:* 387 mph at 23,000 ft *Ceiling:* 38,500 ft *Max take-off weight:* 7500 lb *Armament:* 2×13-mm MG 131 mg, 3×20-mm MG 151 cannon

Messerschmitt Me 309

Intended as a successor to the Bf 109, the Me 309 was cancelled after its development was delayed so long by technical problems – especially with the undercarriage – and the fact that the new generation of Focke-Wulf fighters proved a better proposition

Span: 36 ft 1 in *Length:* 31 ft 4 in *Engine:* Daimler-Benz DB 603A-1, 1750 hp *Max speed:* 496 mph at 26,200 ft *Ceiling:* 39,300 ft *Max take-off weight:* 9050 lb *Armament:* 30-mm MK 103 or MK 108 cannon, 2×13-mm MG 131 mg (light version); 30-mm MK 103 or MK 108 cannon, 2×20-mm MG 151 cannon, 4×13-mm MG 131 mg (heavy version)

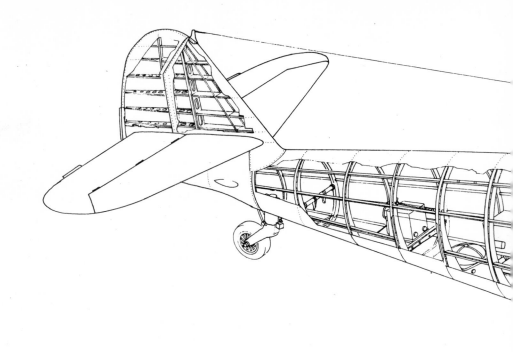

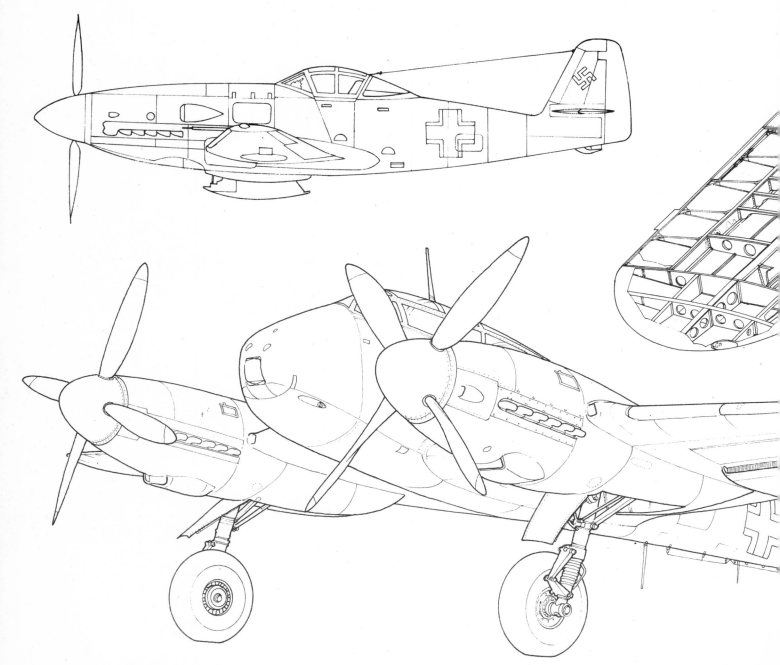

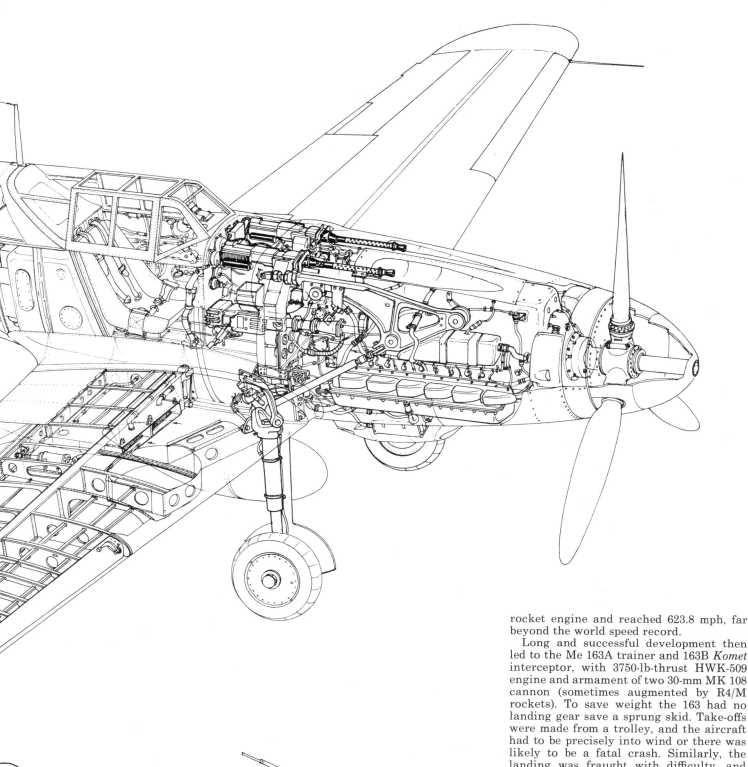

Messerschmitt Me 210
The Me 210, designed as a successor to the Bf 110, had an unhappy career largely as a result of being rushed into production before the basic design deficiencies had been corrected. An order for 1000 Me 210s was placed even before the first prototype had flown, but in the event only 350 were completed and the type was succeeded by the Me 410 Hornisse
Span: 53 ft 7 in *Length:* 40 ft 3 in *Engine:* 2 × Daimler-Benz DB 601F, 1395 hp each *Max speed:* 385 mph *Ceiling:* 23,000 ft *Max take-off weight:* 17,850 lb *Armament:* 2 × 20-mm MG 151 cannon, 2 × 7.9-mm MG 17 mg, 2 × 13-mm MG 131 mg

rocket engine and reached 623.8 mph, far beyond the world speed record.

Long and successful development then led to the Me 163A trainer and 163B *Komet* interceptor, with 3750-lb-thrust HWK-509 engine and armament of two 30-mm MK 108 cannon (sometimes augmented by R4/M rockets). To save weight the 163 had no landing gear save a sprung skid. Take-offs were made from a trolley, and the aircraft had to be precisely into wind or there was likely to be a fatal crash. Similarly, the landing was fraught with difficulty, and any drift or a heavy touchdown caused the residual propellants to slosh together and explode. But in the air the 163 was a dream, with beautiful flying qualities. No other aircraft could get near it, and the 370-odd delivered achieved great success in steep interceptions of US 8th Air Force heavy bombers, followed by a swift glide back to base.

In contrast the Me 262 was a conventional fighter, with the same outstanding flying qualities (quite different from the 163 but exceptionally pleasant and safe) combined with normal range and endurance. What made the 262 different was that it was a jet. Development had begun in late 1938, and the first prototype flew with a nose piston engine in April 1941. In July 1942 it flew with two Jumo 004 turbojets under the wings, eventually receiving a tricycle landing gear, full combat equipment and the

Messerschmitt Me 262

The first jet fighter to enter service, the Me 262 could have altered the course of the Second World War if it had been employed in the role for which it was intended. On Hitler's instructions, however, the type was used primarily as a ground-attack aircraft, and fewer than one-sixth of those built ever saw service.

Span: 40 ft 11½ in *Length:* 34 ft 9½ in *Engine:* 2×Junkers Jumo 004B-1, -2 or -3, 1980 lb thrust each *Max speed:* 583 mph at 30,000 ft *Ceiling:* 37,500 ft *Max take-off weight:* 14,100 lb *Armament:* 4×30-mm MK 108 cannon, 24×R4M rocket projectiles

Cockpit is a totally enclosed unit for pressurisation purposes, although no service machines were ever pressuris

Tank filler cap

Radio loop

Stabiliser adjusting motor

238-gallon tank

132-gallon auxiliary tank

Fla

Radio

Master compass

Variable orifice 'bullet' moves in and out to vary exit area

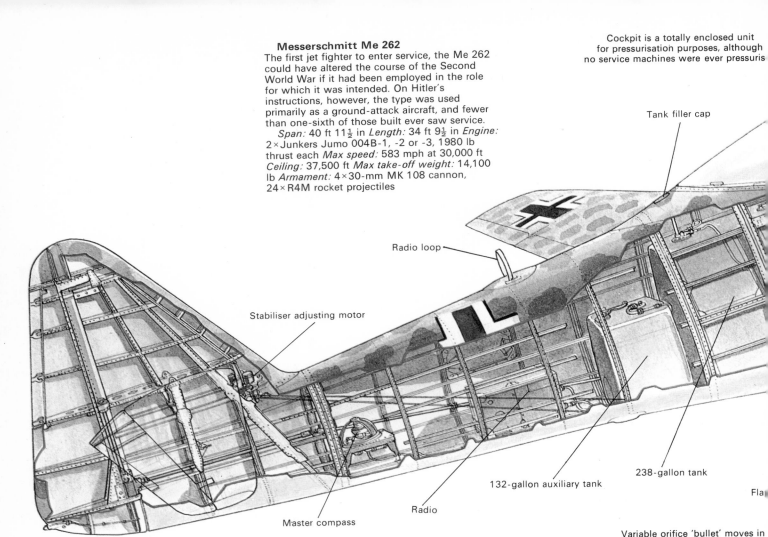

devastating armament of four 30-mm MK 108 cannon. Production was scheduled to get under way in 1943, but Allied bombing, and Hitler's insistence that all the Me 262s should be used as bombers instead of fighters, seriously delayed deliveries. EK 262, the operational-reasearch and development group, received their first aircraft in June 1944, followed in September by III/EJG2 training unit and 8/ZG26 fighter squadron. The first RAF Meteor squadron had been equipped two months previously. There were many variants of the 262, but nearly all the 1433 completed were of the A-1a *Schwalbe* (Swallow) fighter type or the A-2a *Sturmvogel* (Stormbird) bomber with two 551-lb bombs. The A-2a/U2 had a prone bombardier in place of the guns, and among the other versions was the B-family of tandem-seat radar night fighters. All were extremely formidable, though many pilots were killed in training accidents through failure to appreciate that a dual conversion trainer was needed. Most of the Allied victories over these aircraft were gained by patrols orbiting over the Luftwaffe airfields.

Fastest of the non-jets was the Dornier Do 335, which in the only form built in numbers (the A-0 and A-1) attained 477 mph with MW50 boost. Fitted with a 1900-hp DB 603 ahead of and behind the cockpit, driving a propeller at each end, the 335 *Pfeil* (Arrow) was a substantial machine first flown in the autumn of 1943. Many sub-types were planned, including night fighters, big-winged high-altitude versions and the Do 635 twin-fuselage model with 'an engine at each corner'.

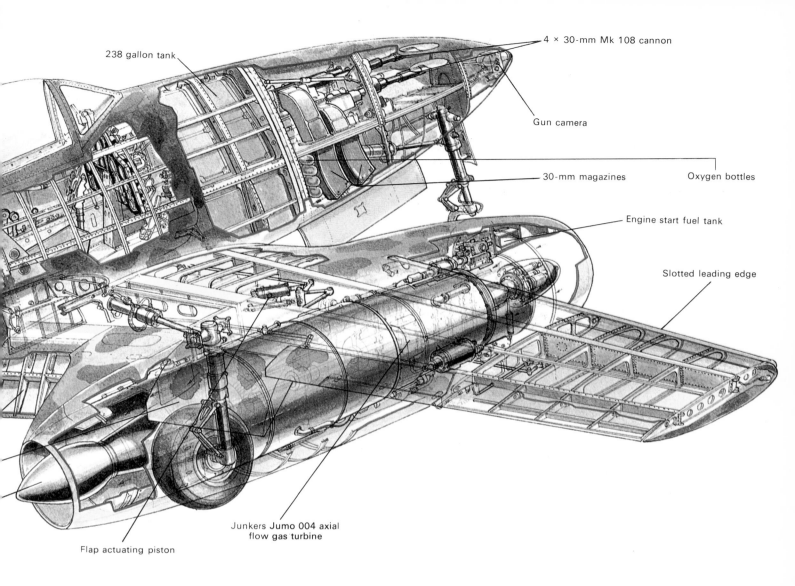

238 gallon tank

4 × 30-mm Mk 108 cannon

Gun camera

30-mm magazines

Oxygen bottles

Engine start fuel tank

Slotted leading edge

Junkers Jumo 004 axial flow gas turbine

Flap actuating piston

Dornier Do 335

The unique push-pull engine configuration of the Do 335 had been patented by Dr Claude Dornier in 1937, but a prototype warplane did not fly until 1943. Performance was exceptional but delays and diversification into night-fighter and reconnaissance variants kept production down

Span: 45 ft 3⅓ in *Length:* 45 ft 5¼ in *Engine:* 2 × Daimler-Benz DB 603G, 1900 hp *Max speed:* 473 mph at 26,200 ft *Ceiling:* 37,400 ft *Max take-off weight:* 25,800 lb *Armament:* 2 × 15-mm MG 151 cannon, 1 × 30-mm MK 103 cannon, 1100 lb bombs

Heinkel He 162 Salamander
The *Volksjäger* (People's Fighter) was a desperate attempt to develop a high-performance fighter which used commonly available materials, could be built by relatively unskilled labour and flown by novice pilots. The planned output of a thousand a month was — hardly surprisingly — not achieved, and total production barely exceeded 100

Span: 23 ft 8 in *Length:* 29 ft 8½ in *Engine:* BMW 003A-1, -2, or E-1, 1760 lb thrust *Max speed:* 522 mph at 19,700 ft *Ceiling:* 39,500 ft *Max take-off weight:* 5940 lb *Armament:* 2×30-mm MK 108 cannon

The RAF's first jet fighter, the Gloster Meteor, entered service on a test basis in mid-1944 and by August one had claimed a victory over a V-1. Tactical sorties began over Europe in April 1945 but no Meteor ever met a Luftwaffe jet fighter

Smithsonian

II P-59 Airacomet

rst turbojet-powered aircraft to be built in
nited States made its maiden flight in
tions of great secrecy in late 1942. Stability
ms made it unsuitable for operational use
e P-59 was used solely for research and
ng
n: 45 ft 6 in *Length:* 38 ft *Engine:* 2×
al Electric J 31-GE-5, 2000 lb thrust *Max
:* 413 mph at 30,000 ft *Ceiling:* 46,200 ft
ake-off weight:* 12,700 lb *Armament:*
-mm cannon, 3×.5-in mg

Focke-Wulf's glued-wood Ta 154 *Moskito*
was a failure; the extraordinary Bachem
Ba 349 *Natter* (Viper) and Blohm und Voss
Bv 40 target-defence interceptors never
reached service; and the impressive Heinkel
He 162A Salamander, popularly called the
Volksjager (People's Fighter) was designed,
flown and put into mass production in the
final three months of 1944, but the Luftwaffe
was by then denuded of pilots and even jet
fuel. Built of wood and metal, the 162 was
an excellent answer to the challenge of
finding a truly modern fighter 'to be built
as a piece of consumer goods' at the rate of
4000 per month. It is also an indication of
the depths to which planning had fallen
that this extremely advanced machine was
to be flown by Hitler Youth previously

Messerschmitt Me 163 Komet
The Me 163 was originally intended as a high-
speed research aircraft, but the encouraging trials
results led to the type being adopted as a home-
defence intercepter. The Me 163B Komet, the

only pure-rocket aircraft to see service in the
Second World War, first went into action against
B-17 Fortresses in August 1944. The type was of
limited operational use, despite its exotic design,
and only about 350 were built
Span: 30 ft 7 in *Length:* 18 ft 8 in *Engine:*
Walter HWK 109-509A-2 bi-fuel rocket motor,
3750 lb thrust *Max speed:* 596 mph at up to
30,000 ft *Ceiling:* 40,000 ft *Max take-off weight:*
9500 lb *Armament:* 2×30-mm MK 108 cannon,
up to 24×R4M rocket projectiles

given a few quick towline hops in primary
gliders.
The last German fighter to fly was the
Gotha Go 229, designed as the Ho IX V2
prototype by the Horten brothers as the
first jet-propelled member of a long family
of flying-wing machines. On two Jumo 004B
engines it reached 497 mph in early trials in
March 1945. A production version would
have had four 30-mm MK 108 or 103 cannon
and two 2205-lb bombs.
In the final year of the war German
designers explored a number of bizarre
configurations for fighters, most of them of
the short-range target-defence type. Several
attempted to save time and resources by
using the Argus 014 impulse-duct engine of
the Fi 103 flying bomb, while others used
a completely new kind of jet engine, the
ramjet. One of the most unusual of all these
experiments was intended to have a ramjet
fuelled by powdered coal, or a mixture of
finely divided carbonaceous fuel and a
liquid hydrocarbon. This was one of the
Lippisch shapes, with wings and fin of delta
(triangular) form. Many projects were tailless, while the Ta 183 had a sharply swept
vertical tail carrying a swept tailplane on
top (today this looks normal, but in 1943 it
was utterly futuristic). Messerschmitt explored many wing shapes, and in the P.1101,
almost ready for flight in 1945, arranged
for the wing sweep to be adjusted to different settings on the ground. In 1951 this

aircraft flew in the United States as the
Bell X-5, with swing-wings adjustable in
flight.
Possibly the strangest fighter of all was
the Focke-Wulf *Triebflügel*, a target-defence
interceptor which stood on its tail and
achieved VTO (vertical take-off) by three
rotary wings mounted on bearings around
the fuselage and spun by tip-ramjets. In
normal flight it was to reach 620 mph with
the fuselage in the conventional attitude,
and two Mk 103 and two MG 151 were to be
fitted in the nose. With skill and luck the
pilot was to regain the vertical attitude,
gently descending onto a landing wheel at
the rear tip of the fuselage with outrigger
wheels extended from the tips of the four
fins. Though scarcely credible, the same
concept was used in 1948–56 by two turbo-
prop VTOL interceptors of the US Navy
intended for use from small ship platforms.
Thus, while the Luftwaffe soldiered on
with the 190 and 109, German research
mapped out tracks leading far into the
future but irrelevant to the defence of the
crumbling Reich during the last two years
of the Second World War.
In contrast, British designers kept their
feet firmly on the ground and seldom built
anything that did not relate directly to the
operating needs of the front-line squadrons.
The outstanding de Havilland 100 'Spider
Crab', later named Vampire, flew in September 1943, but just missed the war. The

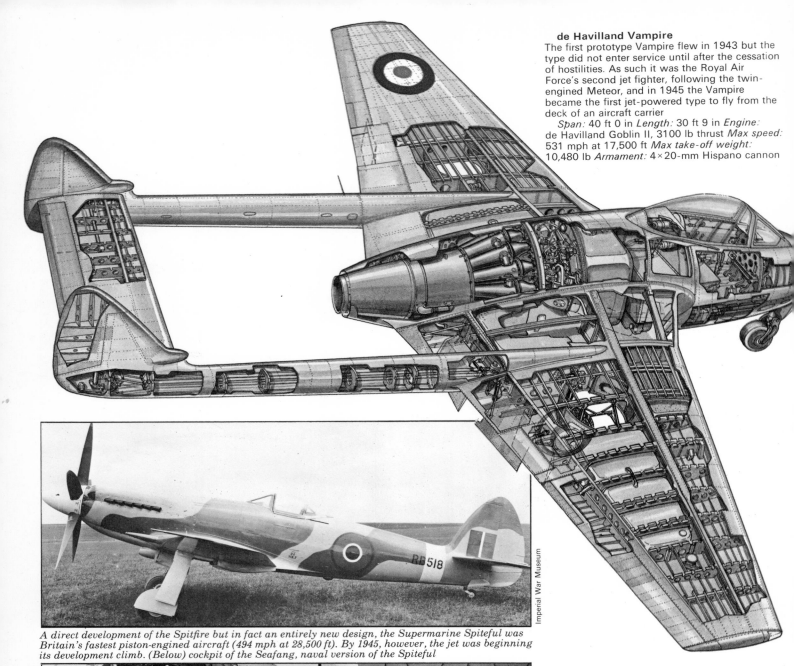

de Havilland Vampire

The first prototype Vampire flew in 1943 but the type did not enter service until after the cessation of hostilities. As such it was the Royal Air Force's second jet fighter, following the twin-engined Meteor, and in 1945 the Vampire became the first jet-powered type to fly from the deck of an aircraft carrier

Span: 40 ft 0 in *Length:* 30 ft 9 in *Engine:* de Havilland Goblin II, 3100 lb thrust *Max speed:* 531 mph at 17,500 ft *Max take-off weight:* 10,480 lb *Armament:* 4×20-mm Hispano cannon

A direct development of the Spitfire but in fact an entirely new design, the Supermarine Spiteful was Britain's fastest piston-engined aircraft (494 mph at 28,500 ft). By 1945, however, the jet was beginning its development climb. (Below) cockpit of the Seafang, naval version of the Spiteful

Gloster F.9/40, however, later named Meteor, flew in March 1943, and after development with seven types of British turbojet entered RAF service with 616 Sqn in July 1944, becoming the first fully operational jet aircraft in the world. The production Meteor I was powered by the 1700-lb Rolls-Royce Welland and reached 410 mph in fighting trim, sufficient to catch and destroy flying bombs, becoming operational on 4 August. By April 1945 the more powerful (2000-lb Derwent I) Meteor III was in service from 2nd Tactical Air Force Continental bases with 616 and 504 Sqns, reaching 493 mph and fitted with an improved canopy that slid instead of being hinged. In the United States the Bell P-59A Airacomet remained a jet conversion trainer, but the outstanding Lockheed YP-80A did see evaluation service in Italy in 1945, but no combat however.

THE SETTING SUN

Fighter development in Japan in the Second World War ran broadly parallel to that in Germany: while the front-line pilots had to make do with improved models of old aircraft, the design teams created numerous exciting fighters which never got into action. In both countries the situation was to a large degree a vicious circle; the need to concentrate on modifications to the old types interfered seriously with development of the new ones, and continuing delay to the replacement types kept the pressure on improvement of the existing aircraft. Nowhere was this more apparent than in the great Mitsubishi company, where not even the brilliance of Jiro Horikoshi could produce a replacement for the *Zero-Sen* in time to save defeat.

Most of the effort went into extremely urgent work on the A6M *Zero-Sen*, which by 1943 was demonstrably hard-pressed, if not outclassed, by such aircraft as the F4U and F6F. By late 1943 the A6M5 family was in production, and like the 109G this late model soon outnumbered all its predecessors. It was little changed at first, having the clipped wings rounded and the engine installation improved with individual ejector exhaust stacks. Along with aerodynamic detail refinement, the 5a then introduced belt-fed cannon, with 25 extra rounds per gun; in the 5b one of the fuselage machine guns was replaced by a 12.7-mm weapon and bullet-proof canopy; and the grossly underpowered 5c received new armament of two 20-mm Type 99 Mk 4 and two 13.2-mm Type 3 in the wings and a 13.2-mm in the fuselage. In late 1944 the

water/methanol-boosted *Sakae* 31 resulted in the 6c version, which also introduced self-sealing wing tanks. The 7 was a fighter-bomber made in trivial numbers in the final desperate weeks of the war, and production did not even begin on the A6M8 with the bigger 1560-hp *Kinsei* engine.

Though the total of 10,049, 10,449 or 10,937 of all models of *Zero-Sen* (the records are confusing) is impressive, this was the only Japanese warplane to be built in anything like such quantity. From the start of 1944 loss of carriers and skilled pilots greatly diminished the effectiveness of the Imperial Navy Air Force, and rapidly changing tactical situations resulted in many fighters being modified as home-defence night fighters (such as the A6M5d-S with oblique 20-mm cannon in the rear fuselage) or *Kamikaze* suicide bombers. Nakajima built 327 of the A6M2-N float-seaplane version, which was intended to

clear the skies for amphibious landings but was forced into defensive duties where it was easy meat for the Allied fighters.

The fighter which failed to replace the Zero was the A7M *Reppu* (Hurricane), which received the code-name 'Sam' though it never got into action. Horikoshi was certain that the required performance demanded the powerful MK9 engine, and tried to scheme his new fighter around it, but the Navy insisted on the lower-powered *Homare* NK9. There is abundant evidence that the Navy did not appreciate the vital need to introduce a much more powerful fighter at the earliest possible date, and at one time decided not to go ahead with development at all until April 1943. As it was, the prototype A7M did not fly until 6 May 1944, and though by the final defeat there were four major versions, the total number of aircraft built was a mere ten. The same pattern can be seen in the great array of new or proposed Japanese fighters. Though of immense technical interest, they never fired a shot against the Allies, except, perhaps, for the Kawasaki Ki-102b (Randy), which during a test flight is alleged to have shot an engine clean out of a B-29 with a single shell from its 57-mm gun! In fact, quite a few of these potent high-altitude, ground-attack and night fighter Ki-102 versions were built, the 102b sub-type reaching operational units.

A development of the Ki-102 was the Ki-108 high-altitude fighter, which demonstrated that the Japanese found the design of pressure cabins as difficult as did engineers in Europe. The Ki-109 was a

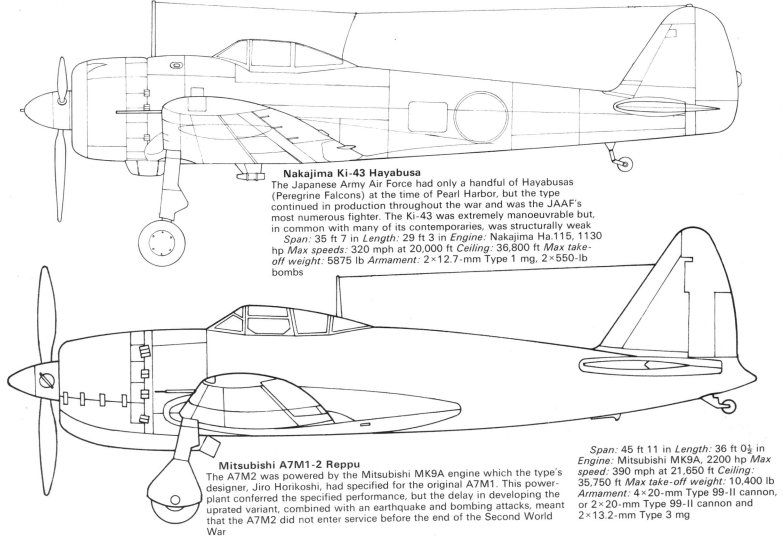

Nakajima Ki-43 Hayabusa
The Japanese Army Air Force had only a handful of Hayabusas (Peregrine Falcons) at the time of Pearl Harbor, but the type continued in production throughout the war and was the JAAF's most numerous fighter. The Ki-43 was extremely manoeuvrable but, in common with many of its contemporaries, was structurally weak
Span: 35 ft 7 in *Length:* 29 ft 3 in *Engine:* Nakajima Ha.115, 1130 hp *Max speeds:* 320 mph at 20,000 ft *Ceiling:* 36,800 ft *Max take-off weight:* 5875 lb *Armament:* 2×12.7-mm Type 1 mg, 2×550-lb bombs

Mitsubishi A7M1-2 Reppu
The A7M2 was powered by the Mitsubishi MK9A engine which the type's designer, Jiro Horikoshi, had specified for the original A7M1. This power-plant conferred the specified performance, but the delay in developing the uprated variant, combined with an earthquake and bombing attacks, meant that the A7M2 did not enter service before the end of the Second World War

Span: 45 ft 11 in *Length:* 36 ft 0½ in *Engine:* Mitsubishi MK9A, 2200 hp *Max speed:* 390 mph at 21,650 ft *Ceiling:* 35,750 ft *Max take-off weight:* 10,400 lb *Armament:* 4×20-mm Type 99-II cannon, or 2×20-mm Type 99-II cannon and 2×13.2-mm Type 3 mg

remarkable conversion of the Ki-67 heavy bomber, resulting in one of the largest fighters of the Second World War. More than 20 of these unusual machines were built, most having the unique but carefully considered armament of a single 75-mm Type 88 anti-aircraft gun firing ahead, with 15 rounds loaded individually by the co-pilot. This enabled the monster interceptor to cruise in formation with a B-29 but out of range of smaller guns. Great efforts were made to increase altitude performance, and one aircraft was flown with a battery of rocket motors to reduce the time taken to reach B-29 altitude. A far more deadly Mitsubishi Army fighter was the Ki-83, one of the best warplanes built in Japan but started so late that only four flew. Powered by two 2200-hp turbocharged Ha-211Ru engines, the -83 ('Steve') looked like a Grumman F7F Tigercat, another design that virtually missed the war, and like the US Navy fighter had both power and punch. With a speed of 438 mph, range exceeding 2000 miles and armament of two 3-mm and two 20-mm, plus light bombs internally, the Ki-83 demonstrated that Japan could create competitive aircraft for the 1945–46 warfare that never came to pass.

Other high-altitude Army fighters include the Nakajima Ki-87 and Tachikawa Ki-94, both powered by the 2400-hp Nakajima Ha-44 with turbocharger and pressurised cockpit. Both were armed with two 30-mm and two 20-mm cannon, plus a heavy bomb, and reached about 440 mph. The only Army fighter that paid off was a conversion of the indifferent Ki-61 'Tony', large numbers of which were lying about without engines in late 1944 because of lack of liquid-cooled power plants. The only available alternative was the 1500-hp Mitsubishi Ha-112-II radial, and though this hardly fitted the slim fuselage, a quick lash-up conversion was flown. It proved to be an amazing success, with comparable speed and significantly improved handling. Over 270 conversions were rushed into service, proving safe in the hands of inexperienced pilots

and able to tackle anything from a Hellcat to a B-29. Production urgently began on a version specially designed to the radial engine, but this did not reach service.

One of the Army fighters was the Kawasaki Ki-64, with two liquid-cooled Ha-40 engines combined in a single 24-cylinder unit driving a contraprop, with the cockpit placed between the front and rear banks of cylinders. Similarly, the Navy Yokosuka R2Y had coupled V-12 engines, but this was an even bigger aircraft and was converted into an attack bomber. A bizarre Navy fighter was the Kyushu J7W, a canard (tail first) with efficient variable-camber foreplane resembling those flown on some fighters of the 1970s. Powered by a 2130-hp MK9D driving a six-blade pusher propeller, the J7W1 *Shinden* (Magnificent Lightning) might have been outstanding, with a speed of 466 mph and armament of four 30-mm cannon, but the prototype did not fly until two weeks before the surrender. Aichi built the S1A *Denko* (Bolt of Light) as a specialised night fighter, with two fan-cooled *Homares* and a radar-operator in a broad but shallow dorsal turret with two 20-mm cannon, presumably to hit whatever the two 30-mm in the nose missed.

The Navy operated Japan's only Second World War jets. The Mitsubishi J8M1 *Shusui* (Swinging Sword) was intended to be a copy of the Me 163B, but the submarine bringing the drawings was sunk and the Mitsubishi team were left with only a Walter rocket engine and a rough idea of the German interceptor's features. Quite quickly a design was prepared, trials begun with gliders and a powered version built (it crashed). Nakajima's *Kikka* (Orange Blossom) was a downgraded Me 262, with only 1047-lb thrust from each Ne-20 turbojet. Influenced by German design, the *Kikka* was conceived as an attack fighter carrying bombs; because payload was limited, the proposed 30-mm guns were then left out. The war was over before the Japanese had made engines with enough thrust (Ne-130 of 1984 lb) for them to be put back.

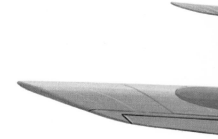

Kawanishi N1K2-J Shiden-Kai
The Shiden-Kai resulted from an extensive redesign of the N1K1-J Shiden (Violet Lightning) and has been described as the Japanese Naval Air Force's finest Second World War fighter. Fewer than 500 were built, however, because teething troubles delayed the build-up of production until late in the war, when extensive US bombing was disrupting the supply of components
Span: 39 ft 4 in *Length:* 30 ft 8 in *Engine:* Nakajima NK9H Homare 21, 1990 hp *Max speed:* 369 mph at 18,400 ft *Ceiling:* 35,300 ft *Max take-off weight:* 9040 lb *Armament:* 4×20-mm Type 99-II cannon, 2×550-lb bombs

Grumman Tigercat
This twin-engined single-seater could be flown off carriers and served with the US Marines flying close-support missions as the Pacific war was ending. Of the 364 machines built, most were post-war night-fighters
Span: 51 ft 6 in *Length:* 46 ft 11 in *Engine:* 2×Pratt & Whitney R-2800-34W, 2800 hp *Max speed:* 429 mph at 22,100 ft *Ceiling:* 37,300 ft *Max take-off weight:* 22,091 lb *Armament:* 4×20-mm cannon, 8×5-in rockets/2000-lb bomb/torpedo

Goodyear FG-1D
Goodyear-built version of the Vought F4U Corsair, the ungainly but powerful fighter-bomber that gained a legendary reputation in the Pacific war
Span: 41 ft *Length:* 32 ft 10 in *Engine:* Pratt & Whitney R-2800-18W Double Wasp, 2000 hp at take-off *Max speed:* 415 mph *Ceiling:* 36,900 ft *Armament:* 6×.5-in mg/2000-lb bombs/rockets

The Grumman F6F Hellcat incorporated the operational recommendations gathered from US Navy pilots who had met the Zero in combat. With excellent speed, climb and manoeuvrability, the Hellcat could outmatch the Zero in a dogfight

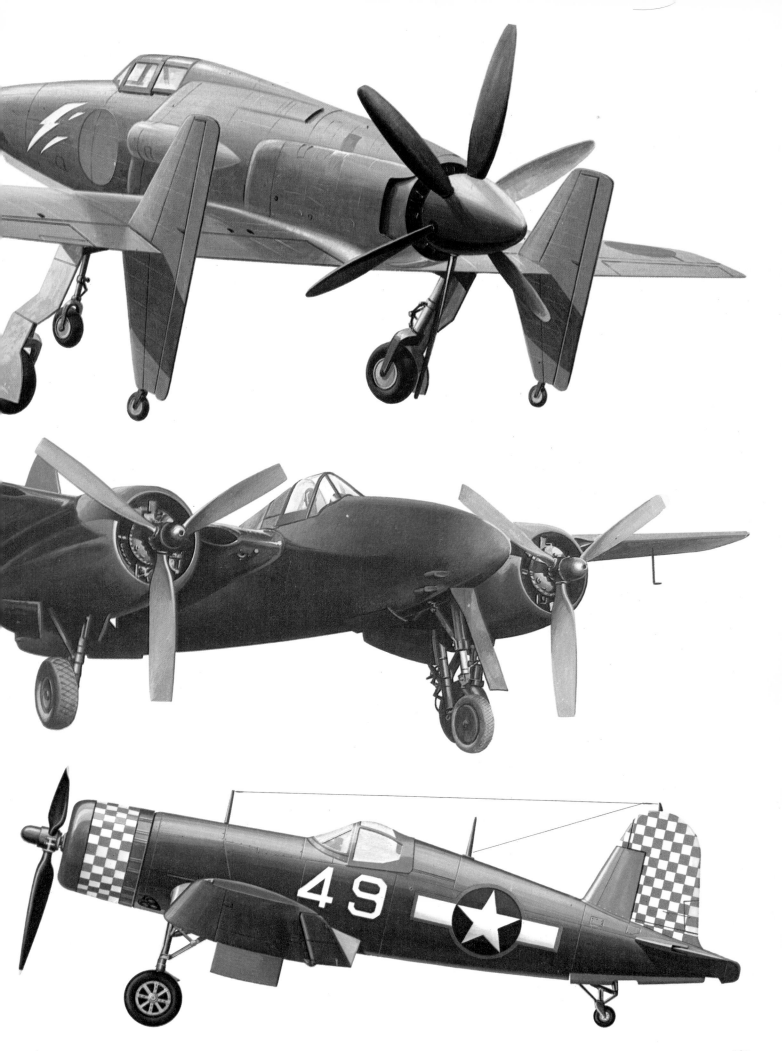

FIGHTER TECHNOLOGY

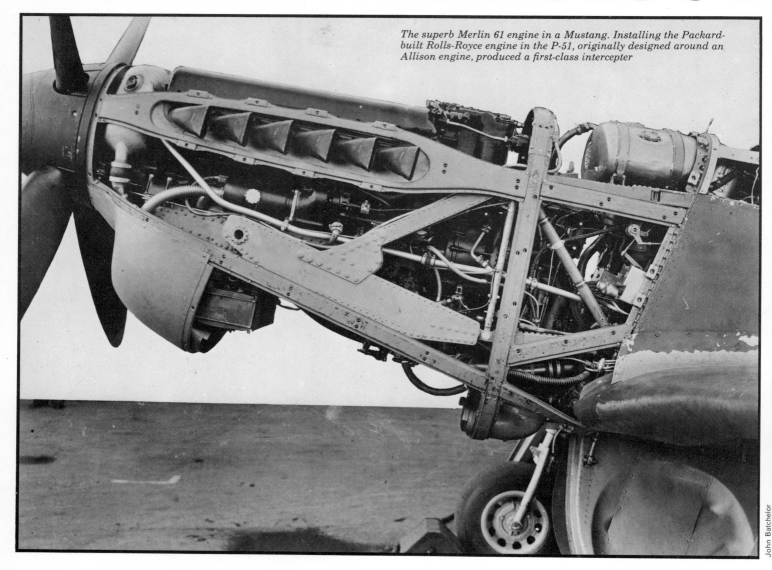

The superb Merlin 61 engine in a Mustang. Installing the Packard-built Rolls-Royce engine in the P-51, originally designed around an Allison engine, produced a first-class intercepter

John Batchelor

Always dictating fighter design, and more often than not success or failure in combat, were the guns and engines around which the fighters of the Second World War were designed. Fighters were often planned in one form and later emerged in another, while many fighters were actually designed as bombers (for example, the Ju 88). Nevertheless, running through most major programmes there was a coherent thread, which may have been occasionally disrupted by technical snags or changes in official requirements but usually resulted in the development taking place in sensible steps. Nowhere in aviation history is this more evident than in the case of the Spitfire, which began with a simple airframe with 242 sq ft of wing and a gross weight of 5800 lb, designed to a load factor of 10, and finished the war with a markedly different airframe with 244 sq ft and a gross weight of 12,750 lb, designed to a load factor of 11. Such a change transformed the character of the aircraft. Unlike most combat aircraft, which over the years progressively became slower and more sluggish as weight increased, the 120% increase in weight of the Spitfire/Seafire was accompanied by dramatic increase in performance, solely because

of Rolls-Royce's impressive progression from the 990-hp Merlin I to the 2375-hp Griffon 85.

Few fighters could enjoy a comparable increase in available power. The power of some aircraft actually decreased, while most increased by about ten per cent. Britain farsightedly planned in 1937 for fighters with engines of 2000 hp, but unfortunately picked the wrong ones. While the Bristol Centaurus radial was ignored, concentration on the Rolls-Royce Vulture (a failure) and Napier Sabre (a success after five costly years of effort) killed the Hawker Tornado and delayed the Hawker Typhoon and Tempest, delaying their operational serviceability until near the very end of the war. In the United States in 1935–40, the emphasis was on the powerful aircooled radial, but the fact that virtually every fighter in the Battle of Britain had a liquid-cooled engine prompted the US Army to launch big liquid-cooled engine programmes at Pratt & Whitney, Curtiss, Lycoming, Chrysler and Continental, backing up existing work by Allison. Many fighters flew with these new engines, but all eventually fell by the wayside. The final winners for US fighter propulsion, apart from the

Packard-built Merlin, were the same big radials that were used at the start, by far the most important of which was the R-2800 Double Wasp. This drove a Corsair at over 400 mph in 1940, no mean achievement for so large a warplane, and by 1945 was driving much heavier versions of the Corsair, Thunderbolt and other American fighters at speeds exceeding 450 mph.

There was no substitute for sheer horse-power. Frequently, in comparisons between 'streamlined' liquid-cooled engines and 'un-streamlined' radials, the powers are dissimilar. For example, the Italian fighters of 1940–41 had radials of around 840-hp, and it is hardly surprising that their performance was improved by fitting German liquid-cooled engines of 1475 hp. A closer comparison was seen in the Curtiss P-36A, of 1150 hp and 327 mph speed, which when re-engined with a 1160-hp Allison, reached 337 mph. Much later a P-47H Thunderbolt reached 490 mph with the Chrysler XIV-2220, one of the experimental liquid-cooled units, but another reached 504 mph with the bluff-fronted Double Wasp. Perhaps the supreme expression of the piston-engined fighter can be seen in two late-wartime models that just failed to see combat duty. Britain's

Supermarine Spiteful XIV was a beautiful little fighter with four 20-mm guns, a new laminar-section wing of only 210 sq ft, and a high-blown 2375-hp Griffon engine, giving a speed of 483 mph. America's Republic XP-72 was equally fine in its lines, armed with various guns including six 0.5-in or four big 37-mm cannon, plus two 1000-lb bombs, and fitted with the same 300-sq-ft wing as the P-47; this had a 3450-hp R-4360-13 Wasp Major and reached 490 mph. They represented different philosophies, but both were supremely effective.

It is popularly supposed that the capture of a Fw 190 in 1942 led to the sudden realisation in Britain that good fighters might have radial engines. There is some truth in this, but the fixation with the liquid-cooled engine was of quite brief duration. Most of the RAF's fighters between the wars – Grebe, Gamecock, Siskin, Bulldog, Gauntlet and Gladiator – had radial engines, and only the Fury had the in-line. The supposed superiority of the in-line may have been reinforced by the lack of top-quality radial-engined fighters in Western Europe in 1938–41, until the emergence into combat of the Focke-Wulf 190. No such attitude afflicted the Soviet Union, where there were good engines of both types. Although the Yak fighters continued to use the VK-105 and -107-type in-line engines, the other mass-produced fighter family, by Lavochkin, did not hit its stride until it switched to a radial.

John Batchelor

RATO (Rocket Assisted Take-Off) installation on a Seafire giving a burst of power for take-offs from escort carriers

German Aero Engines
By the outbreak of war the rearming German aircraft industry had a range of powerful in-line and radial engines available from a variety of manufacturers. Liquid-cooled in-lines were favoured for fighters (with the very notable exception of the Fw 190) and radials for transport and bomber aircraft but the precision products of the German aero-engine industry could not compete in volume output with the industrial might of the United States

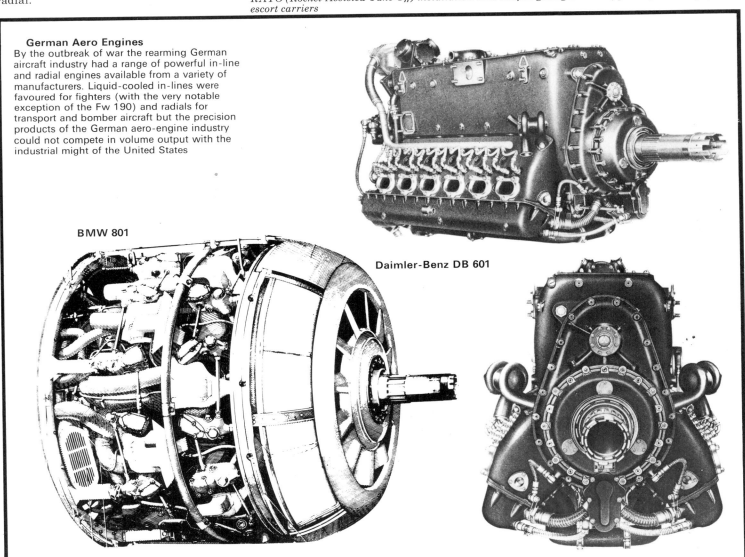

BMW 801

Daimler-Benz DB 601

The evolution of the fighter-bomber was one of the most important developmental themes in Second World War aircraft design. Many types were adapted – some, like the Fw 190G and Hurricane II, with outstanding success. Equally successful was the massive P-47 Thunderbolt, seen here being refuelled and armed with .5-in machine-gun belts and 250-lb bombs on a forward airstrip in France, 1944

Fighter Armament

Except for the Lewis, virtually all the guns used in air combat in the First World War had been originally designed for use by armies or navies. But rifle-calibre weapons are so numerous, and often so closely inter-related, that it is difficult to be dogmatic about which were new designs, or planned from the start for air use. Certainly in the 1920s and 1930s the Vickers, used in fighters all over the world, would have been immediately recognized by Hiram Maxim in the 19th century, and it retained its popularity by refinement and reliability. Few of the other rifle-calibre guns of the period were dramatically different, though some were gas-operated. The American fighters backed up the Lewis with the belt-fed Colt-Browning, an outstanding weapon fitted to a few fighters in 1917, and a variant of it called the Marlin. The Browning was developed in the 1920s with a much harder-hitting calibre of 0.5-in, and in Italy, and several other countries, the same 12.7-mm calibre was adopted as being well worth the extra size and weight; paradoxically, Germany, which had been the pioneer of the 12.7-mm machine gun for tanks and aircraft, stayed with rifle calibre until 1938.

Germany had also done more than any other country to develop fast-firing cannon, fed with explosive or other special types of ammunition. The best cannon actually used in numbers in Second World War air combat was the German 20-mm Becker, which was obviously more lethal than the cumbersome and slow-firing Hotchkiss used by the French. But in 1919 Becker sold his patents to Oerlikon Machine Tool Works in Switzerland, and when the reborn Luftwaffe wanted a cannon in the mid-1930s Rheinmetall had to buy the old German patent back. As the MG FF the Oerlikon was mass-produced in Germany from 1938, at first for the Bf 109 and subsequently for many fighters, bombers and other aircraft. It was a fairly short and light weapon, its main drawback being that it was fed by a 60-round drum. But so was the only other fully developed, and related, aircraft cannon of the pre-1939 era, the 20-mm Hispano. The growing Hispano-Suiza company had developed some of the best and most powerful aircraft engines of the First World War, and their chief designer M Marc Birkigt had spent much time trying to perfect a *moteur canon* with the gun lying between the cylinder blocks and firing through the hub of the propeller. Of course, this could be done only with a geared engine, and the geared Hispano gave a lot of trouble (as related earlier in describing the S.E.5 fighting scout, and the Caudron R.11). The first *moteur canon* in combat was the old 37-mm Hotchkiss, and though Spad XII fighters fitted with this were often deadly (Guynemer achieved four victories in one, and Fonck 11 in another) the heavy slow-firing cannon caused severe recoil problems and choked the pilot with cordite fumes. Birkigt master-minded the design of an extremely efficient new cannon of only 20-mm calibre but firing automatically, and at 550–600 rounds per minute. Moreover, the muzzle velocity was high, so that the trajectory was flat, accuracy high

and hitting power (in terms of kinetic energy of a solid shot) actually greater than for the old Hotchkiss. The new 20-mm cannon was mounted in the traditional propeller-hub position in the Dewoitine D.501 fighters of the early 1930s, and Dewoitine boldly fitted two in the wings of many D.37-series (373) fighters of the same period. The 20-mm *moteur canon* was fitted to the main French fighters of 1940, the M.S.406 and Dewoitine D.520, and two wing-mounted examples were fitted to the Bloch 152. By 1940 there were also manually aimed Hispano installations and the first power turrets in French bombers. After years of delay, the same gun was also adopted by the ailing RAF, to make up for lack of a British cannon, and first used in the twin-engined Whirlwind, designed to carry four in the nose. Later it was the standard British fighter gun in the Second World War.

Curiously, no fighter in operational service had a gun firing through the propeller shaft of a radial engine, though such an arrangement was tried experimentally. With a geared engine having the propeller shaft offset from the crankshaft, a *moteur canon* was not difficult to install, and with a liquid-cooled in-line engine the gun was sometimes mounted on the engine itself. Designers sometimes adopted unconventional aircraft layouts to facilitate the provision of powerful nose armament, examples being the American P-38 and P-39 of 1939. In fact there was no need for unusual layouts, and there were other reasons, in addition to armament, for the unconventionality of the P-38 and -39.

Nevertheless, the variety of armament in the Second World War was exceptional. Some nations adopted more or less standard armament and stuck to it. Britain began with eight rifle-calibre machine guns and quite soon switched to four licence-built 20-mm Hispanos, while the Soviet Union seldom departed far from one 20-mm and one or two 12.7-mm (in Yaks) or two 20-mm (later three) in Lavochkin. In Italy the standard armament of two 12.7-mm machine guns was gradually recognised as hopelessly inadequate and supplemented by three of the excellent German MG 151 cannon. But in Germany and Japan such rigid standardisation did not apply. Though a few aircraft, including the most numerous Japanese Army and Navy fighters, tended to have uniform armament, a great variety of guns and other armaments were available and were fitted in every possible combination.

Originally Japanese guns were based on Western patterns such as the Vickers 0.303-in and Browning 0.5-in, but by 1940 guns of Japanese design were coming into use. One of the first of these was the Army Ho-5 cannon, virtually a Browning scaled up to 20-mm calibre and very soon giving good service. The standard Navy gun of this calibre was the Type 99; this was a large family with many lengths, weights, muzzle velocities and feed systems. Development in Japan had begun in 1930, making use of the original Becker and Oerlikon drawings, but it soon became distinctive and was used in both fixed installations and in many hand-aimed or turreted forms. By 1944 production was beginning on a 30-mm version of the same family, the Type 5, with a muzzle velocity of 2460 ft/sec, high for a weapon of so large a calibre. The Army 30-mm gun was lighter, the Ho-105 having lower velocity. Quite large numbers of

37-mm Ho-203 were used, these being short-barrel, slow-firing, low-velocity guns of ancient origin. The 40-mm Ho-301 was new, but rather cumbersome and limited in range by the low velocity of its rocket-propelled shells. By far the hardest-hitting Japanese gun was the 57-mm Ho-401, with rate of fire of only 90 shots/min but high velocity and with extremely destructive projectiles. The 401 was used on several heavy fighters in 1944–45.

Britain was the only major Second World War power to have virtually no home-developed aircraft guns, apparently because in the vital 1930s nobody thought about producing any. The standard guns were the American Browning of 1916, altered to fire rimmed 0.303-in ammunition, and the hard-hitting Hispano of 1917, which by 1940 was in licence-production by British MARC Ltd and was later developed to have belt-feed, a shorter barrel and other changes. Almost all US fighters were armed with the 0.5-in Browning or M-2 cannon (Hispano-derived), though several almost identical patterns of 37-mm cannon were also used in the P-38, P-39 and some other aircraft.

Soviet guns were almost entirely home-developed from 1931, and their quality and performance were outstanding. In fitness for hard service, ease of mass-production, reliability and firepower they had few equals. The rifle-calibre gun was the ShKAS of 7.62-mm, with rate of fire up to 1800 rds/min and weight appreciably less than the rifle-calibre Browning. The heavy machine gun was the Beresin BS, firing 12.7-mm ammunition similar to the Browning but at 900 rds/min instead of 650–850, and with a gun weight of 55 lb (fighter installation) instead of 64 lb. The 20-mm gun was the ShVAK, much shorter and lighter than a Hispano but with almost as much hitting power and a rate of fire of 800/min instead of 600. The remarkable 23-mm V-Ya had the extremely high muzzle velocity of 3020 ft/sec, coupled with 600/min rate of fire, but this tank-killing gun was seldom fitted to fighters.

German guns were by far the most adventurous. The Rheinmetall MG 17 was the standard machine gun for fighters in 1939, and despite the development from the MG 34 infantry weapon of the simple and light MG 81, the old MG 17 remained the chief fixed machine gun to the end, though it was almost entirely replaced by heavier weapons. The standard heavy machine gun was the excellent Rheinmetall MG 131 of 13-mm calibre, first used in 1938 and soon the most common synchronised fuselage gun on the Bf 109 and Fw 190. Weighing only 38 lb, it was extremely reliable, firing high-velocity ammunition at 900–960/min with detonation accomplished electrically instead of by a mechanical pin fired into the percussion cap; this greatly facilitated synchronisation.

Electrical firing was selected in 1935 by the Mauser company for a completely new gun, the MG 151, firing 15-mm ammunition at the extremely high velocity of 3150 ft/sec. Though a superb gun, it was used in only a few aircraft, being replaced by the most important gun of the Luftwaffe, the MG 151/20. Identical except for calibre, this fired 190 lb/minute at 750 rds/min, compared with only 90 lb/min at a slightly lower rate of fire, and its muzzle velocity of 2600 ft/min gave it excellent ballistics and hitting power. The MG 151 was used in about 80% of all German fighters built after 1941, and some Fw 190s, Ju 88s and Me 410s had as many as six or eight, all firing ahead. It completely replaced the old Ikaria MG FF, of original Oerlikon design, which fired different low-velocity ammunition at a lower rate from a 60-round drum.

By 1939 development was well advanced on a large 30-mm cannon derived from the Solothurn 20-mm S-18 anti-tank gun. It emerged in 1941 as the Rheinmetall MK 101, but with a length of almost 10ft and bare weight of 287–396 lb it was too cumbersome for any except anti-tank aircraft. Rhein-metall's MK 108 was a complete contrast. This was the stubbiest little 30-mm gun imaginable, with length of 45 in, weight of 133 lb and rate of fire of 450/min of low-velocity (1640 ft/sec) ammunition by simple

The quest for a heavy concentrated nose armament brought many design solutions, but the twin-engined single-seat Westland Whirlwind with four 20-mm Hispano cannon in the nose had only a modestly successful career

126

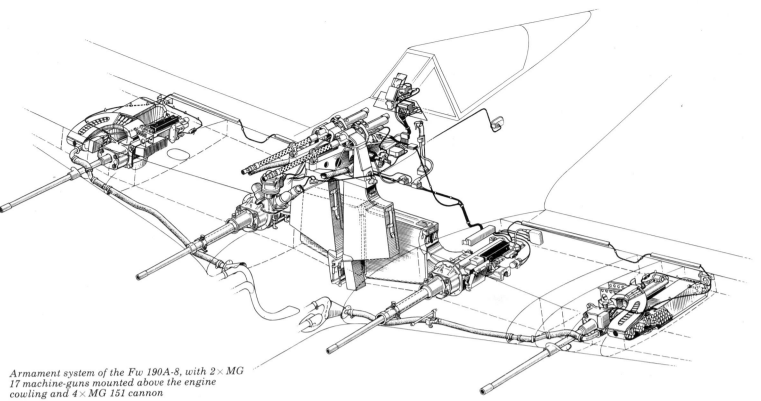

Armament system of the Fw 190A-8, with 2 × MG 17 machine-guns mounted above the engine cowling and 4 × MG 151 cannon

blow-back action. Easily made from sheet stampings, it was mass-produced for the Bf 109G, Fw 190, Ta 152, Me 163, Me 262 and many other fighters, making up for its low velocity (which limited effective range except with a very experienced pilot) by the devastating explosive power of its HE ammunition. In 1944 a third, and again totally different, 30-mm cannon completed development and came into service on selected fighters. The Rheinmetall MK 103 was a large (91-in, 320-lb) high-velocity gun with gas operation and rate of fire of some 420 rds/min. Among the aircraft fitted with this tremendous weapon were the Ta 152C-3, the Bf 109K (selected models), most types of single-seat Do 335 and several sub-types of He 219.

Mauser's brilliant MG 213 revolver

cannon, with five-chambered feed drum allowing rates of fire up to 1200 rds/min, did not see action in the Second World War but served as the basis for almost all the aircraft cannon of the immediate post-war era such as the British Aden, French DEFA, American M-39 and certain Soviet cannon. Still further off were a great array of recoilless cannon, rocket launchers and other unconventional weapons. The SG 116, for example, was a gun which fired inert masses to the rear to counteract the kinetic energy of the projectile, as in the British Davis gun of 1915. The more promising MK 115 was a 55-mm cannon firing large rounds with thick paper cases which burned through, allowing gas to escape from recoil-neutralising ejector nozzles at the rear; rate of fire was 300 rds/min.

One weapon which was received into large-scale service was the R4/M spin-stabilised air-to-air rocket, with calibre of 55-mm (about 2.2-in), fired from underwing racks on several kinds of fighter including the Me 163B and 262A (the Ba 349 *Natter* would have had a battery of 24 in the nose). This folding-fin projectile spurred development of the post-war American Mighty Mouse of 2.75-in calibre.

A weapon which just failed to complete its development was the Ruhrstahl X-4 air-to-air guided missile, with spools of wire to transmit command signals. With this, as in so many other aspects of air combat, the Germans were years ahead of their enemies. Had their basic planning been better, the outcome of the war might have been very different.

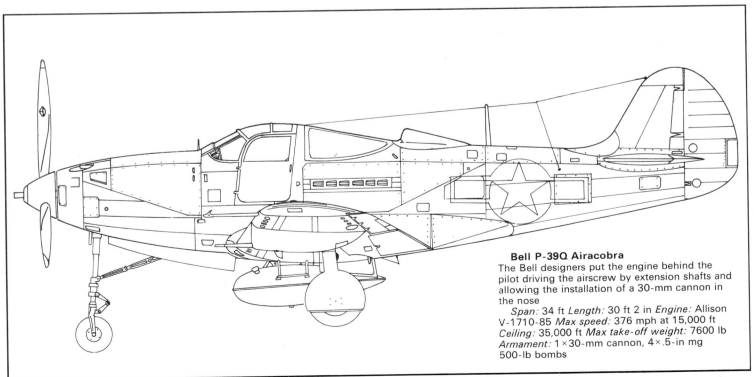

Bell P-39Q Airacobra
The Bell designers put the engine behind the pilot driving the airscrew by extension shafts and allowing the installation of a 30-mm cannon in the nose
Span: 34 ft *Length:* 30 ft 2 in *Engine:* Allison V-1710-85 *Max speed:* 376 mph at 15,000 ft *Ceiling:* 35,000 ft *Max take-off weight:* 7600 lb *Armament:* 1 × 30-mm cannon, 4 × .5-in mg 500-lb bombs

Select Bibliography

Bruce J M *British Aeroplanes 1914-18* (Putnam 1969)

Gray P & Thetford O *German Aircraft of the First World War* (Putnam 1970)

Green W *Fighters* Vols 1-4 (Macdonald 1960)

Green W *Warplanes of the Third Reich* (Macdonald & Janes 1970)

King H F *The Worlds' Fighters* (Putnam 1971)

Lambermont W *Fighter Aircraft of the 1914-18 War* (Harleyford 1961)

Lewis P *The British Fighter Since 1912* (Putnam 1965)